Building Serverless Python Web Services with Zappa

Build and deploy serverless applications on AWS using Zappa

Abdulwahid Abdulhaque Barguzar

BIRMINGHAM - MUMBAI

Building Serverless Python Web Services with Zappa

Commissioning Editor: Aaron Lazar
Acquisition Editor: Karan Sadawana
Content Development Editor: Akshada Iyer
Technical Editor: Adhithya Haridas
Copy Editor: Safis Editing
Project Coordinator: Prajakta Naik
Proofreader: Safis Editing
Indexer: Rekha Nair
Graphics: Jisha Chirayil
Production Coordinator: Deepika Naik

First published: July 2018

Production reference: 1280718

Published by Packt Publishing Ltd.
Livery Place
35 Livery Street
Birmingham
B3 2PB, UK.

ISBN 978-1-78883-761-3

www.packtpub.com

*To my mother, **Kadiza**, and my father, **Abdulhaque**, for their sacrifices and restless
dedication.
I pray to my Lord, "Bestow on them thy mercy even as they cherished me in childhood."
To my wife, **Samreen**, for being my loving partner and a best friend throughout our joint life
journey.
To my son, **Abdulahad**, and my daughter **Aminah**, for their unconditional love and for giving
me a joyful life.
To my cousin, **Sufiyan**, for his support and motivation.*

`mapt.io`

Mapt is an online digital library that gives you full access to over 5,000 books and videos, as well as industry leading tools to help you plan your personal development and advance your career. For more information, please visit our website.

Why subscribe?

- Spend less time learning and more time coding with practical eBooks and Videos from over 4,000 industry professionals

- Improve your learning with Skill Plans built especially for you

- Get a free eBook or video every month

- Mapt is fully searchable

- Copy and paste, print, and bookmark content

PacktPub.com

Did you know that Packt offers eBook versions of every book published, with PDF and ePub files available? You can upgrade to the eBook version at `www.PacktPub.com` and as a print book customer, you are entitled to a discount on the eBook copy. Get in touch with us at `service@packtpub.com` for more details.

At `www.PacktPub.com`, you can also read a collection of free technical articles, sign up for a range of free newsletters, and receive exclusive discounts and offers on Packt books and eBooks.

Contributors

About the author

Abdulwahid Abdulhaque Barguzar is a software architect and an active contributor in the open source community. He has developed a deep understanding of architecting software product development through Python web frameworks and JavaScript frameworks.
He is passionate about implementing and mastering new technologies. In his free time, he researches innovative approaches to rapidly developing and designing a software product and automation testing, aiming to become a master software architect.

About the reviewer

Bhagvan Kommadi has around 18 years of experience in the software industry and has done master's in industrial systems engineering at Georgia Institute of Technology and bachelor's in aerospace engineering from IIT, Madras. He is currently working as Chief Technology Officer of Crystal Delta Solutions, based in Chennai. He has reviewed *Beyond Software Architecture: Creating and Sustaining Winning Solutions* by Luke Hohmann and *Algorithms of the Intelligent Web* by Dr. Haralambos Marmanis.

Packt is searching for authors like you

If you're interested in becoming an author for Packt, please visit `authors.packtpub.com` and apply today. We have worked with thousands of developers and tech professionals, just like you, to help them share their insight with the global tech community. You can make a general application, apply for a specific hot topic that we are recruiting an author for, or submit your own idea.

Table of Contents

Preface

This book is based on the modern way of developing a serverless Python-based web or microservices. Being serverless involves a serverless infrastructure provided by the cloud service provider. This book shows how to use Amazon Web Services to implement the serverless infrastructure. Also, it covers the deployment process using Zappa. Zappa eliminates manual intervention, gives you an automated way to proceed deployment, and helps you maintain multiple deployment stages.

Who this book is for

This book is for beginner to experienced Python developers who want to understand the way to develop Python web services or microservices on the serverless infrastructure. Experienced Python developers can enhance their skills by learning about the serverless technology and understanding serverless deployment.

What this book covers

Chapter 1, *Amazon Web Services for Serverless*, covers understanding the basics of AWS Lambda and API Gateway services. Also, the manual process of creating a serverless service by interacting with the AWS console and CLI tool is covered.

Chapter 2, *Getting Started with Zappa*, explains the concept of the Zappa tool and elaborates the benefits of using Zappa over the manual process of AWS services.

Chapter 3, *Building a Flask Application with Zappa*, explores basic Flask application development and deployment using Zappa as a serverless application.

Chapter 4, *Building a Flask-Based REST API with Zappa*, presents the Flask-based RESTful API development and deployment process with Zappa.

Chapter 5, *Building a Django Application with Zappa*, discusses Django core application development and deploying the application as a serverless over AWS Lambda using Zappa.

Chapter 6, *Building a Django REST API with Zappa*, focuses on RESTful API implementation using the Django REST framework and the deployment process using Zappa.

Chapter 7, *Building a Falcon Application with Zappa*, takes you through developing a RESTful API as a microservice using the Falcon framework and the deployment process using Zappa.

Chapter 8, *Custom Domain with SSL*, explains how to configure a custom domain with Zappa and also covers SSL generation using AWS.

Chapter 9, *Asynchronous Task Execution on AWS Lambda*, showcases the implementation of asynchronous operations for the time-consuming task of using Zappa.

Chapter 10, *Advanced Zappa Settings*, familiarizes you with the additional settings of the Zappa tool to enhance the application deployment process.

Chapter 11, *Securing Serverless Applications with Zappa*, outlines the security aspect of a serverless application over AWS Lambda using Zappa.

Chapter 12, *Zappa with Docker*, presents application development with AWS Lambda context environment using Docker containerization.

To get the most out of this book

Before starting, there are some prerequisites that readers require. Readers should have the following:

- Good understanding of the virtual environment
- Understanding of Python package installation
- Knowledge of traditional deployment using Apache or NGINX
- A basic knowledge of web services or microservices

Download the example code files

You can download the example code files for this book from your account at www.packtpub.com. If you purchased this book elsewhere, you can visit www.packtpub.com/support and register to have the files emailed directly to you.

You can download the code files by following these steps:

1. Log in or register at `www.packtpub.com`.
2. Select the **SUPPORT** tab.
3. Click on **Code Downloads & Errata**.
4. Enter the name of the book in the **Search** box and follow the onscreen instructions.

Once the file is downloaded, please make sure that you unzip or extract the folder using the latest version of:

- WinRAR/7-Zip for Windows
- Zipeg/iZip/UnRarX for Mac
- 7-Zip/PeaZip for Linux

The code bundle for the book is also hosted on GitHub at `https://github.com/PacktPublishing/Building-Serverless-Python-Web-Services-with-Zappa`. In case there's an update to the code, it will be updated on the existing GitHub repository.

We also have other code bundles from our rich catalogue of books and videos available at `https://github.com/PacktPublishing/`. Check them out!

Download the colour images

We also provide a PDF file that has colour images of the screenshots/diagrams used in this book. You can download it here: `https://www.packtpub.com/sites/default/files/downloads/BuildingServerlessPythonWebServiceswithZappa_ColorImages.pdf`.

Conventions used

There are a number of text conventions used throughout this book.

`CodeInText`: Indicates code words in the text, database table names, folder names, filenames, file extensions, pathnames, dummy URLs, user input, and Twitter handles. Here is an example: "Zappa deployment requires the `zappa_settings.json` file, which generates the `zappa init` command."

A block of code is set as follows:

```
client = boto3.client('lambda')
response = client.invoke(
    FunctionName='MyFunction',
    InvocationType='Event'
)
```

When we wish to draw your attention to a particular part of a code block, the relevant lines or items are set in bold:

```
$ curl https://quote-api.abdulwahid.info/daily
{"quote": "May the Force be with you.", "author": "Star Wars", "category":
"Movies"}
```

Any command-line input or output is written as follows:

```
$ pip install awscli
```

Bold: Indicates a new term, an important word, or words that you see onscreen. For example, words in menus or dialogue boxes appear in the text like this. Here is an example: "Click on the **Create a function** button."

 Warnings or important notes appear like this.

 Tips and tricks appear like this.

Get in touch

Feedback from our readers is always welcome.

General feedback: Email `feedback@packtpub.com` and mention the book title in the subject of your message. If you have questions about any aspect of this book, please email us at `questions@packtpub.com`.

Errata: Although we have taken every care to ensure the accuracy of our content, mistakes do happen. If you have found a mistake in this book, we would be grateful if you would report this to us. Please visit www.packtpub.com/submit-errata, selecting your book, clicking on the Errata Submission Form link, and entering the details.

Piracy: If you come across any illegal copies of our works in any form on the Internet, we would be grateful if you would provide us with the location address or website name. Please contact us at copyright@packtpub.com with a link to the material.

If you are interested in becoming an author: If there is a topic that you have expertise in and you are interested in either writing or contributing to a book, please visit authors.packtpub.com.

Reviews

Please leave a review. Once you have read and used this book, why not leave a review on the site that you purchased it from? Potential readers can then see and use your unbiased opinion to make purchase decisions, we at Packt can understand what you think about our products, and our authors can see your feedback on their book. Thank you!

For more information about Packt, please visit packtpub.com.

1
Amazon Web Services for Serverless

In this chapter, we are going to learn about Amazon Web Services for managing a serverless infrastructure. We will be exploring the AWS workflow to create a serverless application. We will learn about the manual process for creating a basic serverless application and an automated process using the AWS **CLI** (**command line interface**).

Topics we will cover in this chapter include:

- Transitioning from the traditional server to serverless
- Getting started with AWS Lambda
- How AWS Lambda works
- Executing a Lambda function
- Creating Lambda triggers
- Creating a serverless RESTful API
- AWS Lambda interaction by the AWS CLI

Technical requirements

There are some technical prerequisites before moving ahead. We are going to demonstrate AWS through a web console and the AWS CLI. The following prerequisites should be considered:

- All the demonstration has been tested on a Linux machine with Ubuntu 16.04. We have shared the links to each library used in this book. You can get the detailed information about the installation and configuration with a specific platform.
- We are using open source libraries and software. Hence, for each library, we are going to share its official documentation links. You can refer to those links for detailed information about a specific library.

Transitioning from traditional server to serverless

Web hosting has changed drastically since it started. Physical server machines were shared among many web applications, and it was a really big challenge when it came to scale. It proved to be very expensive for any individual or company to afford an entire server machine to host their web application.

But, thanks to **virtualization**, the need for a physical server for any web application has been eliminated. Virtualization provides the ability to create many virtual servers as opposed to a single physical server.

Now, the new era of serverless is making the developer's life easier, as we can focus our hard work on development instead of investing time and money on deployment.

Amazon introduced **Amazon Elastic Compute Cloud** (**Amazon EC2**) as a cloud computing solution. Amazon EC2 makes it possible to create an array of virtual servers or instances the Amazon Cloud without investing in hardware. You can scale it as per your requirements in terms of networking, computing, and storage.

The serverless approach is nothing but the process of eliminating the manual workload of setting up the hosting environment. Cloud service providers provide serverless services, and so you never actually own any server. Instead, the cloud service provider executes your code in a high-availability infrastructure.

Getting started with AWS Lambda

Many cloud service providers introduced different services for the serverless infrastructure. Amazon introduced AWS Lambda as a compute service, where you just provide your code and AWS Lambda executes the code in a highly scalable infrastructure by itself. You don't need to worry about managing the services manually. You need to pay for the compute time of your code execution, and there are no charges when your code is not running.

AWS Lambda executes the code as needed in response to events such as data storage events on an S3 bucket, Amazon DynamoDB events, and HTTP request events via the API Gateway. AWS Lambda is able to execute the code based on scheduled time events via AWS CloudWatch Events. AWS Lambda supports Python, Node.js, C#, and Java.

 Amazon **Simple Storage Service (S3)** is a storage service provided by Amazon. It has a simple web interface to store the data. Amazon S3 has associated services events that can be used by other services.

How AWS Lambda works

You need to write a function, which will be executed by AWS Lambda on your behalf.

AWS Lambda is implemented on a container-based model that supports a runtime environment and executes the code as per the Lambda function configuration. When the Lambda function is invoked, it launches the container (an execution environment) based on the AWS Lambda configuration and enables the basic runtime environment, which is required to execute the code.

Let's start with some practical work:

1. To create a Lambda function, you must have an AWS account. If you don't have an AWS account, then you need to sign up on AWS (`https://aws.amazon.com/`) by providing some basic contact and payment information, as it's essential information required by Amazon.

2. Go to the Lambda home page (`https://console.aws.amazon.com/lambda/home`). Click on the **Create a function** button. This will redirect you to the **Create function** page, which is described in the next step. Take a look at the following screenshot:

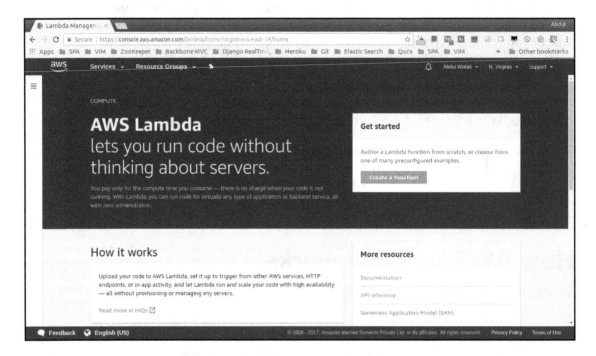

3. AWS provides three different options to create a Lambda function, such as **Author from scratch**, **Blueprints**, and **Serverless Application Repository**. We will be using the **Blueprint** option, which has some built-in Lambda functions. We can choose these blueprints based on our requirements from the search bar, where you can filter by tag and attributes or search by keywords:

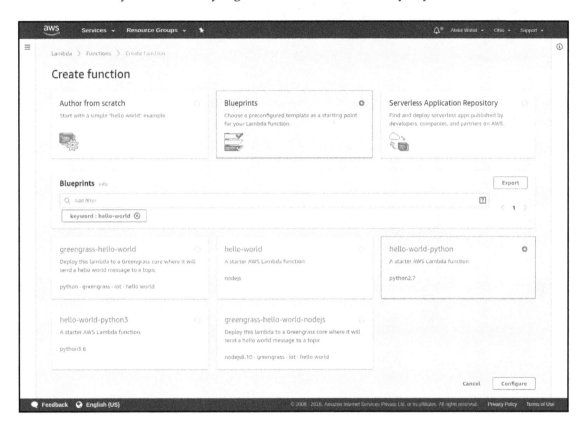

4. Let's choose a **hello-world-python** blueprint. Once we choose the blueprint, we need to set up the basic information about the Lambda function. This information includes the Lambda function's **Name and Role,** as shown in the following screenshot:

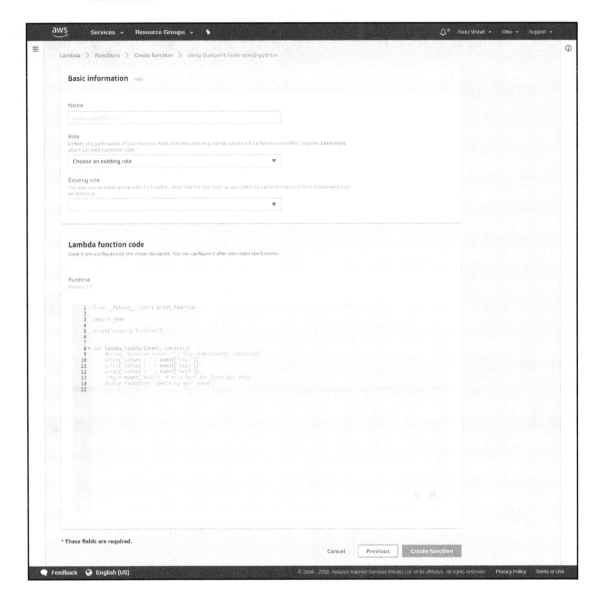

5. Here, **Name** will be a unique identification for your Lambda function and **Role** defines the permissions of your Lambda function.

   There are three options available for creating a role:

- **Choose an existing role**
- **Create new role from template(s)**
- **Create a custom role**
  Let's look at them in more detail:

  - **Choose an existing role**: This allows you to select the previously created role.
  - **Create new role from template(s)**: Here, you need to define a role name. AWS Lambda provides ready-made built-in role policy templates that have pre-configured permissions. These are based on other AWS services-related permissions required by the AWS Lambda function. On any role selection, Lambda will automatically add the logging permission to CloudWatch (AWS logging service), as this is the basic permission required by Lambda.
  - **Create a custom role**: AWS provides an additional privilege to create a customized role to access AWS Lambda. Here, you can define the role based on your requirement.

6. Let's create the `HelloWorld` Lambda function with some role. Here, I chose the S3 object read-only permission policy template.

7. The following screenshot describes the newly created `HelloWorld` Lambda function:

HelloWorld Lambda function

The Lambda function includes three sections:

- **Configuration**
- **Triggers**
- **Monitoring**

Let's look at detailed information about the configuration and monitoring. We will have a separate section for triggers.

Configuration

Lambda execution depends on the configuration setting. Configuring the Lambda function requires the following details:

- Function code
- Environment variables
- Tags
- Execution role
- Basic settings
- Network
- Debugging and error handling

Function code

Here, you are required to write the code. The Lambda function has a predefined pattern for writing the code. While writing the code, you need to understand the context. Lambda provides three kinds of feasibility, which decides your runtime execution for the code:

- **Code entry type**: This section provides three options to decide the entry type for your code, such as editing code inline, uploading a ZIP file, and uploading a file from Amazon S3.
- **Runtime**: This section provides options to decide the runtime programming language context for your code, such as Python, C#, NodeJS, and Java.
- **Handler**: A handler defines the path to your method/function, such as `<filename>.<method_name>`. For example, if you want to execute a function named as a `handler`, which is defined in `main.py`, then it would be `main.handler`.

Let's get back to our newly created hello world function named `lambda_handler`.

Here, the handler value is defined as `lambda_function.lambda_handler`, where `lambda_function.py` is the filename and `lambda_handler` is the method name:

```python
def lambda_handler(event, context):
    print("value1 = " + event['key1'])
    print("value2 = " + event['key2'])
```

`Lambda_handler` accepts two positional arguments, `event` and `context`:

- `event`: This argument contains event-related information. For example, if we configure the Lambda function with Amazon S3 bucket events, then we would get S3 bucket information in event arguments, such as bucket name, region, and so on.
- `context`: This argument contains the context-related information that may be required during runtime for code execution.

Environment variables

You can set the environment variables in key-value pairs, which can be utilized in your code.

Tags

You can use tags for grouping and filtering your Lambda functions. You may have multiple Lambda functions with different regions, so tags help make Lambda functions more manageable.

Execution role

As we previously discussed the role and permission while creating the Lambda function, Lambda provides the capability to edit the existing role that you chose at the time of the Lambda function creation.

Basic settings

Under basic settings, you can configure the memory and execution timeout. Lambda supports memory from 128 MB to 1,536 MB. Timeout execution is in seconds; the default timeout execution Lambda supports is 300 seconds. This setting helps you to control the code execution performance and cost for your Lambda function.

Network

In the network section, you can configure the network access to your Lambda function.

AWS provides a **VPC** (**Virtual Private Cloud**) service to create a virtual network, which allows access to AWS services. You can also configure the networking as per your requirements.

We will discuss the Lambda function with VPC in the upcoming chapters. As of now, we will choose **No VPC** in the network section.

Debugging and error handling

AWS Lambda automatically retries the failed asynchronous invocation. But you can also configure the **DLQ** (**Dead Letter Queue**), such as the SQS queue or SNS topic. To configure the DLQ, the Lambda function must have permission to access DLQ resources.

Now that we understand the configuration, let's go ahead with the execution of the Lambda function.

Let's look at the *Monitoring* section, which describes the activity related to our Lambda function. It can be used to analyze the performance of our Lambda function execution.

Monitoring

AWS CloudWatch is a monitoring service for AWS resources and manages all activity logs. It creates metric data to generate statistical data. CloudWatch enables real-time monitoring of AWS resources. It also monitors hardware information related to AWS EC2 or RDS database instances and other resources.

Lambda monitoring sections display the last 24 hours' analytics data related to the Lambda function's activity and performance. The following screenshot shows the monitored analytics information about our hello world Lambda function:

Let's move on to the next section, where we are going to look at the Lambda function execution.

Executing the Lambda function

AWS Lambda supports several methods of execution. Let's start with the basic execution from its own web console interface. AWS Lambda provides the capability to test the function manually, where you can define the test event context. If you want to test against some other Amazon services, then there are built-in event templates available.

The following screenshot demonstrates the test event creation:

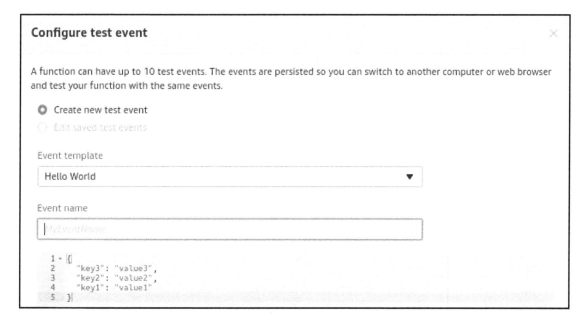

As shown in the preceding screenshot, a single Lambda function can have a maximum of 10 test events and the test events are persisted, so you can reuse them whenever you want to test your Lambda function.

I created the test event with the event name as `HelloWorld` and now I am going to execute the `HelloWorld` function, when converting the Lambda function as a Python microservice, as shown in the following code:

```
from __future__ import print_function
import json
```

```
print('Loading function')

def lambda_handler(event, context):
    print("Received event: " + json.dumps(event, indent=2))
    print("value1 = " + event['key1'])
    print("value2 = " + event['key2'])
    print("value3 = " + event['key3'])
    return "Hello World"
```

Here, we are printing the event data and then returning back to the `Hello World` string:

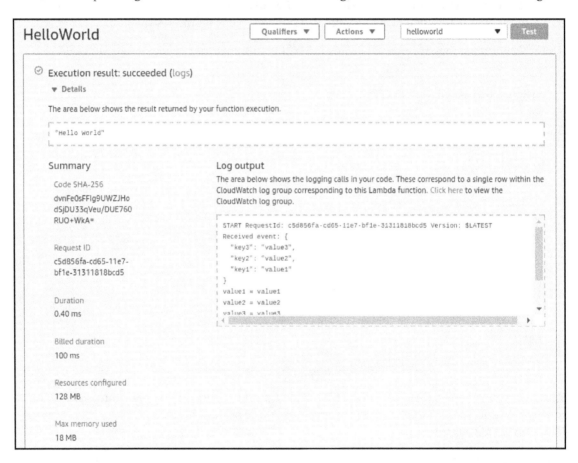

Lambda manages some information on every request execution, such as a request ID and billing information. The Lambda price model is based on the time consumption on request processing, whereas the request ID is the unique identification of every request.

In the **Log output**, you can see all the print statements output. Now, let's raise an error and see how Lambda responds and returns the logs.

We are going to replace the current code with the following snippet:

```
from __future__ import print_function
import json

print('Loading function')


def lambda_handler(event, context):
    print("Received event: " + json.dumps(event, indent=2))
    raise Exception('Exception raised manually.')
```

The following screenshot is the log snippet of the execution result:

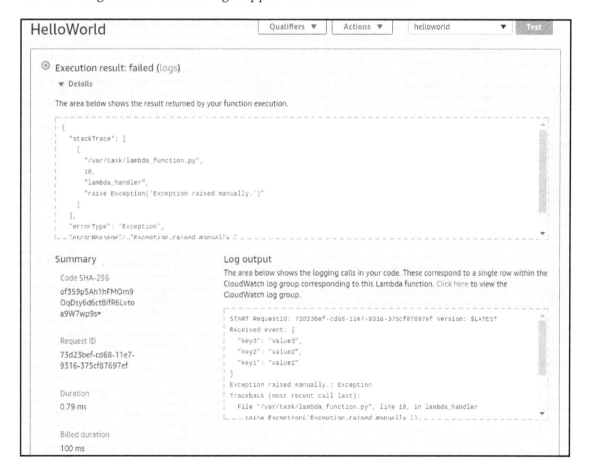

Here, Lambda responded with the complete stack trace information and logged it as well. You can check the CloudWatch logs, as CloudWatch is preconfigured with the AWS Lambda execution.

We learned about the Lambda function execution from the Lambda console, and now it's time to execute the Lambda function from a schedule trigger. In our project, we often need to have a cron job schedule to execute some functionality at a particular time period.

Lambda triggers will help us to set up the triggers based on events. Let's move ahead to introduce the trigger to our hello world function.

Creating Lambda triggers

The Lambda function can be configured in response to events. AWS provides a list of triggers that support lots of events. These triggers belong to their associated AWS services.

You can add a trigger to your Lambda function from the triggers section.

I am going to slightly modify the hello world Lambda function. Here, we are printing the request ID, which is received in the context object as an `aws_request_id` attribute. It also prints the timestamp:

```
lambda_function.py
 1   from __future__ import print_function
 2
 3   import json
 4   from datetime import datetime
 5
 6   print('Loading function')
 7
 8
 9   def lambda_handler(event, context):
10       current_time = datetime.now()
11       print ('Hello World with Request ID {0}'.format(context.aws_request_id))
12       print ("Function executed on {0}"\
13           .format(current_time.strftime('%d-%b-%Y at %H:%M:%S') ))
14   
```

Now, we are going to add a trigger to our Lambda function that will execute our Lambda function every minute.

The following screenshot shows the **Add trigger** flow, where you can easily configure any trigger from the left-hand panel with your Lambda function:

We are going to configure the **CloudWatch Events** trigger. **CloudWatch Events** deliver near real-time system events that describe the changes in AWS resources.

You can set up simple event rules with operational events in AWS resources as they occur, and you can also schedule automated events that self-trigger based on cron or the rate expression.

 The cron and rate expression are two different methods to define a schedule expression. The cron expressions have six required fields, such as cron (fields), and the rate expressions have two required fields, such as rate (value unit). These methods help us to define a schedule expression. You can find detailed information at `http://docs.aws.amazon.com/AmazonCloudWatch/latest/events/ScheduledEvents.html`.

Here, we are going to schedule a rate expression to execute our hello world Lambda function every minute. We need to select **CloudWatch Events** from the triggers dropdown.

To create the CloudWatch event rule, we are going to create a new rule. We need to set up the rule with some required information, such as the rule name, which is a unique identifier. So, we are going to name the rule as `hello-world-every-minute` and the rule type as either the event pattern or schedule expression. In our case, it would be a schedule expression as the rate (1 minute), as shown in the preceding screenshot.

Once we set the trigger and enable it, the scheduled event would get triggered as per the schedule expression. Let's see our hello world Lambda logs after five minutes.

To view the logs related to any services, you need to do the following:

1. Open the CloudWatch console at `https://console.aws.amazon.com/cloudwatch/`
2. In the navigation pane, choose **Logs**
3. Select the log group related to the `HelloWorld` Lambda function

The following screenshot describes the **CloudWatch** log access:

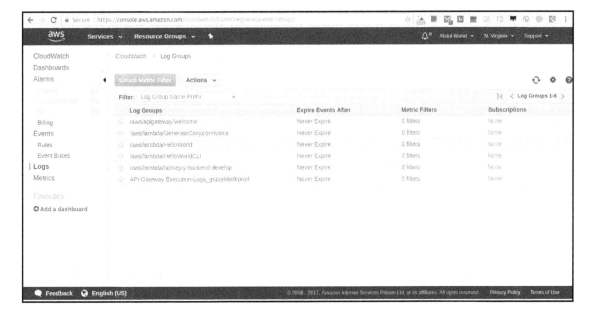

By selecting the HelloWorld Lambda function log groups, you see the logging activity related to our HelloWorld Lambda function. The following screenshot shows the logs of the HelloWorld function:

Here, you can see that our hello world Lambda function is executed exactly every minute since the time we have enabled the trigger.

Now, let's move ahead to create a serverless RESTful API.

Serverless RESTful API

Let's understand the microservice scenario where we are going to deploy a serverless hello world function that will respond to HTTP events through the API Gateway.

The Amazon API Gateway service enables you to create, manage, and publish a RESTful API to interact with AWS resources at any scale. The API Gateway provides an interface where you expose the backend through the REST application programming interface.

To enable the AWS serverless infrastructure, the API Gateway plays an important role, as it can be configured to execute the Lambda functions.

Now, we are going to configure an API Gateway service to executes the Lambda function

Here is the hello world function:

```python
lambda_function.py
 1   from __future__ import print_function
 2
 3   import json
 4
 5   print('Loading function')
 6
 7
 8 ▾ def lambda_handler(event, context):
 9       data = {"message": "Hello World returned in JSON"}
10       headers = {"Content-Type": "application/json"}
11       return {"statusCode": 200, \
12              "headers": headers, \
13              "body": json.dumps(data)}
```

When we integrate the AWS Lambda function with the API Gateway, the Lambda function must return a dictionary object with the required keys as statusCode, headers, and body. The value of the body attribute must be in a JSON string. Hence, we converted the Python dictionary into a JSON string.

It's time to integrate the API Gateway with the Lambda function. As we have seen in our previous discussion about triggers, we are going to add a trigger with the API Gateway:

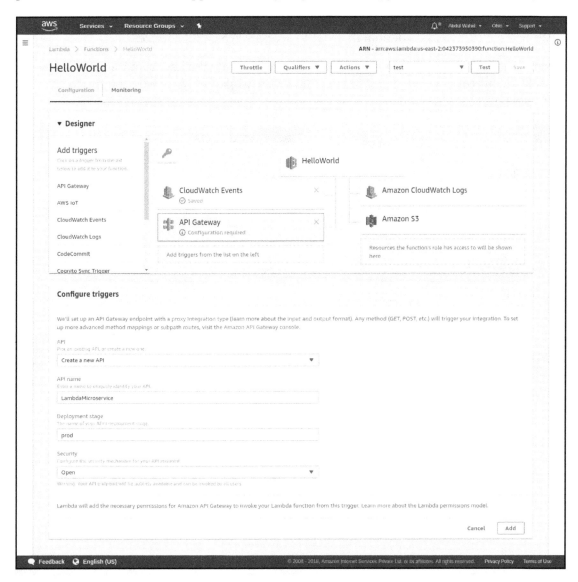

We are going to create an API Gateway service with the name as `LambdaMicroservice`. The API Gateway enables you to create and maintain a deployment stage as per your requirement.

If you want to secure your API then you have two options—using AWS IAM and opening it with the access key, or keeping it as open, making it publicly available.

AWS **IAM** (**Identity Access Management**) is an AWS cloud service that is helpful in creating a secure access credential in order to access AWS cloud services.

Opening with the access key feature allows you to generate the key from the API Gateway console. In our case, we are going to keep the security open only, as we need to access our API publicly:

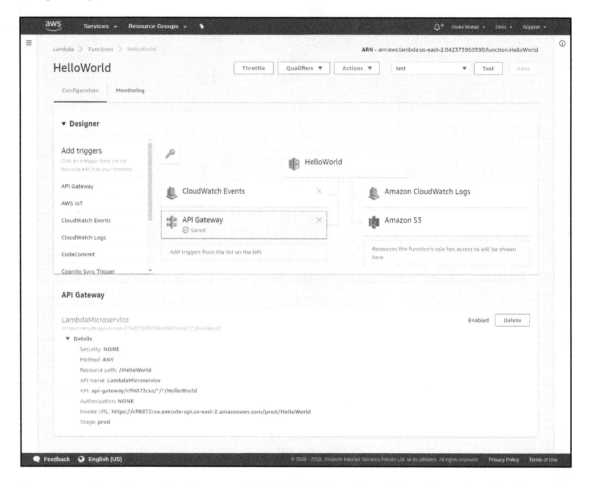

Once you add and save the changes, the REST API is ready within a few seconds. The invoke URL is our REST API endpoint.

Let's hit the invoke URL using the `curl` command-line tool and see what happens:

```
$ curl
https://cfi6872cxa.execute-api.us-east-2.amazonaws.com/prod/HelloWorld
{"message": "Hello World returned in JSON"}
```

That's it. We are done with creating a serverless RESTful API using AWS Lambda and the API Gateway. Now, we are going to see how we can interact with the AWS services using the AWS CLI.

AWS Lambda interaction with theAWS CLI

The AWS CLI is an open source tool developed on top of AWS SDK for Python using the Boto library, which provides commands to interact with AWS services. With the very minimum configuration, you can manage any AWS services from the CLI. It provides direct access to AWS services and you can develop shell scripts to manage your resources.

For example, if you want to upload the file to the S3 bucket, then you can do so by just a single command from the CLI:

```
$ aws s3 cp index.html s3://bucket-name/
```

`aws s3 cp` is a shell-like command that performs the multi-part file upload operation in order to complete the operation.

It also supports customization for some of the AWS services. You can see the list of AWS services supported by `aws-cli` by using the `--help` command.

Installing the AWS CLI

`awscli` is available to as a Python distributor package. You can easily install it with the `pip` command, as described in the following code:

```
$ pip install awscli --upgrade
```

Here are the prerequisites:

- Python 2 with version 2.6.5+ or Python 3 with version 3.3+
- Unix, Linux, macOS, or Windows

Configuring the AWS CLI

`awscli` directly accesses AWS services but we need to configure and authenticate it in order to access AWS services.

Run the `aws configure` command to configure the AWS CLI with your Amazon account:

```
(.env) abdulw@ULTP-711:~/workspace/lambda_poc$ aws configure
AWS Access Key ID [****************QAPA]:
AWS Secret Access Key [****************u98V]:
Default region name [ap-south-1]:
Default output format [json]:
(.env) abdulw@ULTP-711:~/workspace/lambda_poc$
```

You can get the AWS access key ID and AWS secret access key from the **My Security Credentials** option, as shown in the following screenshot:

Let's configure the AWS Lambda function using AWS CLI.

Configuring Lambda function with the AWS CLI

Let's configure our hello world Lambda function and triggers using the `awscli utility` command.

The AWS CLI supports all available AWS services. You can see a detailed description of the `aws` command using `aws help` and it will also list all the available services.

We are interested in Lambda, as we are going to create a Lambda function with a simple hello world context:

```
$ aws lambda help
```

This will list a complete description of the Lambda service and all the available commands that are required to manage the AWS Lambda service.

Creating a Lambda function

Here, we are going to create a new Lambda function with the `aws lambda create-function` command. To run this command, we need to pass the required and optional arguments.

Make sure you have a role with permission for the `lambda:CreateFunction` action.

Previously, in the AWS Lambda console, we chose the code entry point as inline editing. Now, we will be using a ZIP file as a deployment package.

Before creating the Lambda function, we should create a Lambda function deployment package.

This deployment package will be a ZIP file consisting of your code and any dependencies.

If your project has some dependencies, then you must install the dependencies in the root directive of the project. For example:

```
$ pip install requests -t <project-dir> OR
$ pip install -r requirements.txt  -t <project-dir>
```

Here, the `-t` option indicates the target directory.

Create a simple `lambda_handler` function in a file named as `handler.py`, as shown in the following screenshot:

```
handler.py  ✕
1    from __future__ import print_function
2
3    print('Loading function')
4
5
6    def lambda_handler(event, context):
7        return "Hello World ! Response by lambda function."
8
```

Now, let's make a deployment package as a ZIP file consisting of the preceding code:

```
abdulw@ULTP-711:~/workspace/lambda_poc$ ls
handler.py
abdulw@ULTP-711:~/workspace/lambda_poc$ cat handler.py
from __future__ import print_function

print('Loading function')


def lambda_handler(event, context):
    return "Hello World ! Response by lambda function."


abdulw@ULTP-711:~/workspace/lambda_poc$ zip -r hello_world_package.zip  handler.py
  adding: handler.py (deflated 22%)
abdulw@ULTP-711:~/workspace/lambda_poc$ ls
handler.py   hello_world_package.zip
abdulw@ULTP-711:~/workspace/lambda_poc$ ▊
```

Now, we are ready to create the Lambda function. The following screenshot describes the command execution:

```
abdulw@ULTP-711:~/workspace/lambda_poc$ aws lambda create-function --function-name HelloWorldCLI
 --description 'Hello world lambda function created from AWS CLI' --runtime python2.7 --handler
'handler.lambda_handler' --role arn:aws:iam::042373950390:role/service-role/SimpleMicroservicePe
rmission --zip-file fileb://hello_world_package.zip
{
    "FunctionName": "HelloWorldCLI",
    "Role": "arn:aws:iam::042373950390:role/service-role/SimpleMicroservicePermission",
    "LastModified": "2017-11-22T15:53:43.821+0000",
    "Description": "Hello world lambda function created from AWS CLI",
    "Version": "$LATEST",
    "CodeSize": 297,
    "Timeout": 3,
    "FunctionArn": "arn:aws:lambda:us-east-1:042373950390:function:HelloWorldCLI",
    "MemorySize": 128,
    "Runtime": "python2.7",
    "CodeSha256": "UQU7I97Ldui98qE9NIGm4KoyBHk7vYXgAUWKvLDEhdk=",
    "Handler": "handler.lambda_handler"
}
abdulw@ULTP-711:~/workspace/lambda_poc$ ▮
```

You can see that, in the AWS Lambda console, the Lambda function immediately got created:

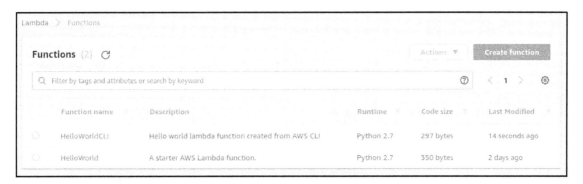

Let's discuss the required and optional parameters that we used with the `aws lambda create-function` command:

- `--function-name` (required): The name is self-explanatory. We need to pass the Lambda function name that we are intending to create.
- `--role` (required): This is a required parameter where we need to use the AWS role ARN as a value. Make sure this role has permissions to create the Lambda function.

- `--runtime` (required): We need to mention the runtime environment for the Lambda function execution. As we mentioned earlier, AWS Lambda supports Python, Node.js, C#, and Java. So these are the possible values:
  - `python2.7`
  - `python3.6`
  - `nodejs`
  - `nodejs4.3`
  - `nodejs6.10`
  - `nodejs4.3-edge`
  - `dotnetcore1.0`
  - `java8`

- `--handler` (required): Here, we mention the function path that will be an execution entry point by the AWS Lambda. In our case, we used `handler.lambda_function`, where the handler is the file that contains the `lambda_function`.

- `--description`: This option lets you add some text description about your Lambda function.

- `--zip-file`: This option is used to upload the deployment package file of your code from your local environment/machine. Here, you need to add `fileb://` as a prefix to your ZIP file path.

- `--code`: This option helps you upload the deployment package file from the AWS S3 bucket.

You should pass a string value with a pattern, such as the one shown here:

```
"S3Bucket=<bucket-name>,S3Key=<file-name>,S3ObjectVersion=<file-version-id>".
```

There are many other optional parameters available that you can see with the `help` command, such as `aws lambda create-function help`. You can use them as per your requirement.

Now we will see the Lambda function invocation using the command $ `aws lambda invoke`.

Invoking the function

The Lambda CLI provides a command to directly invoke the Lambda function:

```
$ aws lambda invoke --function-name <value> <outfile>
```

Let's look at the parameters:

- `--function-name` (required): This parameter asks for a Lambda function name
- `outfile` (required): Here, you need to mention a filename where the returned output or response by the Lambda function will be stored

Here are other optional parameters available that you can list by the `help` command.

Let's invoke our recently created `HelloWorldCLI` function:

```
abdulw@ULTP-711:~/workspace/lambda_poc$ ls
handler.py  hello_world_package.zip
abdulw@ULTP-711:~/workspace/lambda_poc$ aws lambda invoke --function-name HelloWorldCLI lambda_output.txt
{
    "StatusCode": 200
}
abdulw@ULTP-711:~/workspace/lambda_poc$ ls
handler.py  hello_world_package.zip  lambda_output.txt
abdulw@ULTP-711:~/workspace/lambda_poc$ cat lambda_output.txt && echo
"Hello World ! Response by lambda function."
abdulw@ULTP-711:~/workspace/lambda_poc$ █
```

When we invoked the Lambda function, it immediately responded with a status code and the Lambda function returned the output data stored in the newly created `lambda_output.txt` file by the `lambda invoke` command.

Create-event-source-mapping

This is a subcommand of the `aws lambda` command and is used to create event mapping for your Lambda function. `$ aws lambda create-event-source-mapping` supports only Amazon Kinesis stream and Amazon DynamoDB stream events mapping. We will discuss event mapping with the Amazon API Gateway and CloudWatch event using Zappa in the upcoming chapters.

Summary

In this chapter, we learned about the manual process of creating a simple AWS Lambda and configuring some triggers against it. Also, we looked at the AWS Lambda configuration using the AWS CLI. It's really amazing to implement a serverless application. These AWS services play an essential part in creating a serverless infrastructure, where you can develop your application and deploy it as serverless.

Questions

1. What would be the benefits of being serverless?
2. What is the role of Amazon S3 in the serverless infrastructure?

Getting Started with Zappa

2

Previously, we learned about creating a serverless application using the AWS Web Console and AWS CLI. Now, we are going to learn about Zappa and automating operations for creating a serverless application.

In this chapter, we are going to cover the following topics:

- What is Zappa?
- Installing and configuring Zappa
- Building, testing, and deploying a Python web service using Zappa
- Zappa's uses

Technical requirements

Before moving ahead, let's ensure we fulfill the technical requirements. The following subsections will go over the hardware and software requirements for this chapter.

Hardware

For demonstration purposes, we used a basic configured machine with the following specification:

- Memory—16GB
- Processor—Intel Core i5
- CPU—2.30GHz x 4
- Graphics—Intel HD Graphics 520

Software

The following are the software specifications:

- OS—Ubuntu 16.04 LTS
- OS-Type—64 bit
- Python 3.6
- Python development packages: `build-essential`, `python-dev`, and `python-virtualenv`
- AWS credentials and AWS CLI
- Zappa

We will go over a detailed description for setting up the environment in the upcoming sections. In the meantime, you can configure essential packages such as `python3.6` and `awscli`.

What is Zappa?

Zappa is an open source tool that was developed and designed by Rich Jones, founder/CTO of Gun.io (`https://www.gun.io/`). Zappa was mainly designed to build and deploy serverless Python applications on AWS Lambda and API Gateway.

Zappa is great for deploying serverless Python microservices with frameworks such as Flask and Bottle for hosting large web applications and CMSes with Django. You can also deploy any Python WSGI application as well.

In the previous chapter, we implemented the basic hello world microservice, using AWS Lambda and API Gateway. Zappa automates all these manual processes and gives us a handy tool to build and deploy Python applications.

It's as easy as this:

```
$ pip install zappa
$ zappa init
$ zappa deploy
```

As we described earlier, the tradition of web hosting is where the server needs to be always online, listening to HTTP requests and processing the requests one by one. If the queue of incoming HTTP requests grows, then a timeout error will occur as the server will have failed to serve that many requests per second.

API Gateway serves each request with a virtual HTTP server with auto scalability. That's the reason it can serve a single request to millions of requests without fail. Hence, we get the infinite scaling with zero downtime infraction of your current deployment cost.

Now, we are going to go through an app demonstration, but, before we do that, let's configure Zappa on your machine, which we will go through in the upcoming section.

Installing and configuring Zappa

Installing Zappa is a straightforward task, but before we move ahead, we need to configure the prerequisites. Make sure you have Python 2.7 or Python 3.6 and have a valid AWS account. Now, you need to configure the AWS credentials on your machine with `help` `awscli`:

```
$ pip install awscli
```

Configure the AWS credentials using the `aws` `configure` command, as shown in the following screenshot:

```
(.env) abdulw@ULTP-711:~/workspace/lambda_poc$ aws configure
AWS Access Key ID [****************QAPA]:
AWS Secret Access Key [****************u98V]:
Default region name [ap-south-1]:
Default output format [json]:
(.env) abdulw@ULTP-711:~/workspace/lambda_poc$ ▮
```

The configuration for AWS credentials requires that you have an **AWS Access Key ID**, **AWS Secret Access Key**, **Default region name**, and a **Default output format**.

You can get AWS credential information from your **My Security Credentials** page, as shown in the following screenshot:

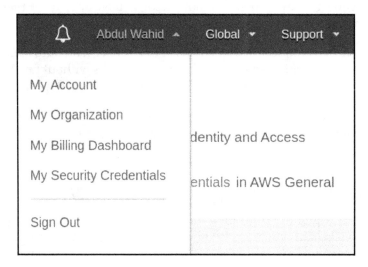

Once you've configured your AWS credentials, we can move ahead with Zappa's installation.

Zappa must be installed in a virtual environment. It's strongly recommended that you create a virtual environment and activate it before installing Zappa. I prefer to use the virtualenv tool. There are other tools available to manage your virtual environments:

```
$ virtualenv env -p python3.6
```

Here, we are creating a virtual environment named env and using python3.6, where -p indicates the Python version. Now, activate the virtual environment as follows:

```
$ source env/source/bin
```

We are set to go now, so let's install Zappa using pip:

```
$ pip install zappa
```

Now, we are ready to launch Zappa. In the following sections, we will be creating a small program to demonstrate how we can make Zappa's deployment serverless.

Building, testing, and deploying a Python web service using Zappa

We are going to create a simple hello world program as a microservice using Python's Bottle framework. Let's follow some basic steps to configure a small project using the Bottle framework:

1. First, we will create a new project directory named `lambda_bottle_poc`:

    1. `$ mkdir lambda_bottle_poc`

2. Let's create a virtual environment inside the `lambda_bottle_poc` directory:

    1. `$ virtualenv env -p python3.6`

2. Here is the basic hello world program using the Bottle framework:

```
hello.py    ✕
1    from bottle import Bottle, run
2
3    app = Bottle()
4
5    @app.route('/hello')
6    def hello():
7        return "Hello World!\n"
8
```

Now it's time to deploy the program as serverless on AWS Lambda and expose the /hello API via API Gateway. In the previous chapter, we described the manual process to deploy the Python application, using AWS console and AWS CLI, which was a really big challenge.

But with the help of Zappa, all manual processes of the AWS console and AWS CLI are automated and provides a rapid process to deploy and maintain your application in a serverless environment.

Building the deployment package

Let's initialize Zappa using the `zappa init` command. This command helps you to create and deploy Python applications. This command runs in a user interactive mode with some basic questions required so that we can set up the deployment process.

By the end of the questionnaire, Zappa creates a JSON file named `zappa_settings.json`. This file is nothing but the backbone of Zappa as it maintains the mapping information that's used by Zappa internally.

We will discuss the Zappa `init` command process in detail in a few moments. Before that, just have a look at following screenshot, which describes the flow of the `zappa init` command:

As you can see, `zappa init` starts up user interactive mode with some questions. Let's look at some information about each question.

What do you call this environment? (default dev)

Amazon API Gateway provides a mechanism to maintain different environment stages of your hosted API. For example, you can create environment stages for development, staging, and production.

With the help of Zappa, you can manage environment stages in a very easy way. In answer to the preceding question, you can define your own environment stage name or leave it empty to consider the default stage name as `dev`.

What do you want to call your bucket? (default zappa-2o2zd8dg4)

Zappa deployments will need to be uploaded to a private Amazon S3 bucket. AWS Lambda requires two types of code entry, such as inline code and uploading the ZIP. If the ZIP file size exceeds 10 MB, then consider uploading the ZIP onto Amazon S3. This is why Zappa, by default, creates a bucket which will be used to upload the deployment ZIP file and refer to AWS Lambda.

You can provide your own existing bucket name or choose the default, as suggested by Zappa. If the bucket doesn't exist, then Zappa will automatically create one for you.

What's your modular path to your app function? (default dev)

The AWS Lambda function requires an attribute, such as `lambda_handler`, which points to a function as an entry point for Lambda execution. Hence, we need to provide information about the function name with a modular path such as `<filename>.<function_name/app_name>` to Zappa.

In our case, we have a file named `hello.py` and an app object that was created using the `Bottle` class of Python's Bottle framework. Hence, the answer to this question is `hello.app`.

Would you like to deploy the application globally? (default n)

AWS provides a feature to extend the Lambda services to all available regions. That's what you should do if you want to make your service available globally with much less latency. Zappa supports this feature, which will enable you to extend the Lambda service in all regions without any manual effort.

Finally, you would get a `zappa_settings.json` file, which will have all configurations related to your deployments. Let's have a look at the `zappa_settings.json` file in the next section.

The zappa_settings.json file

Once you've finished the questionnaire session, Zappa creates a basic `zappa_settings.json` file based on your input. `zappa_settings.json` plays an important role in configuring Zappa with your project. If you initialize Zappa in your existing project (`Django`/`Flask`/`Pyramid`/`Bottle`), then Zappa automatically detects the type of project and creates the `zappa_settings.json` file accordingly.

The following is the content of our newly created `zappa_settings.json` file for the hello world program:

```
{
    "dev": {
        "app_function": "hello.app",
        "aws_region": "ap-south-1",
        "profile_name": "default",
        "project_name": "lambda-bottle-p",
        "runtime": "python3.6",
        "s3_bucket": "zappa-2o2zd8dg4"
    }
}
```

For a Django project, it uses `django_settings` instead of `app_function`. `django_settings` needs to be initialized with the path to your Django settings:

```
{
    "dev": {
        "django_settings": "your_project.settings",
        "aws_region": "ap-south-1",
        "profile_name": "default",
        "project_name": "lambda-bottle-p",
        "runtime": "python3.6",
```

```
        "s3_bucket": "zappa-2o2zd8dg4"
    }
}
```

The preceding configuration is enough to deploy a basic Python web application. Let's move on and deploy hello world as a serverless application.

Deploying and testing hello world

Zappa deployment is super easy, as you only need to run a single command in order start the deployment:

```
$ zappa deploy <stage_name>
```

That's it! We are done with deployment. Now, let's deploy the hello world program. The following screenshot describes the deployment process:

Once the deployment completes, we get the API URL endpoint. Let's test the hello world application by hitting the API URL with the /hello endpoint:

```
$ curl -l
https://071h4br4e0.execute-api.ap-south-1.amazonaws.com/dev/hello
```

After running the preceding command, you will see the following output:

```
Hello World!
```

It's really amazing to be able to configure the service and deploy it in a few seconds. Now, we will see its basic uses related to the zappa_settings.json file in detail.

Basic uses

Zappa covers each and every deployment process. Let's have a detailed discussion regarding the deployment flow with Zappa.

Initial deployments

Once you are done with initializing Zappa, then you can deploy the application on to the `production` stage in a single command, as shown in the following code snippet:

```
$ zappa deploy production
   .
   .
   .

Deployment complete !
https://071h4br4e0.execute-api.ap-south-1.amazonaws.com/production
```

When you call the `$ zappa deploy` command, Zappa performs some tasks to complete the deployment. The following is the internal flow and process of Zappa regarding deployment:

1. Compress the application code in your local environment into a ZIP archive by replacing any dependencies with versions in a precompiled Lambda package.
2. Set up the Lambda `handler` function with the required WSGI middleware based on your application's type.
3. Upload the generated archive from the preceding two steps into the Amazon S3 bucket.
4. Create and manage the necessary AWS IAM policies and roles.
5. Creates the AWS Lambda function with reference to the uploaded ZIP archive file on the AWS S3 bucket.
6. Create the AWS API Gateway resources along with the different stages as per Zappa configuration.
7. Create the WSGI compatible routes for the API Gateway resources.
8. Link the API Gateway routes to the AWS Lambda functions.
9. Finally, remove the ZIP file from AWS S3.

Note: `lambda-packages` (https://github.com/Miserlou/lambda-packages) is an open source repository that's maintained by the Zappa community. This repository contains the most essential Python libraries as precompiled binaries, which will be compatible with AWS Lambda.

This is how Zappa deals with the deployment process—It completes all of these tasks on its own and gives you the honor of deploying your application with a single command.

Update

If you have already deployed your application, then you are required to update your latest application code on AWS Lambda by simply using the following command:

```
$ zappa update production
.
.
.
Your updated Zappa deployment is live!:
https://071h4br4e0.execute-api.ap-south-1.amazonaws.com/production
```

We can compare this to using `zappa deploy`, which only updates a few tasks. They are mentioned here:

- It creates an archive ZIP with the latest application code; the local environment is a precompiled Lambda package
- It uploads the archived ZIP on to AWS S3
- It updates the AWS Lambda

That's it! We're done with updating the existing deployment, and it only took a couple of seconds.

Status

You can simply check the status of your application deployment by running the following:

```
$ zappa status production
```

This will print detailed information about the AWS Lambda function, schedule events, and the API Gateway.

Tailing logs

Zappa provides a facility for watching the logs related to your deployment. You can simply use the following command:

```
$ zappa tail production
```

This will print all logs related to HTTP requests and AWS events. If you want to print logs related to HTTP requests, you can simply pass the `--http` argument:

```
$ zappa tail production --http
```

You can reverse the preceding command with non-HTTP events and log messages by simply using the following code::

```
$ zappa tail production --non-http
```

You can also limit the log with respect to time using the `--since` argument:

```
$ zappa tail production --since 1h # 1 hour
$ zappa tail production --since 1m # 1 minute
$ zappa tail production --since 1mm # 1 month
```

You can also filter the logs with the `--filter` argument, for example:

```
$ zappa tail production --since 1h --http --filter "POST"
```

This will show only HTTP `POST` requests for the last hour. This uses the AWS CloudWatch log-filter pattern (`http://docs.aws.amazon.com/AmazonCloudWatch/latest/logs/FilterAndPatternSyntax.html`).

Rollback

AWS Lambda maintains the revision of your deployments. You can rollback to the previously deployed version by providing a revision number, as shown here:

```
$ zappa rollback production -n 3
```

This will simply revert the Lambda code with the previously uploaded archived ZIP.

Undeploy

If you wanted to remove your deployed application completely, then you simply use the following command:

```
$ zappa undeploy production
```

This will remove the published AWS Lambda and API Gateway. If you want the logs related to your application from AWS CloudWatch, then you simply pass the argument along with the preceding command, as shown here:

```
$ zappa undeploy production --remove-logs
```

This will purge the logs from AWS CloudWatch.

Package

Zappa provides a command to generate a build package archive locally without deploying the application:

```
$ zappa package production
```

When you run this command, Zappa automatically packages your active virtual environment into an AWS Lambda compatible package.

Internally, it replaces any local dependencies with AWS Lambda compatible, precompiled versions. These dependencies are included in the following order:

- Lambda compatible many Linux wheels from the local cache
- Lambda compatible many Linux wheels from PyPi
- Lambda-specific versions from Lambda packages (`https://github.com/Miserlou/lambda-packages`)
- Archive the active virtual environment
- Archive the project directory

While processing, packaging, and packing, Zappa ignores some unnecessary files such as `.pyc` files. If they are available, then `.py` will get ignored. Zappa also sets the correct execution permissions, configures package settings, and creates a unique, auditable package manifest file.

The generated package archive will be Lambda compatible. You can set a callback function that will be invoked once the archive is created:

```
{
    "production": {
        "callbacks": {
            "zip": "my_app.zip_callback"
        }
    }
}
```

Here, production is your stage name and under callback, you can set the callback method by mapping to `"zip"`. This can help you write your own custom deployment automation.

We have seen the basic uses of Zappa. Now it's time to do some practical work. We are going to build some Python application developments with Zappa, so stay tuned!

Summary

Zappa provides flexible features so that you can perform the deployment process. We covered the basic uses of Zappa and gained an understanding of the packaging and deployment process. Zappa makes it very simple and easy for developers to configure and perform the deployment of an application to a serverless environment.

Questions

1. What is Zappa?
2. How can we secure the application in AWS?

3
Building a Flask Application with Zappa

In the last chapter, we learned about automating the deployment process using Zappa, since Zappa helps us to deploy a Python application on the AWS Serverless infrastructure. We used this to develop a Python application using some of the Python web frameworks. In this chapter, we going to develop a Flask-based application as a serverless application on AWS Lambda.

In the previous chapter, we saw how Zappa is useful for performing serverless deployments and how it makes it easy to deploy with a single command. Now, it's time to see the larger application deployed by Zappa, since it's really important to see how an application is configured and moved to AWS Lambda.

In this chapter, we'll be covering the following topics:

- What is Flask?
- Minimal Flask application
- Configuring with Zappa
- Building, testing, and deploying on AWS Lambda
- A complete Flask Todo application

Technical requirements

Before making headway, let's understand the technical requirements and configure the development environment. This chapter does have a conceptual demonstration of an application development. Hence, there are some prerequisites:

- Ubuntu 16.04/macOS/Windows
- Python 3.6
- Pipenv tool
- Zappa
- Flask
- Flask Extensions

Once you have configured Python 3.6 and installed the Pipenv tool, you can create a virtual environment and install these packages. We are going to explore the installation and configuration of this in a later section. Let's move on and understand some basic concepts of Python-based frameworks and their related implementation.

What is Flask?

Flask is a well-known Python micro web framework in the Python community. It's adopted and preferable because of its extensible nature. Flask aims to keep the code simple but extensible.

By default, Flask does not include any database abstraction layer, form validation, or any other specific functionality. Instead, Flask supports extensions to add any well-defined functionality to your application. Numerous extensions are available to provide database integration, form validation, file upload handling, authentication, and more. The Flask core team reviews extensions and ensures that they won't break the future release.

Flask allows you to define the design as per your application needs. You are not bound to follow some strict rule by Flask. You can write your application code in a single file or in a modular manner. Flask supports built-in development servers and fast debuggers, unit testing, RESTful request dispatching, Jinja2 templating, and secure cookies (for client-side sessions), all of which are WSGI 1.0-compliant and Unicode-based.

That's why many in the Python community prefer to use the Flask framework as their first choice. Let's make headway and explore the Flask-based application development process with actual implemention along with a serverless approach.

Installing Flask

Flask mainly depends on two external libraries such as Werkzeug and Jinja2. Werkzeug provides a Python standard **WSGI** (**Web Server Gateway Interface**) that enables a Python application to interact with HTTP. Jinja2 is a templating engine that enables you to render an HTML template with your own customized context.

Now, let's move on and install Flask. All its dependencies will be automatically installed; you don't need to install dependencies manually.

It's recommended that you use `virtualenv` to install Flask, since `virtualenv` enables you to install Python packages in parallel for different Python projects.

If you don't have `virtualenv`, then you can simply install it by using the following code:

```
$ sudo apt-get install python-virtualenv
```

Once you have installed `virtualenv`, you need to create a new environment for your Flask project, as shown in the following screenshot:

```
abdulw@ULTP-711:~$ mkdir flask_todo
abdulw@ULTP-711:~$ cd flask_todo/
abdulw@ULTP-711:~/flask_todo$ virtualenv .env -p python3.6
Running virtualenv with interpreter /usr/bin/python3.6
Using base prefix '/usr'
New python executable in /home/abdulw/flask_todo/.env/bin/python3.6
Also creating executable in /home/abdulw/flask_todo/.env/bin/python
Installing setuptools, pip, wheel...done.
abdulw@ULTP-711:~/flask_todo$ 
```

We will be using `virtualenv` in the upcoming sections. Now, let's install Flask:

```
$ pip install flask
```

We are ready to have fun with Flask. We will be creating a minimal Flask application to demonstrate the Flask application workflow.

A minimal Flask application

Let's see what a minimal Flask application looks like:

```
from flask import Flask
app = Flask(__name__)
@app.route('/')
def index():
  return 'Hello World!'
```

That's it, we are done with the minimal Flask application. It's very simple to configure and create a microservice with Flask.

Let's discuss what exactly the preceding code is doing and how we would run the program:

1. First, we imported a Flask class.
2. Next, we created an instance of the Flask class. This instance will be our WSGI application. This first argument will be the name of the module or package. Here, we created a single module, hence we used __name__. This is needed so that Flask knows where to look for templates, static, and other directories.
3. Then, we used app.route as a decorator with a URL name as a parameter. This will define and map the route with the specified function.
4. The function will be invoked to the HTTP request with the URL specified in the route decorator.

To run this program, you can either use the flask command or python -m flask, but before that, you need to set an environment variable as FLASK_APP with a module file name of where the Flask instance was defined:

```
$ export FLASK_APP=hello_world.py
$ flask run
* Serving Flask app "flask_todo.hello_world"
* Running on http://127.0.0.1:5000/ (Press CTRL+C to quit)
```

This launches a built-in server that is good enough for testing and debugging locally. The following is a screenshot of the localhost running in the browser:

Of course, it wouldn't work with production, but Flask provides numerous options for deployment. You can have a look at http://flask.pocoo.org/docs/0.12/deploying/ #deployment for more information, but in our case, we are going to deploy to a serverless environment on AWS Lambda and API Gateway using Zappa.

Configuring with Zappa

In order to configure Zappa, it's required that you have Zappa installed, as mentioned in the previous chapter. Zappa provides the zappa init command, which enables a user interactive mode initialization so that we can configure the Python application.

I followed the default configuration settings that were suggested by the zappa init command. This generates the zappa_settings.json file, which is the backbone for configuring any Python application with Zappa.

Here is the content of the zappa_settings.json file:

```
{
  "dev": {
      "app_function": "hello_world.app",
      "aws_region": "ap-south-1",
      "profile_name": "default",
      "project_name": "flask-todo",
      "runtime": "python3.6",
      "s3_bucket": "zappa-yrze3w53y"
  }
}
```

Now, during initialization, Zappa has the ability to identify the type of your Python application and generate the set attributes accordingly. In our case, Zappa detected the Python program as a Flask application. Hence, it asked for the Flask instance path, which we initialized as `app = Flask(__name__)` in the `hello_world.py` file.

Now that the Zappa configuration has been completed as per our basic needs, it's time to deploy it on AWS Lambda.

Building, testing, and deploying on AWS Lambda

We described the basic uses of Zappa with some basic commands in the previous chapter. Using these commands, we can build the deployment package, deploy the application, and perform other basic operations.

Once you have the `zappa_settings.json` file in place with all of the valid attributes, you can start the deployment process by using the `zappa deploy <stage_name>` command. As per our `zappa_settings.json` file, we have one stage defined as `dev`, so, to start the deployment, we can run the `deploy` command, as shown in the following code:

```
$ zappa deploy dev
```

The following screenshot describes the deployment flow:

```
(.env) abdulwali@LTP-711:~/flask_todo$ zappa deploy dev
Calling deploy for stage dev..
Creating flask-todo-dev-ZappaLambdaExecutionRole IAM Role..
Creating zappa-permissions policy on flask-todo-dev-ZappaLambdaExecutionRole IAM Role.
Downloading and installing dependencies..
 - sqlite==python36: Using precompiled lambda package
Packaging project as zip.
Uploading flask-todo-dev-1514664256.zip (5.6MiB)..
100%|                                                                        | 5.86M/5.86M
 [00:02<00:00, 2.52MB/s]
Scheduling..
Scheduled flask-todo-dev-zappa-keep-warm-handler.keep_warm_callback with expression rate(4 minutes)!
Uploading flask-todo-dev-template-1514664316.json (1.6KiB)..
100%|                                                                        | 1.62K/1.62K
 [00:00<00:00, 4.40KB/s]
Waiting for stack flask-todo-dev to create (this can take a bit)..
100%|                                                                        | 4/4 [
00:12<00:00,  4.29s/res]
Deploying API Gateway..
Deployment complete!: https://gxwjhwp91i.execute-api.ap-south-1.amazonaws.com/dev
(.env) abdulwali@LTP-711:~/flask_todo$ ▮
```

Once the Zappa deployment is complete, it generates a random API gateway endpoint. Zappa configures AWS Lambda with API Gateway based on the `zappa_settings.json` file.

Now, the Flask application is available through the previously generated API. Let's test it to see the **Hello World!** response from the Flask application. You can hit the URL in the browser, as shown in the following screenshot:

Now, let's move on to the next section to see an application development using the Flask framework.

A complete Flask Todo application

As we have seen how Zappa makes it super easy to deploy the Flask application, it's time to see the complete workflow that we may need while developing a Flask-based application. We are going to develop a Flask-based modularized application, where each functionality will be an independent module, such as authentication, Todo application, and so on.

The authentication module will be responsible for maintaining the authentication and authorization mechanism. It will also include the implementation of the login and sign up process.

Whereas the todo module will have a basic implementation of todo operations, this operation flow will be authorized by the authentication module. With the help of Flask extensions, we are going to manage and configure these modules. Apart from these core modules, we are also going to see the implementation related to the user interface, database configuration, and static file integration.

Prerequisite

In order to set up the development environment, we need to perform some configurations related to virtualenv and the required packages.

Virtualenv

Before we start working on the project, let's create a virtual environment and enable it, as shown in the following screenshot:

```
abdulw@ULTP-711:~/workspace/flask_todo(master)$ virtualenv .env -p python3.6
Running virtualenv with interpreter /usr/bin/python3.6
Using base prefix '/usr'
New python executable in /home/abdulw/workspace/flask_todo/.env/bin/python3.6
Also creating executable in /home/abdulw/workspace/flask_todo/.env/bin/python
Installing setuptools, pip, wheel...done.
abdulw@ULTP-711:~/workspace/flask_todo(master)$ source .env/bin/activate
(.env) abdulw@ULTP-711:~/workspace/flask_todo(master)$
```

Flask extensions

Flask is a microframework, but it has an extensible nature wherein you can add more features as per your needs. To develop a Todo application, we may need some basic features such as data persistence and a user authentication mechanism. So, while working on a Flask application, we are going to use some Flask extensions.

The Flask registry provides numerous extensions, which are standalone packages, and you can easily configure them with your Flask application instance. You can see the complete list of Flask extensions at: http://flask.pocoo.org/extensions/.

We are going to use the following Flask and Flask extensions packages:

- Flask==0.12.2
- Flask-Login==0.4.0
- Flask-SQLAlchemy==2.3.2
- Flask-WTF==0.14.2
- Flask-Migrate==2.1.1

I would recommend listing these packages in a separate file named requirements.txt and then installing them in one go, as follows:

```
pip install -r requirements.txt
```

This will install all of the listed packages with their dependencies.

Scaffolding

While implementing any project from scratch, you are free to design the scaffolding of your project. We are going to follow the scaffolding shown in the following screenshot:

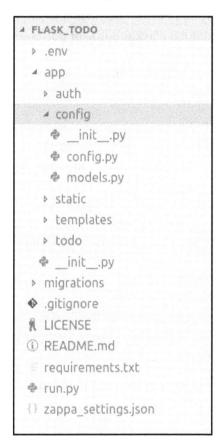

Let's look at each directory and its uses in detail:

- .env: This is our virtualenv directory, which has been created by the virtualenv command.
- auth: We are going to create a standalone generic authentication module using the Flask-Login and Flask-SqlAlchemy extensions.
- config: Here, we are going to create some configuration and generic database models, which may be needed by other modules.

- `static`: It's Flask standard practice to put the static content under the `static` directory. Hence, we will be using this directory for all required static content.
- `templates`: Flask has built-in support for the Jinja2 template engine and follows the standard layout for the template files based on the modules' names. We will see a detailed description of this later, when we actually utilize the templates.
- `todo`: This is a standalone Flask module or package which has the basic to-do functionality.
- `__init__.py`: This is Python's standard file that is required under a directory to build a Python package. We are going to write code here to configure our application.
- `migrations`: This directory is autogenerated by `Flask-Migrate`. In a future section, we will see how `Flask-Migrate` works.
- `.gitignore`: This contains a list of files and directories that should be ignored by Git versioning.
- `LICENSE`: I have created a Git repository using GitHub and included an MIT license for our `flask_todo` repository.
- `README.md`: This file is used to describe information about the repository on GitHub.
- `requirements.txt`: This is the file where we listed all the required packages mentioned in the preceding section.
- `run.py`: Here, we are going to create the final instance of our Flask application.
- `zappa_settings.json`: This file gets generated by Zappa and has Zappa-related configurations.

We will look at a detailed explanation of the code in the upcoming sections.

Configuration

While implementing any project, we may be required to have some configurations that are specific to different environments, such as toggling the debug mode in the development environment and monitoring in the production environment.

Flask has a flexible way of overcoming the configuration handling mechanism. Flask provides a `config` object on its instance. This `config` object is built by extending the Python `dictionary` object but with some additional features such as loading the configuration from a file, object, and default built-in configurations. You can look at a detailed description of the `config` mechanism at `http://flask.pocoo.org/docs/0.12/config/`.

In order to maintain the configuration based on environments, we are going to create a file called `config/config.py` with the following code:

```
import os
from shutil import copyfile

BASE_DIR = os.path.dirname(os.path.dirname(__file__))


def get_sqlite_uri(db_name):
    src = os.path.join(BASE_DIR, db_name)
    dst = "/tmp/%s" % db_name
    copyfile(src, dst)
    return 'sqlite:///%s' % dst


class Config(object):
    SECRET_KEY = os.environ.get('SECRET_KEY') or os.urandom(24)
    SQLALCHEMY_COMMIT_ON_TEARDOWN = True
    SQLALCHEMY_RECORD_QUERIES = True
    SQLALCHEMY_TRACK_MODIFICATIONS = False

    @staticmethod
    def init_app(app):
        pass

class DevelopmentConfig(Config):
    DEBUG = True
    SQLALCHEMY_DATABASE_URI = get_sqlite_uri('todo-dev.db')


class ProductionConfig(Config):
    SQLALCHEMY_DATABASE_URI = get_sqlite_uri('todo-prod.db')


config = {
    'dev': DevelopmentConfig,
    'production': ProductionConfig,
}
```

Here, we created a `Config` object as a base class that has some generic configuration and `Flask-SqlAlchemy` configurations. Then, we extended the base `Config` class with environment-specific classes. Finally, we created a mapping object, which we will use from the aforementioned keys.

Base model

SQLAlchemy is most famous for its **object-relational mapper (ORM)**, an optional component that provides the data mapper pattern, where classes can be mapped to the database in open-ended, multiple ways, allowing the object model and database schema to develop in a cleanly decoupled way from the beginning. We are using the Flask-SQLAlchemy extension here, which extends the support of SQLAlchemy. Flask-SQLAlchemy enhances the features that may need to be integrated with the Flask application.

We are going to combine the generic SQL operations which are required to interact by using Flask-SQLAlchemy. Hence, we are going to create a base model class and will use this class for other modules' model classes. That's the reason we are putting it under the config directory. Here is the models.py file.

File—config/models.py:

```python
from app import db


class BaseModel:
    """
    Base Model with common operations.
    """

    def delete(self):
        db.session.delete(self)
        db.session.commit()

    def save(self):
        db.session.add(self)
        db.session.commit()
        return self
```

You can see here that we group the database operations that are required by all models. The db instance was created in the app/__init__.py file using the Flask-SQLAlchemy extension.

Here, we have implemented the save and delete methods. db.Model defines a generic pattern to create a model class that represents the database table. In order to save and delete, we need to follow some predefined operations such as db.session.add(), db.session.delete(), and db.session.commit().

So, we grouped the generic operations under the `save` and `delete` methods. These methods will be called from a model class that will inherit them. We will look at this later when we create a model class by extending `BaseModel`.

Authentication

In order to develop an authentication module, we are going to use the `Flask-Login` extension. The `Flask-Login` extension provides a user session management mechanism. It handles the common tasks for managing user sessions such as logging in, logging out, and remembering the user.

To integrate `Flask-Login`, you need to create the instance and define some default parameters, as described in the following code snippet:

```
from flask_login import LoginManager
app = Flask(__name__)
login_manager = LoginManager()
login_manager.session_protection = 'strong'
login_manager.login_view = 'auth.login'
login_manager.login_message_category = "info"
login_manager.init_app(app)
```

We are going to create an authentication module as an `auth` package. An `auth` package will have basic scaffolding, as shown here:

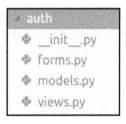

Blueprint

Before diving into a detailed description of each file, let's have a look at the instantiation Flask mechanism. As you already know, we are creating a submodule as an independent module under the `root` module. Flask introduces the concept of blueprint for making the submodule components under a common pattern.

The Flask blueprint instance is very similar to a Flask instance, but it's not an application object. Instead, it has the ability to construct and extend the parent application. With the help of blueprint, you can design a modular application.

The following is a code snippet of the `Blueprint` instantiation in the `auth/__init__.py` file:

```
from flask import Blueprint
auth = Blueprint('auth', __name__)
from . import views
```

As you can see, it has very similar characteristics to the `Flask` class and follows a similar pattern. Now, we will be using the `auth` instance of the `blueprint` in views to register routes. To execute the application, we need to bind the `blueprint` object with the Flask application instance.

The following is the code snippet from the `app/__init__.py` file where we are going to create the Flask application instance:

```
from .auth import auth as auth_blueprint
from app.config import config

app = Flask(__name__)
app.config.from_object(config[environment])

app.register_blueprint(auth_blueprint, url_prefix='/auth')
```

With the help of the `register_blueprint` method, we are registering the `auth` module blueprint and we can add the URL prefix as well. We will have the complete description of this file after we look at the `todo` module explanation.

Models

Let's start by creating the `User` model with basic functionality. The following is a code snippet of the user model.

File—`auth/models.py`:

```
import re
from datetime import datetime

from app.config.models import BaseModel
from flask_login.mixins import UserMixin
from sqlalchemy.orm import synonym
from werkzeug.security import generate_password_hash, check_password_hash
```

```
from app import db
from app import login_manager


class User(UserMixin, BaseModel, db.Model):
    __tablename__ = 'user'
    id = db.Column(db.Integer, primary_key=True)
    _email = db.Column('email', db.String(64), unique=True)
    password_hash = db.Column(db.String(128))


    def __init__(self, **kwargs):
        super(User, self).__init__(**kwargs)

    def __repr__(self):
        return '<User {0}>'.format(self.email)

    @property
    def email(self):
        return self._email

    @email.setter
    def email(self, email):
        if not len(email) <= 64 or not bool(re.match(r'^\S+@\S+\.\S+$',
email)):
            raise ValueError('{} is not a valid email
address'.format(email))
        self._email = email

    email = synonym('_email', descriptor=email)

    @property
    def password(self):
        raise AttributeError('password is not a readable attribute')

    @password.setter
    def password(self, password):
        if not bool(password):
            raise ValueError('no password given')

        hashed_password = generate_password_hash(password)
        if not len(hashed_password) <= 128:
            raise ValueError('not a valid password, hash is too long')
        self.password_hash = hashed_password

    def verify_password(self, password):
        return check_password_hash(self.password_hash, password)
```

```
        def to_dict(self):
            return {
                'email': self.email
            }


    @login_manager.user_loader
    def load_user(user_id):
        return User.query.get(int(user_id))
```

Now, we have created the `User` model, but how does it relate or map with the `Flask-Login` extension? The answer to this is the `load_user` method, which is wrapped by the `login_manager.user_loader` decorator. Flask provides this method to load the user into the session. This method is called with the `user_id` that's present in the session.

We can persist the user's data into the database with the help of the `User` model. As a web application, user data needs to enter through a user interface such as HTML. As per our requirements, we need two types of HTML forms for login and sign up functionality.

Let's move on to the next section and learn about rendering HTML forms through Flask.

Forms

`Flask-WTF` extensions provide the ability to develop forms in Flask and render them through Jinja2 templates. `Flask-WTF` extends the `WTForms` library, which has standard patterns to design a form.

We need two forms for this, such as `SignupForm` and `LoginForm`. The following is the code for creating forms classes.

File—`auth/forms.py`:

```
from flask_wtf import FlaskForm
from wtforms import StringField, PasswordField, SubmitField
from wtforms.validators import Required, Length, Email, EqualTo

class LoginForm(FlaskForm):
    email = StringField(
        'Email', validators=[Required(), Length(1,64), Email()]
    )
    password = PasswordField(
        'Password', validators=[Required()]
    )
    submit = SubmitField('Log In')
```

```
class SignupForm(FlaskForm):
    email = StringField(
        'Email', validators=[Required(), Length(1,64), Email()]
    )
    password = PasswordField(
        'Password', validators=[
            Required(),
            EqualTo('confirm_password', message='Password must match.')]
    )
    confirm_password = PasswordField(
        'Confirm Password', validators=[Required()]
    )
    submit = SubmitField('Sign up')
```

Here, we create the forms with some validations. Now, we are going to use these forms in the views section, where we are going to render the templates along with the forms context.

Views

Flask implemented the views in a very flexible way, where you can define the routes along with them. Flask's generic views implementation is inspired by Django's generic views. We will look at a detailed description of method views in a further section, but here, we are going to use simple views.

The following is the views snippet.

File—auth/views.py:

```
from flask import render_template, redirect, url_for
from flask_login import login_user, login_required, logout_user

from app.auth import auth
from app.auth.forms import LoginForm, SignupForm
from app.auth.models import User

@auth.route('/login', methods=['GET', 'POST'])
def login():
    form = LoginForm()
    if form.validate_on_submit():
        user_by_email = User.query.filter_by(email=form.email.data).first()
        if user_by_email is not None and
user_by_email.verify_password(form.password.data):
            login_user(user_by_email)
            return redirect(url_for('todo.list'))
    return render_template('auth/login.html', form=form)
```

```
@auth.route('/signup', methods=['GET', 'POST'])
def signup():
    form = SignupForm()
    if form.validate_on_submit():
        if not User.query.filter_by(email=form.email.data).scalar():
            User(
                email = form.email.data,
                password = form.password.data
            ).save()
            return redirect(url_for('auth.login'))
        else:
            form.errors['email'] = 'User already exists.'
            return render_template('auth/signup.html', form=form)
    return render_template('auth/signup.html', form=form)


@auth.route('/logout')
@login_required
def logout():
    logout_user()
    return redirect(url_for('auth.login'))
```

Here, we created the /login, /signup, and /logout routes, which we invoke based on HTTP requests. We are rendering an empty form instance on the HTTP GET request and processing the data on the POST request by using the Flask-WTF method and the validate_on_submit() method. While rendering the template, we are passing the form instance and redirect based on required actions.

Let's have a look at the templates mechanism in the next section.

Templates

Flask has built-in support for Jinja2 templating. Jinja2 templating has a standard defined pattern for rendering the HTML. We can place dynamic content by passing the context argument. Jinja2 gives an ability to render HTML with some expressions and conditions, extending and including template features.

Flask follows a standard templating scaffolding structure to lay out all template files. The following is the scaffolding we followed by creating a templates directory under the project's root directory and then creating subdirectories based on other module names:

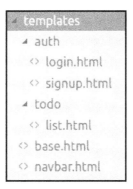

Here, we have created templates as per the module and put the generic templates under the root directory.

Similarly, we have maintained the static file's scaffolding:

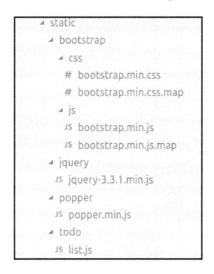

We kept the static libraries and modules-related files. With the help of the `url_for` method, we can get the relative path of any static files and routes. Hence, in the following template, we included all static files using a `url_for` method, such as `<link rel="stylesheet" href="{{ url_for('static', filename='bootstrap/css/bootstrap.min.css')}}">`.

In the same way, we are going to include all static files in the base template.

File—`templates/base.html`:

```
<!DOCTYPE html>
<html lang="en">
<head>
    <meta charset="UTF-8">
    <meta name="viewport" content="width=device-width, initial-scale=1.0">
    <meta http-equiv="X-UA-Compatible" content="ie=edge">
    <meta name="csrf-token" content="{{ csrf_token() }}">
    <meta name="author" content="AbdulWahid AbdulHaque">
    <title>Flask Todo App</title>

    <link rel="stylesheet" href="{{ url_for('static',
filename='bootstrap/css/bootstrap.min.css') }}">
    <link rel="stylesheet" href="{{ url_for('static',
filename='bootstrap/css/bootstrap.min.css.map') }}">
    {% block css %}{% endblock %}

    <script type="text/javascript" src="{{ url_for('static',
filename='jquery/jquery-3.3.1.min.js')}}"></script>
    <script type="text/javascript" src="{{ url_for('static',
filename='bootstrap/js/bootstrap.min.js')}}"></script>
    <script type="text/javascript" src="{{ url_for('static',
filename='popper/popper.min.js')}}"></script>
    {% block js %}{% endblock %}
</head>
<body>
    {% include 'navbar.html' %}
    {% block body %}{% endblock %}
    <script type="text/javascript">
        $('.dropdown-toggle').dropdown();
    </script>
</body>
</html>
```

We defined all generic HTML that is required on all other templates. We also created a basic bootstrap navbar and kept this in `navbar.html`, which is included in the `base.html` template by `{% include 'navbar.html' %}`. As you can see, Jinja2 templating makes it super easy to maintain the templates and provide a standard pattern.

The following is a code snippet of the `navbar.html` template where we created a navbar using Bootstrap CSS classes.

File—`templates/navbar.html`:

```
<nav class="navbar navbar-expand-lg navbar-light bg-light">
    <a class="navbar-brand" href="#">Todo's</a>
    <button class="navbar-toggler" type="button" data-toggle="collapse"
data-target="#navbarNavDropdown" aria-controls="navbarNavDropdown" aria-
expanded="false" aria-label="Toggle navigation">
        <span class="navbar-toggler-icon"></span>
    </button>
    <div class="collapse navbar-collapse" id="navbarNavDropdown">
        {% if current_user.is_authenticated %}
        <ul class="navbar-nav ml-auto">
            <li class="nav-item dropdown ml-auto">
                <a class="nav-link dropdown-toggle" href="#"
id="navbarDropdownMenuLink" data-toggle="dropdown" aria-haspopup="true"
aria-expanded="false">
                    Welcome <i>{{ current_user.email }}</i>
                </a>
                <div class="dropdown-menu" aria-
labelledby="navbarDropdownMenuLink">
                    <a class="dropdown-item"
href="../auth/logout">Logout</a>
                </div>
            </li>
        </ul>
        {% endif %}
    </div>
</nav>
```

While designing `navbar.html`, we added some conditional statements to display the logged-in user's information and logout options when the user is logged in.

Let's move on to the sign up and login page. The following is the code snippet for the sign up page.

File—`templates/auth/signup.html`:

```
{% extends "base.html" %}

{% block body %}
<div class="container align-middle mx-auto" style="width:30%; margin-
top:5%">
    <div class="card bg-light mb-3">
        <div class="card-header"><h3>Sign Up</h3></div>
        <div class="card-body">
            <form method="post">
                {{ form.hidden_tag() }}
                {% if form.errors %}
                    {% for error in form.errors.values() %}
                        <div class="alert alert-danger" role="alert">
                            {{error}}
                        </div>
                    {% endfor %}
                  {% endif %}
                <div class="form-group">
                    <label for="exampleInputEmail1">Email address</label>
                    {{ form.email(class_="form-control",
id="exampleInputEmail1", placeholder="Email", maxlength=128)}}
                    <small id="emailHelp" class="form-text text-
muted">We'll never share your email with anyone else.</small>
                </div>
                <div class="form-group">
                    <label for="exampleInputPassword1">Password</label>
                    {{ form.password(class_="form-control",
placeholder="Password") }}
                </div>
                <div class="form-group">
                    <label for="exampleInputPassword">Confirm
Password</label>
                    {{ form.confirm_password(class_="form-control",
placeholder="Confirm Password") }}
                </div>
                <div class="form-group">
                    {{ form.submit(class_="btn btn-primary btn-lg") }}
                    <a class="float-right" href="login">Already have
account.</a>
                </div>
            </form>
        </div>
    </div>
</div>
{% endblock %}
```

Here is the output of the **Sign Up** page:

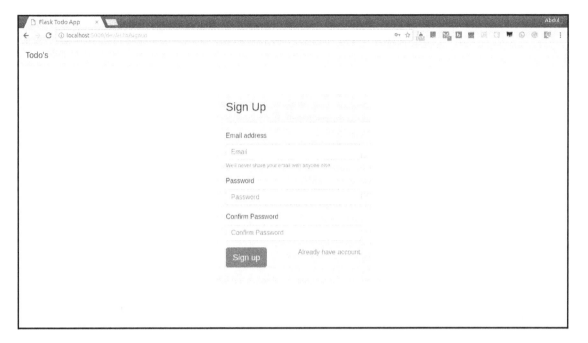

On the HTTP GET request on the `auth.signup` view, this will return an empty form and render it through the `signup.html` template. We also added code to receive the sign up data on the HTTP POST request in the sign up view. We persist the user data on the sign up process using the `User` model.

Here is the login template.

File—templates/auth/login.html:

```
{% extends "base.html" %}

{% block body %}
<div class="container align-middle mx-auto" style="width:30%; margin-
top:5%">
    <div class="card bg-light mb-3">
        <div class="card-header"><h3>Login</h3></div>
        <div class="card-body">
            <form method="post">
                {{ form.hidden_tag() }}
                {% if form.errors %}
                    <div class="has-error"><strong>Unable to login.
Typo?</strong></div>
                {% endif %}
                <div class="form-group">
                    <label for="exampleInputEmail1">Email address</label>
                    {{ form.email(class_="form-control",
id="exampleInputEmail1", placeholder="Email", maxlength=128)}}
                    <small id="emailHelp" class="form-text text-
muted">We'll never share your email with anyone else.</small>
                </div>
                <div class="form-group">
                    <label for="exampleInputPassword1">Password</label>
                    {{ form.password(class_="form-control",
id="exampleInputPassword1", placeholder="Password") }}
                </div>
                <div class="form-group">
                    {{ form.submit(class_="btn btn-primary btn-lg") }}
                    <a class="float-right" href="signup">New around here?
Sign up</a>
                </div>
            </form>
        </div>
    </div>
</div>
{% endblock %}
```

Now, the user can proceed and log in to the system, For login, we have created the login form and rendered it through the auth.login view. The following is a screenshot of the **Login** page:

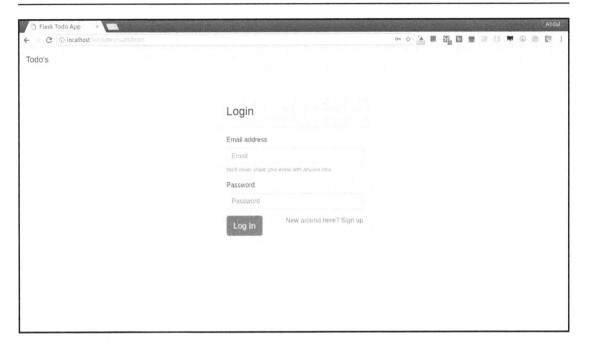

On the HTTP POST request, we are processing the user login mechanism using the Flask-Login extension, which provides a function called login_user and performs the login process. It creates a session and adds user_id into the session to remember the user for the further request until we remove the user from the session or perform the logout with the logout_user method, as mentioned in the auth.logout view.

The authentication process completes here, as the user login executes successfully and redirects the user to another page or template. Now, it's time to move on to the todo module.

Todo

The Todo program is considered to be a straightforward and simple application, and it is widely used to explain any language or framework after hello world!. We follow the same scaffolding structure for the todo module as well.

The following is a screenshot of the scaffolding for the todo module:

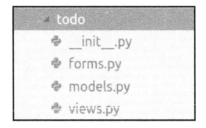

Let's see the detailed description for each file in the todo module.

Blueprint

Flask introduces the concept of blueprint for developing application components and command patterns in an application or across multiple applications. It helps to comprehend large-scale applications by centralizing the root Flask application object. Blueprint acts as a separate Flask application without creating an actual Flask application object, and is able to instantiate application objects, initialize several extensions, and register a collection. It also provides template filters, static files, templates, and other utilities.

As explained in the auth module, we will also create the Blueprint instance for the Todo application. This will be configured in the app.__init__.py file, which is where we created the Flask application instance.

The following is a code snippet of the todo module's blueprint.

File—todo/__init__.py:

```
from flask import Blueprint

todo = Blueprint('todo', __name__)

from . import views
```

Once we have created the blueprint object of the todo module, we can use it to add routes in views and register the blueprint with the Flask application instance.

The following is the code snippet of app/__init__.py, which is where we are going to register blueprint:

```
from .auth import auth as auth_blueprint
from app.config import config

app = Flask(__name__)
app.config.from_object(config[environment])

app.register_blueprint(todo_blueprint, url_prefix='/todos')
```

Model

We are going to use Flask-SQLAlchemy to create a todo model. It will have a relationship with the User model with a backward reference, so that we can query the todo data that's related to the User model.

The following is the code snippet for the todo model.

File—todo/models.py:

```
from datetime import datetime
from app import db
from app.config.models import BaseModel


class Todo(db.Model, BaseModel):
    __tablename__ = 'todo'
    id = db.Column(db.Integer, primary_key=True)
    title = db.Column(db.String(128))
    is_completed = db.Column(db.Boolean, default=False)
    created_by = db.Column(db.String(64), db.ForeignKey('user.email'))
    user = db.relationship('User', backref=db.backref('todos', lazy=True))

    def __init__(self, title, created_by=None, created_at=None):
        self.title = title
        self.created_by = created_by
        self.created_at = created_at or datetime.utcnow()

    def __repr__(self):
        return '<{0} Todo: {1} by {2}>'.format(
            self.status, self.title, self.created_by or 'None')

    @property
    def status(self):
        return 'finished' if self.is_completed else 'open'
```

```
def finished(self):
    self.is_completed = True
    self.finished_at = datetime.utcnow()
    self.save()

def reopen(self):
    self.is_completed = False
    self.finished_at = None
    self.save()

def to_dict(self):
    return {
        'title': self.title,
        'created_by': self.created_by,
        'status': self.status,
    }
```

Here, we created the todo model with basic functionality and validation. Now, we will use this model to persist the `todo` data. However, we also need to have a UI for users to enter the `todo` data and perform some actions.

Forms

We will have a simple todo form in which we have a textbox with a **Submit** button. It should also contain the list view to display the todo data.

The following is a code snippet of the Todo form.

File—`todo/forms.py`:

```
from flask_wtf import FlaskForm
from wtforms import StringField, SubmitField
from wtforms.validators import Required, Length


class TodoForm(FlaskForm):
    title = StringField(
        'What needs to be done?', validators=[Required(), Length(1, 128)]
    )
    submit = SubmitField('Submit')
```

As you can see, our Todo form is straightforward with some basic validation. It's time to use this form in views to render them into HTML template.

Views

We created the instance of a blueprint for todo, and we will use this instance to create the routes in views. The following is the code snippet for views.

File—`todo/views.py`:

```python
import json

from flask import render_template, redirect, url_for, jsonify, request
from flask_login import login_required, current_user
from app.todo import todo
from app.todo.forms import TodoForm
from app.todo.models import Todo


@todo.route('/', methods=['GET', 'POST'])
@login_required
def list():
    context = dict()
    form = TodoForm()
    if form.validate_on_submit():
        Todo(form.title.data, created_by=current_user.email).save()
        return redirect(url_for('todo.list'))
    context['form'] = form
    context['todos'] = current_user.todos
    context['items_left'] = len([todo for todo in current_user.todos if not
todo.is_completed])
    return render_template('todo/list.html', **context)


@todo.route('/<todo_id>', methods=['DELETE'])
@login_required
def remove(todo_id):
    Todo.query.filter_by(id=int(todo_id)).delete()
    return jsonify({'message': 'Todo removed successfully'})


@todo.route('/<todo_id>', methods=['PATCH'])
@login_required
def update(todo_id):
    data = json.loads([k for k in request.form.keys()][0])
    todo = Todo.query.filter_by(id=int(todo_id)).scalar()
    if data.get('status'):
        todo.finished()
    else:
        todo.reopen()
    return jsonify({'message': 'Todo updated successfully'})
```

We defined three routes here. We have already used `todos` as the prefix while registering the todo blueprint on the Flask application object. Keeping that in mind, we have decided to use the route URLs.

To persist the todo data, we need to perform four types of action, which are—create a todo item, list todo items, update any specific item, and delete any specific todo item. These actions are nothing but a standard form of **CRUD** (**Create**, **Retrieve**, **Update**, **Delete**) operations.

CREATE

For creating an action, we decided to have the URL as `/`, but with the prefix, it would become `todos/`. On the HTTP `POST` request, we expect the todo data from the user, and based on the submitted data, we will create the todo data using the todo model, for example, `Todo(form.description.data, creator=current_user.email).save()`.

RETRIEVE

On the HTTP `GET` request, we would render the template `todo/list.html` with a context that would include the form instance, list of todo data, and todos count. As described in the preceding code snippet, we get the user-related todo data such as `current_user.todos` and filter the data using list compensation. Then, we prepare the context and pass it to the `render_template` method to display the data in HTML.

UPDATE

To update the todo data, we would use the HTTP `PATCH` request for the route `todos/<todo_id>`. But, this time, we don't have any form and we are required to pass the data, hence we are using jQuery to make an Ajax query for the `PATCH` request.

We defined some attributes and methods to mark the todo data as finished, so based on the update data, we would use these methods to update the todo record.

DELETE

Similarly to deleting the todo record from the database, we need to use the todo model's query methods, such as `Todo.query.filter_by(id=int(todo_id)).delete()`. As you can see, the routing views are straightforward. Now, let's have a look at templates.

Templates

A lot of work needs to be done to accomplish the todo workflow. We defined the `templates/todo/list.html` template to display the todo form and a list of todo records. In a previous section, we described how we rendered and passed the context data.

The following is the code snippet for the todo list template.

File—`templates/todo/list.html`:

```
{% extends "base.html" %}
{% block js %}
    <script src="{{url_for('static', filename='todo/list.js')}}"></script>
{% endblock %}
{% block body %}
<div class="container align-middle mx-auto" style="width:30%; margin-
top:5%">
    <div class="card mb-3">
        <div class="card-header" align="center"><h3>todo's</h3></div>
        <div class="card-body">
            <form method="post" class="form-inline">
                {{ form.hidden_tag() }}
                {% if form.errors %}
                    <div class="has-error"><strong>Invalid task.
Typo?</strong></div>
                {% endif %}
                <div class="form-group ml-3">
                    {{ form.title(class_="form-control", placeholder="What
needs to be done?", maxlength=128)}}
                </div>
                <div class="form-group">
                    {{ form.submit(class_="btn btn-primary ml-2") }}
                </div>
            </form>
            <div class="badge badge-pill badge-info ml-3 mt-2">
                {{items_left}} items left
            </div>
            <ul class="list-group list-group-flush mt-3" id="todolist">
                {% for todo in todos %}
                <li class="list-group-item" id="{{todo.id}}">
```

```html
                        <input type="checkbox" aria-label="Checkbox for
following text input" {% if todo.is_completed %} checked {% endif %}>
                        {{todo.title}}
                        <span class="badge badge-danger badge-pill float-
right">X</span>
                    </li>
                    {% endfor %}
                </ul>
            </div>
        </div>
</div>

<script>

</script>
{% endblock %}
```

We used the context data to display the todo form and list of records. There are some operations that we need to write jQuery code for, such as updating the todo based on the checkbox action, and removing the todo based on the **delete** button action.

The following is the jQuery code snippet.

File—`static/todo/list.js`:

```javascript
var csrftoken = $('meta[name=csrf-token]').attr('content');
function csrfSafeMethod(method) {
// these HTTP methods do not require CSRF protection
return (/^(GET|HEAD|OPTIONS|TRACE)$/.test(method));
}

$.ajaxSetup({
    beforeSend: function(xhr, settings) {
        if (!csrfSafeMethod(settings.type) && !this.crossDomain) {
          xhr.setRequestHeader("X-CSRFToken", csrftoken);
        }
    }
  });

$(document).ready(function(){

    // Update todo
    $('#todolist li>input[type="checkbox"]').on('click', function(e){
        var todo_id = $(this).parent().closest('li').attr('id');
        $.ajax({
            url : todo_id,
            method : 'PATCH',
            data : JSON.stringify({status: $(this).prop('checked')}),
```

```
        success : function(response){
            location.reload();
        },
        error : function(error){
            console.log(error)
        }
    })
})

// Remove todo
$('#todolist li>span').on('click', function(e){
    var todo_id = $(this).parent().closest('li').attr('id');
    $.ajax({
        url : todo_id,
        method : 'DELETE',
        success : function(response){
            location.reload();
        },
        error : function(error){
            console.log(error)
        }
    })
})
})
})
```

While making the Ajax request, we also added support for CSRF. Ajax requests are simple and straightforward as these are requests that are being served through the previously mentioned todo routes. The following is a screenshot of the todo list page:

Now, we are done with the `todo` module, and it's time to configure the todo blueprint with a Flask application object.

FLASK_APP

In any Flask project, we create the Flask application object and refer to the file path with a value to the `FLASK_APP` argument or environment variable. In our case, we created a modular application that has separate modules defined for specific operations, but now we need to combine all of these modules in one place. We have already seen the `blueprint` objects and their integration. Here, we will look at the actual process of combining the blueprint and other required extensions.

The following is the code snippet for the Flask application object.

File—`app/__init__.py`:

```
from flask import Flask
from flask_sqlalchemy import SQLAlchemy
from flask_login import LoginManager
from flask_migrate import Migrate
from flask_wtf.csrf import CSRFProtect

from app.config import config

db = SQLAlchemy()
migrate = Migrate()
csrf = CSRFProtect()

login_manager = LoginManager()
login_manager.session_protection = 'strong'
login_manager.login_view = 'auth.login'
login_manager.login_message_category = "info"

def create_app(environment):
    app = Flask(__name__)
    app.config.from_object(config[environment])

    csrf.init_app(app)
    db.init_app(app)
    migrate.init_app(app, db=db)
    login_manager.init_app(app)

    from .auth import auth as auth_blueprint
    app.register_blueprint(auth_blueprint, url_prefix='/auth')
```

```
from .todo import todo as todo_blueprint
app.register_blueprint(todo_blueprint, url_prefix='/todos')

return app
```

Here, we are configuring the extensions and blueprints, but under a method called `create_app`. This method needs an argument to set up the environment-specific configuration, hence it's really good to have this function and get the Flask application instance for a specific configuration.

The following is the code snippet for `run.py`, where we will be using the `create_app` method.

File—`flask_todo/run.py`:

```
from app import create_app

app = create_app('dev')
```

Here, we used the `dev` environment configuration. You can use this file as your `FLASK_APP` parameter, for example, `FLASK_APP=run.py flask run`.

We are done with the todo app development, so now it's time to proceed with deployment using Zappa.

Deployment

We are going to initiate the deployment using Zappa. To configure Zappa, you need to have Zappa installed and configured with your AWS credentials by using AWS CLI. Once we have installed Zappa and dealt with the AWS CLI configuration, we can move ahead and deploy the Todo application.

The following is a screenshot of the `zappa init` command process:

When we run the `zappa init` command, Zappa automatically identifies the framework type and suggests the required parameters. In our case, we kept the `app_function` name as `run.app` because we are initiating the `flask app` object through the `create_app` method in `run.py`.

The `zappa init` command creates the `zappa_settings.json` file, which has all the configured parameters. You are free to modify it as per your needs.

Now, it's time to execute the deployment process using the `zappa deploy <stage_name>` command. Initially, we would use the `zappa deploy` command. Once our app has been deployed, we can't use the `zappa deploy` command. Instead, we need to use the `zappa update <stage_name>` command.

The following is the code for the `zappa deploy dev` command:

```
$ zappa deploy dev
Calling deploy for stage dev..
Creating chapter-3-dev-ZappaLambdaExecutionRole IAM Role..
Creating zappa-permissions policy on chapter-3-dev-ZappaLambdaExecutionRole
IAM Role.
Downloading and installing dependencies..
 - sqlite==python36: Using precompiled lambda package
Packaging project as zip.
Uploading chapter-3-dev-1529318192.zip (9.4MiB)..
100%|

                        | 9.87M/9.87M [00:05<00:00, 1.89MB/s]
Scheduling..
Scheduled chapter-3-dev-zappa-keep-warm-handler.keep_warm_callback with
expression rate(4 minutes)!
Uploading chapter-3-dev-template-1529318886.json (1.6KiB)..
100%|

                        | 1.62K/1.62K [00:00<00:00, 4.87KB/s]
Waiting for stack chapter-3-dev to create (this can take a bit)..
50%|                                        | 2/4 [00:09<00:10,
5.29s/res]
Deploying API Gateway..
Deployment complete!:
https://m974nz8zld.execute-api.ap-south-1.amazonaws.com/dev
```

We are done with deployment and are able to access the Todo application on a generated URL, as shown in the following screenshot.

Here is the output after visiting the URL (`https://m974nz8zld.execute-api.ap-south-1.amazonaws.com/dev/auth/signup`):

I am going to keep the `flask_todo` Lambda function live so that you can try it anytime. I have created a GitHub repository (`https://github.com/PacktPublishing/Building-Serverless-Python-Web-Services-with-Zappa/tree/master/chapter_3`) and pushed all of the code base to it for future reference.

Summary

In this chapter, we covered the workflow of creating a Flask-based application and deploying it over a serverless environment using Zappa. With the help of Zappa, we moved the application to AWS Lambda and performed operations to maintain the deployment. While deploying the application, we don't need to configure the traditional server software; instead, we just use a JSON file to configure the deployment with multiple environments.

In the next chapter, we are going to see REST API's implementation.

Questions

1. What is Amazon API Gateway?
2. What is the use of `function_name` in `zappa_settings.json`?

Building a Flask-Based REST API with Zappa

4

So far, we have seen how we can develop a Flask-based application and deploy it over a serverless infrastructure, we have created a complete web application along with a HTML rendering process, and we have used various Flask extensions to build the application in a very efficient way.

In this chapter, we are going to develop a Flask-based RESTful API. This will cover the REST API implementation using Flask and deploying it using Zappa. In Chapter 1, *Amazon Web Services for Serverless,* we saw the manual process of integrating the AWS Lambda and API Gateway, so now we will be deploying the REST API in an automated way using Zappa. Zappa will take care of the Flask REST API integration with API Gateway by configuring the proxy settings to pass the request to invoke Lambda functions.

Let's move on in our journey and develop a REST API over a serverless architecture.

In this chapter, we will cover the following topics:

- Installing and configuring Flask
- Designing a REST API
- Integrating Zappa
- Building, testing, and deploying the REST API using Zappa

Technical requirements

We are going to create a Flask-based REST API, and therefore we have some prerequisites before starting the practical implementation:

- Ubuntu 16.04 LTS
- Python 3.6

- Virtual environment
- Flask 0.12.2
- Flask-JWT 0.3.2
- Flask-SQLAlchemy 2.3.2
- Flask-Migrate 2.1.1
- Flask-RESTful 0.3.6
- Zappa 0.45.1
- Flask
- Flask extensions

Installing and configuring Flask

We are going to develop a Flask-based REST API that will be deployed as serverless on AWS Lambda. So, here, installing and configuring Flask would be in a virtual environment.

We are going to be creating a virtual environment and enabling it to install all the required packages. This can be done using the following command:

```
virtualenv .env -p python3.6
source .env/bin/activate
```

Now, we are going to list all of the required packages in the requirements.txt file and we will install all of the packages at once. The following describes the content of the requirements.txt file:

```
Flask==0.12.2
Flask-JWT==0.3.2
Flask-SQLAlchemy==2.3.2
Flask-Migrate==2.1.1
flask-restful==0.3.6
zappa==0.45.1
```

Now, we can install all of these packages using the following command:

```
$ pip install -r requirements.txt
```

That's all of packages that will be installed in the virtual environment. Now, let's have a detailed explanation of these packages in the next section.

Flask extensions

Flask has a variety of extensions available that enhance the ability specific to any required feature. In our application, we are going to use multiple extensions, as mentioned in the previous section. These extensions follow a common pattern so that we can integrate them with Flask application objects.

We are going to design a Flask-based REST API application that will have a basic authentication, authorization, and CRUD operation on the Todo model by following the REST API communication standard and validation.

Let's have a look at the usages of these extensions in the upcoming sections.

Flask-JWT

The Flask-JWT extension enables the feature of **JWT** (**JSON Web Token**) functionality in the Flask environment. While designing the REST API, the JWT token plays an important role to authenticate and authorize the API access. We'll look at a detailed description about JWT in the next section.

Learning about JWT

JWT stands for **JSON Web Token**. It's a standard pattern in order to implement security and authenticity access for REST API interfaces. The JWT token is an encoded form of data issued by the server application and is used to authenticate the client access. The client is required to add the JWT token in a HTTP request as an authorization header.

We will be using the JWT token to authenticate the REST API's access. In case you need to understand the JWT mechanism in detail, I recommend reading the JWT documentation at: `https://jwt.io/introduction/`.

Flask-RESTful

The Flask-RESTful extension is designed to implement the REST API with the Flask framework. This extension follows the standard REST API implementation pattern and provides an easy way of REST API implementation. Before implementing the REST API, you must have a basic understanding of REST API standards, so let's have a look at the REST API basics.

Begining with REST

REST stands for **REpresentational State Transfer.** It is a well-defined standard that's used to implement server-client communication in order to persist data. REST follows the **JSON (JavaScript Object Notation)** data representation format to exchange the data.

REST defines some verbs on the HTTP method to perform CRUD operations, such as:

- GET: To retrieve the list of records and specific records with postfix ID parameters in the root URL, which also return a response with a 200 status code
- POST: To create the record on the server and return a response with a 201 status code
- PUT: To update all record fields on the server and returns a response with a 200 status code
- PATCH: To update a specific field in the record set on the server and return a response with a 200 status code
- DELETE: To delete the entire record set with the help of a record-specific ID in the URL, and return a response with a 204 status code

Now, it's time to see some practical work. Let's move on to the next section.

Designing the REST API

We are going to design a REST API for performing CRUD operations on our todos model. Our application will have a basic authentication and authorization workflow in order to secure the REST API endpoints.

The following is the scaffolding for our application:

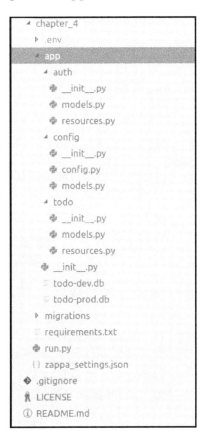

Here, we will have three individual packages called `config`, `auth`, and `todo` under the `app` module. We will configure and create the Flask application object in the `app` module's init file. The following is the code snippet of __init__.py, where we configured the Flask application object with extensions and the `config` object.

File—app/__init__.py:

```
from flask import Flask
from flask_sqlalchemy import SQLAlchemy
from flask_migrate import Migrate
from flask_jwt import JWT, jwt_required, current_identity

from app.config import config

db = SQLAlchemy()
```

```
migrate = Migrate()

def create_app(environment):
    app = Flask(__name__)
    app.config.from_object(config[environment])

    db.init_app(app)
    migrate.init_app(app, db=db)

    from .auth.models import User

    def authenticate(email, password):
        data = request.json
        user = User.query.filter_by(email=data['email']).first()
        if user is not None and user.verify_password(data['password']):
            return user

    def identity(payload):
        user_id = payload['identity']
        return User.query.filter_by(id=user_id).first()

    jwt = JWT(app, authenticate, identity)


    from .auth import auth as auth_blueprint
    app.register_blueprint(auth_blueprint, url_prefix='/auth')

    from .todo import todo as todo_blueprint
    app.register_blueprint(todo_blueprint)

    return app
```

We configured the Flask extensions such as Flask-SQLAlchemy and Flask-Migration, which are straightforward. Flask-JWT integration requires a little bit more work as we need to define the `authenticate` and `identity` methods and use them as parameters while initializing the JWT object. These methods are responsible for authenticating the user and identifying the user.

Apart from extension integration, we are going to create auth and todo apps as Flask blueprint objects and register them with the Flask application object using the `register_blueprint` method.

Let's have a detailed description of each package and it's uses.

Configuring the application settings

In the `config` package, we defined the application level configuration, which would be isolated as per the defined environment. The following is the content of the `config.py` file.

File—`config/config.py`:

```python
import os
from shutil import copyfile

BASE_DIR = os.path.dirname(os.path.dirname(__file__))


def get_sqlite_uri(db_name):
    src = os.path.join(BASE_DIR, db_name)
    dst = "/tmp/%s" % db_name
    copyfile(src, dst)
    return 'sqlite:///%s' % dst


class Config(object):
    SECRET_KEY = os.environ.get('SECRET_KEY') or os.urandom(24)
    SQLALCHEMY_COMMIT_ON_TEARDOWN = True
    SQLALCHEMY_RECORD_QUERIES = True
    SQLALCHEMY_TRACK_MODIFICATIONS = False

    @staticmethod
    def init_app(app):
        pass

class DevelopmentConfig(Config):
    DEBUG = True
    BUNDLE_ERRORS = True
    SQLALCHEMY_DATABASE_URI = get_sqlite_uri('todo-dev.db')


class ProductionConfig(Config):
    SQLALCHEMY_DATABASE_URI = get_sqlite_uri('todo-prod.db')


config = {
    'dev': DevelopmentConfig,
    'prod': ProductionConfig,
}
```

The `config` file exposes the `config` object, which contains different configuration objects as per your environment. In a similar fashion, you can add more environment as per your requirements.

 The `get_sqlite_uri` method is defined to set the `db` file in the `tmp` directory because AWS Lambda requires the SQLite `.db` file in memory at the time of execution.

We will conclude on all the configurations required by the application. So, we also defined a `BaseModel`, which combines all repeated operations needed by an SQL-Alchemy model query set object. The following code snippet is our `BaseModel`, which was inspired by Django's standard pattern to perform save, update, and delete operations. We can add more generic features if required.

File—`config/models.py`:

```
from app import db


class BaseModel:
    """
    Base Model with common operations.
    """

    def delete(self):
        db.session.delete(self)
        db.session.commit()

    def save(self):
        db.session.add(self)
        db.session.commit()
        return self
```

Here, we combined the `db` session operations in order to perform specific transactions such as save, update, and delete. This will help us extend the features of a model class.

Implementing authentication

Authentication is an essential feature to secure the REST API from unauthorized access. So, in order to implement the authentication layer, we are going to use the JWT mechanism. Here, we are going to design two REST APIs for registering a user and for login access.

To persist the data related to users, we would need to define a user model. The following is the code snippet of the `User` model.

File—`auth/models.py`:

```
import re
from datetime import datetime

from app.config.models import BaseModel
from sqlalchemy.orm import synonym
from werkzeug.security import generate_password_hash, check_password_hash
from app import db


class User(BaseModel, db.Model):
    __tablename__ = 'user'
    id = db.Column(db.Integer, primary_key=True)
    _email = db.Column('email', db.String(64), unique=True)
    password_hash = db.Column(db.String(128))


    def __init__(self, **kwargs):
        super(User, self).__init__(**kwargs)

    def __repr__(self):
        return '<User {0}>'.format(self.email)

    @property
    def email(self):
        return self._email

    @email.setter
    def email(self, email):
        if not len(email) <= 64 or not bool(re.match(r'^\S+@\S+\.\S+$',
email)):
            raise ValueError('{} is not a valid email
address'.format(email))
        self._email = email

    email = synonym('_email', descriptor=email)

    @property
    def password(self):
        raise AttributeError('password is not a readable attribute')

    @password.setter
    def password(self, password):
        if not bool(password):
```

```
        raise ValueError('no password given')

    hashed_password = generate_password_hash(password)
    if not len(hashed_password) <= 128:
        raise ValueError('not a valid password, hash is too long')
    self.password_hash = hashed_password

def verify_password(self, password):
    return check_password_hash(self.password_hash, password)

def to_dict(self):
    return {
        'email': self.email
    }
```

This is a basic `User` model with only two fields, which are `email` and `password`. Now, we are going to design a signup API and a login API. The signup API will only accept two parameters, email and password, and will create a user record in the database. The login API will be used to authenticate the user's credentials and will return a JWT token which will be used with other APIs as an authorization header.

Let's create the signup and login APIs. The following is the code snippet of the resource file that includes the contents of the API implementation logic.

File—`auth/resources.py`:

```
from flask import request, jsonify
from flask_restful import Resource, reqparse, abort
from flask_jwt import current_app
from app.auth.models import User


def generate_token(user):
    """ Currently this is workaround
    since the latest version that already has this function
    is not published on PyPI yet and we don't want
    to install the package directly from GitHub.
    See:
    https://github.com/mattupstate/flask-jwt/blob/9f4f3bc8dce9da5dd8a567dfada08
    54e0cf656ae/flask_jwt/__init__.py#L145
    """
    jwt = current_app.extensions['jwt']
    token = jwt.jwt_encode_callback(user)
    return token


class SignUpResource(Resource):
    parser = reqparse.RequestParser(bundle_errors=True)
```

```
    parser.add_argument('email', type=str, required=True)
    parser.add_argument('password', type=str, required=True)

    def post(self):
        args = self.parser.parse_args()
        if not User.query.filter_by(email=args['email']).scalar():
            User(
                email = args['email'],
                password = args['password']
            ).save()
            return {'message': 'Sign up successfully'}
        abort(400, message='Email already exists.')


class LoginResource(Resource):
    parser = reqparse.RequestParser(bundle_errors=True)
    parser.add_argument('email', type=str, required=True)
    parser.add_argument('password', type=str, required=True)

    def post(self):
        args = self.parser.parse_args()
        user = User.query.filter_by(email=args['email']).first()
        if user is not None and user.verify_password(args['password']):
            token = generate_token(user)
            return jsonify({'token': token.decode("utf-8")})
        abort(400, message='Invalid credentials')
```

Flask-RESTful provides a `Resource` class, which is used to define the API resource. It follows the REST standard and provides an easy way to create an API. As we are going to use the signup API on the HTTP most `request` method, we created a `post` method. Similarly, we designed the login API, where we are authenticating the user's credentials and returning a token.

 We have to return the custom method to generate the token since, at the time of writing, the Flask-JWT `PyPI` repository doesn't have an updated release, even though this feature has been added to the GitHub repository.

It's time to configure these resources classes with the `Blueprint` object. The following is the previously mentioned code snippet of the `auth/__init__.py` file.

File—`auth/__init__.py`:

```
from flask import Blueprint
from flask_restful import Api
from .resources import SignUpResource, LoginResource
```

```
auth = Blueprint('auth', __name__)
auth_api = Api(auth, catch_all_404s=True)

auth_api.add_resource(SignUpResource, '/signup', endpoint='signup')
auth_api.add_resource(LoginResource, '/login', endpoint='login')
```

Here, we have created the `Blueprint` object and configured it. Flask-RESTful provides an `API` class, and, using this class, we have registered our signup and login resources. That's it. Now, we can hit the signup and login URL with JSON data to perform the operation. We will have a complete demonstration of these REST APIs after the deployment process.

Implementing the todo API

Let's start the todo API implementation. We need to have a todo REST API endpoint to perform the CRUD operations. As per the REST standard, there would be only one endpoint URL, such as `/todos/<todo_id>/`. This endpoint will be used to persist the todo data into the database. We will need to have a Todo model to persist the data. The following is the code snippet of the Todo model.

File—`todo/models.py`:

```
from datetime import datetime
from app import db
from app.config.models import BaseModel


class Todo(db.Model, BaseModel):
    __tablename__ = 'todo'
    id = db.Column(db.Integer, primary_key=True)
    title = db.Column(db.String(128))
    is_completed = db.Column(db.Boolean, default=False)
    created_by = db.Column(db.String(64), db.ForeignKey('user.email'))
    user = db.relationship('User', backref=db.backref('todos', lazy=True))

    def __init__(self, title, created_by=None, created_at=None):
        self.title = title
        self.created_by = created_by

    def __repr__(self):
        return '<{0} Todo: {1} by {2}>'.format(
            self.status, self.title, self.created_by or 'None')

    @property
    def status(self):
```

```
        return 'completed' if self.is_completed else 'open'

    def completed(self):
        self.is_completed = True
        self.save()

    def reopen(self):
        self.is_completed = False
        self.save()

    def to_dict(self):
        return {
            'id': self.id,
            'title': self.title,
            'created_by': self.created_by,
            'status': self.status,
        }
```

Here, we have created the Todo model with some basic functionality. Now, we are going to use it in the API resource in order to persist the data from the REST endpoint. The following is the code snippet of resources.py, which contains the todo's REST API.

File—todo/resources.py:

```
from flask import request
from flask_restful import Resource, reqparse
from flask_jwt import current_identity, jwt_required

from .models import Todo


class TodoResource(Resource):

    decorators = [jwt_required()]

    def post(self):
        parser = reqparse.RequestParser(bundle_errors=True)
        parser.add_argument('title', type=str, required=True)

        args = parser.parse_args(strict=True)
        todo = Todo(args['title'],
created_by=current_identity.email).save()
        return todo.to_dict(), 201

    def get(self, todo_id=None):
        if todo_id:
            todos = Todo.query.filter_by(id=todo_id,
created_by=current_identity.email)
```

```
        else:
            todos = Todo.query.filter_by(created_by=current_identity.email)
        return [todo.to_dict() for todo in todos]

    def patch(self, todo_id=None):
        parser = reqparse.RequestParser(bundle_errors=True)
        parser.add_argument(
            'status',
            choices=('open', 'completed'),
            help='Bad choice: {error_msg}. Valid choices are \'open\' or
\'completed\'.',
            required=True)

        if not todo_id:
            return {'error': 'method not allowed'}, 405
        args = parser.parse_args(strict=True)
        todo = Todo.query.filter_by(id=todo_id,
created_by=current_identity.email).scalar()
        if args['status'] == "open":
            todo.reopen()
        elif args['status'] == 'completed':
            todo.completed()
        else:
            return {'error':'Invalid data!'}, 400
        return todo.to_dict(), 202

    def delete(self, todo_id=None):
        if not todo_id:
            return {'error': 'method not allowed'}, 405
        Todo.query.filter_by(id=int(todo_id),
created_by=current_identity.email).delete()
        return {}, 204
```

Here, we defined the `TodoResource` class, which will handle GET, POST, PUT, and DELETE HTTP requests. Based on the request type, we are performing the CRUD operation. We also used `reqparse` to defined the validation on the required data from the HTTP requests.

In order to secure `TodoResource`, we have added the `jwt_required` methods in the list of decorators of the `TodoResource` class, which will apply to all associated methods. Now, the `TodoResource` API will only be available with a valid authorization header, otherwise it will respond with the unauthorized access error.

We will see the complete working of this in an upcoming section.

Building, testing, and deploying the REST API using Zappa

We are done with development, and now it's time to deploy the app as serverless in AWS Lambda. We already described the prerequisites to configure Zappa and its associated configuration in the preceding chapter, so here I assume that you have a configured Zappa along with an AWS configuration.

Configuring Zappa

Once you have configured Zappa, you can initialize Zappa for your project. You need to run the `zappa init` command and follow the CLI questionnaire to configure your project with Zappa. I followed the default configuration settings suggested by Zappa. The `zappa init` command will generate the `zappa_settings.json` file, and we are free to modify this file as per our needs.

The following is a code snippet of the `zappa_settings.json` file.

File—`zappa_settings.json`:

```
{
    "dev": {
        "app_function": "run.app",
        "aws_region": "ap-south-1",
        "profile_name": "default",
        "project_name": "chapter-4",
        "runtime": "python3.6",
        "s3_bucket": "zappa-5xvirta98"
    }
}
```

Zappa maintains this JSON file in order to perform the deployment process. Now, we will move on to deploying the application.

Initiating deployment using Zappa

Once you are done with Zappa initialization, it's time to deploy the application. Zappa provides a `zappa deploy` command to deploy the application. This command will perform the deployment process, where it will create the deployment package as a ZIP file, push it onto AWS S3, and configure the AWS Lambda with the API Gateway. We described the complete deployment process in detail in the first chapter.

Once we run this with the `zappa deploy dev` command, our application will be hosted as a serverless application on AWS Lambda. If you wanted to redeploy the same application, then you would need to run the `zappa update dev` command, which will update the existing application.

Let's have a look at demonstrating the deployed application in the next section.

Demonstrating the deployed application

Zappa generates a random URL for the deployed application, and, on every new deployment, it will generate the URL. However, if you are just updating the deployment, then it won't change the URL. This is the URL we got from the Zappa deployment process: `https://jrzlw1zpdi.execute-api.ap-south-1.amazonaws.com/dev/`. We have written the auth and todo APIs with some endpoints, so you won't see anything on the base URL. We will be using our API endpoints as defined in the resources.

Sign up API

We designed the signup API with the endpoint as `/auth/signup`, which expects two parameters—`email` and `password`. This endpoint is responsible for creating the user record in the database. Once we get the successful response, we can use the same user credentials to perform the login and access other APIs.

The following is a screenshot of the signup API:

Here, we use the Advanced REST Client application to test the API. As you can see, we are creating the user record with the signup API. The signup API responds with a 200 status.

Login API

Now, we have a user record available in the database and we can use it to perform a login operation. The login API is responsible for validating the user's credentials and returning a JWT token. This JWT token will be used to authorize the todos API. The following is a screenshot of the login API being used through the REST client:

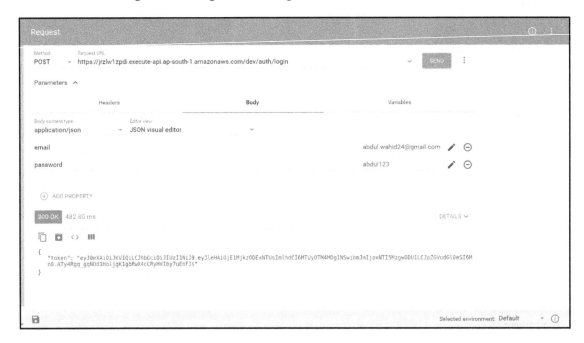

Here, you can see the login API execution, as we got the JWT token that will be used to authorize access to the todo API.

Todo API

Now that we have the JWT token through the login API, let's execute the Todo API. However, here, we will be looking at different scenarios on the Todo API. Our Todo API has an endpoint called `todos/<todo_id>`.

Todo API without authorization

Let's try the todo API without providing the authorization header:

As you can see, we got an unauthorized error from our application. Now, we are going to provide the authorization header with a JWT token.

Todo API with the authorization header

We will use the JWT token returned by the login API and set the authorization header. The value of the authorization header will be `JWT <token>`. Now, let's execute the API with CRUD operations.

The GET request looks as follows:

Here, we got the list of all todo records available in the database. We gained access as we set the authorization header.

The POST request looks as follows:

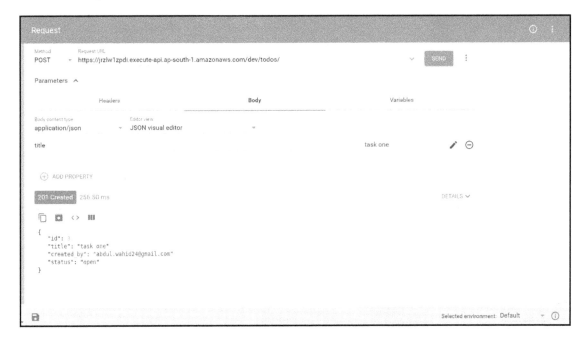

Here, we created a new todo record and got the response with a status code of 201. Now, with the base URL, we can execute the GET and POST requests, but, to perform the GET, PUT, and DELETE functions on specific records, we are required to mention the todo_id in the URL.

The POST request without payload data looks as follows:

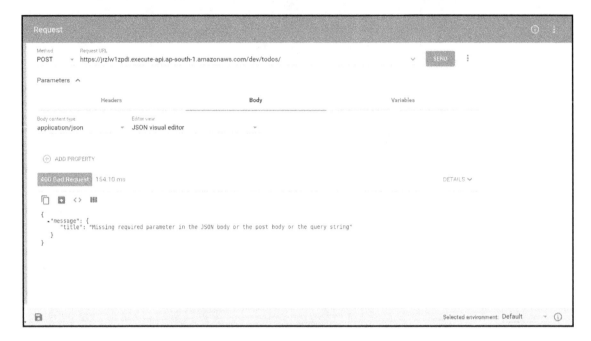

Here, we got the validation error as we haven't provided any payload. We managed this validation with the help of the reqparse module of the flask_restful library.

The GET request with the todo ID looks as follows:

You can see that we have used the todo ID in the URL to view a specific record set.

The PATCH request looks as follows:

Here, we updated the todo status and marked the todo records as finished.

The PATCH request with invalid data looks as follows:

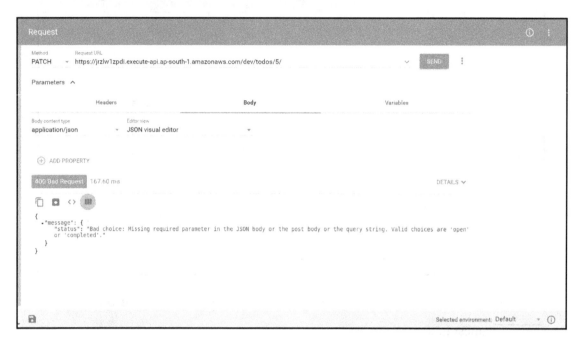

Here, we got the validation error as we defined the required choices using the
reqparse module, as mentioned here:

```
parser = reqparse.RequestParser(bundle_errors=True)
        parser.add_argument(
            'status',
            choices=('open', 'completed'),
            help='Bad choice: {error_msg}. Valid choices are \'open\' or
\'completed\'.',
            required=True)
```

The DELETE request looks as follows:

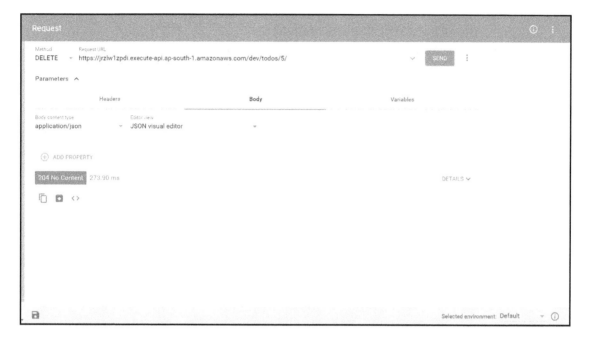

Finally, we deleted the record with the HTTP DELETE request. That's it! We are done with the REST API implementation.

Summary

In this chapter, we learned how to create a Flask-based REST API and configured it with some extensions. With the help of the Flask-JWT extension, we implemented security. The Flask-RESTful extension provides an easy interface to design the REST API. Finally, we configured Zappa to deploy the application in a serverless environment.

In the next chapter, we are going to see the Django application development as a serverless application on AWS Lambda. Stay tuned for it.

Questions

1. Why do we need JWT implementation?
2. What is the `function_name` parameter in the Zappa settings file?

Building a Django Application with Zappa

5

In this chapter, we are going to create a Django based image gallery app where a user can create a photo album and upload images. While working in Django, it's really interesting and challenging to serve the static and media content. Usually, developers store the images in file storage and servers via the URL. Here, we are going to store images in AWS S3 and serve via the CDN network provided by the AWS CloudFront service.

Topics we will cover in this chapter include the following:

- Installing and configuring Django
- Designing an image gallery application
- Serving static and media files via AWS CloudFront CDN
- Setting up static and media files
- Integrating Zappa
- Building, testing, and deploying the Django application using Zappa
- Django management command

Technical requirements

Before moving ahead, let's fulfill some prerequisites required for this chapter. We are going to develop a Django based serverless application, so we need to meet the following requirements, which are being used for developing this application:

- Ubuntu 16.04/Mac/Windows
- Pipenv tool
- Django
- Django Storage
- Django Imagekit
- Boto3
- Zappa

These packages are the required packages for this chapter, and we will be installing and configuring these packages using the pipenv tool. Now we will explore the configuration in detail.

Installing and configuring Django

Configuring any Python project requires following a standard for maintaining the necessary package's versions. Many developers prefer to maintain the `requirements.txt` file, which helps them to keep the application stable. Any version upgrade of specific packages as mentioned in the `requirements.txt` may break the whole application. That's the reason developers strictly follow this standard to maintain a stable version of their application.

Setting up a virtual environment

I was following the traditional pattern until I came across a very cool tool that changed my traditional approach to maintaining the `requirements.txt` file. Now you won't need the `requirements.txt` anymore. It's called **pipenv**; I love to use it.

Pipenv is a Python package management tool inspired by numerous package management tools of different languages, such as npm, Yarm, cargo, composer, builder, and so on. Pipenv is officially recommended by Python.org (`https://www.python.org/`). This tool entitled the standard to manage Python packages.

Installing pipenv

You can initialize the virtual environment from anywhere and it will keep track of every package installation.

Firstly, we need to install `pipenv` at the system level. So, if you are using macOS then you can simply install the `pipenv` using Homebrew as shown here:

```
$ brew install pipenv
```

If you are using Ubuntu 17.10, then you can simply add a PPA repository and install using the `apt` command, such as the following:

```
$ sudo apt install software-properties-common python-software-properties
$ sudo add-apt-repository ppa:pypa/ppa
$ sudo apt update
$ sudo apt install pipenv
```

You can simply install it via `pip` at the system level, instead of using `pip` from an active virtual environment. Take a look at this code line:

```
pip install pipenv
```

The system-level installation will be the installation without using any virtual environment. It installed in the system's `bin` directive and should be executable from the Terminal console.

Now, you can see the detailed information on the pipenv commands by just executing the pipenv command at the Terminal console:

```
abdulw@ULTP-711:~/workspace/book/chapter_5(master)$ pipenv
Usage: pipenv [OPTIONS] COMMAND [ARGS]...

Options:
  --update          Update Pipenv & pip to latest.
  --where           Output project home information.
  --venv            Output virtualenv information.
  --py              Output Python interpreter information.
  --envs            Output Environment Variable options.
  --rm              Remove the virtualenv.
  --bare            Minimal output.
  --completion      Output completion (to be eval'd).
  --man             Display manpage.
  --three / --two   Use Python 3/2 when creating virtualenv.
  --python TEXT     Specify which version of Python virtualenv should use.
  --site-packages   Enable site-packages for the virtualenv.
  --jumbotron       An easter egg, effectively.
  --version         Show the version and exit.
  -h, --help        Show this message and exit.


Usage Examples:
   Create a new project using Python 3.6, specifically:
   $ pipenv --python 3.6

   Install all dependencies for a project (including dev):
   $ pipenv install --dev

   Create a lockfile containing pre-releases:
   $ pipenv lock --pre

   Show a graph of your installed dependencies:
   $ pipenv graph

   Check your installed dependencies for security vulnerabilties:
   $ pipenv check

   Install a local setup.py into your virtual environment/Pipfile:
   $ pipenv install -e .

Commands:
  check       Checks for security vulnerabilities and against PEP 508 markers
              provided in Pipfile.
  graph       Displays currently-installed dependency graph information.
  install     Installs provided packages and adds them to Pipfile, or (if none
              is given), installs all packages.
  lock        Generates Pipfile.lock.
  open        View a given module in your editor.
  run         Spawns a command installed into the virtualenv.
  shell       Spawns a shell within the virtualenv.
  uninstall   Un-installs a provided package and removes it from Pipfile.
  update      Uninstalls all packages, and re-installs package(s) in [packages]
              to latest compatible versions.
```

Here, you can see there are several commands available that provide a very flexible way to deal with the virtual environment.

Configuring and installing packages

Now, we are going to create a virtual environment for our project and install the required packages.

The following screenshot mentions the virtual environment creation process:

```
abdulw@ULTP-711:~/workspace/book/chapter_5(master)$ pipenv --python python3.6
Virtualenv already exists!
Removing existing virtualenv…
Creating a virtualenv for this project…
Using /usr/bin/python3.6 to create virtualenv…
Running virtualenv with interpreter /usr/bin/python3.6
Using base prefix '/usr'
New python executable in /home/abdulw/.local/share/virtualenvs/chapter_5-N1x3-kJk/bin/python3.6
Also creating executable in /home/abdulw/.local/share/virtualenvs/chapter_5-N1x3-kJk/bin/python
Installing setuptools, pip, wheel...done.

Virtualenv location: /home/abdulw/.local/share/virtualenvs/chapter_5-N1x3-kJk
Creating a Pipfile for this project…
```

As you can see from the preceding screenshot, we have created a virtual environment with the following command:

```
$ pipenv --python python3.6
```

We explicitly mentioned the Python version that would be required; you can mention any Python version as well. If you are in hurry and just wanted to initialize with Python version 2 or 3, then you can just run the command as follows:

```
$ pipenv --two
```

You can also use this one:

```
$ pipenv --three
```

After successful execution of the preceding command, `pipenv` creates a virtual environment automatically and creates a `Pipfile` that maintains all installed packages information, similar to `requirements.txt`, but in a very smart way. Look at the following snippet of `Pipfile`:

```
[[source]]

url = "https://pypi.python.org/simple"
verify_ssl = true
```

```
name = "pypi"

[dev-packages]

[packages]

[requires]

python_version = "3.6"
```

It has different sections for managing all packages. Now you can install any package using the following command:

```
pipenv install <package-name>
```

As we are going to use the Django framework, we will install Django using pipenv as shown in the following screenshot:

```
abdulw@ULTP-711:~/workspace/book/chapter_5(master)$ pipenv install django
Installing django…
Collecting django
  Downloading Django-2.0.3-py3-none-any.whl (7.1MB)
Collecting pytz (from django)
  Using cached pytz-2018.3-py2.py3-none-any.whl
Installing collected packages: pytz, django
Successfully installed django-2.0.3 pytz-2018.3

Adding django to Pipfile's [packages]…
Locking [dev-packages] dependencies…
Locking [packages] dependencies…
Updated Pipfile.lock (374a8f)!
```

Once we install any package, then `pipenv` creates a `Pipfile.lock` file. The `Pipfile.lock` file maintains the commit hashes and dependencies of each installed package.

Now, if you were thinking of activating the virtual environment, don't worry about it. You can relay everything to `pipenv` itself. The `pipenv` provides a command named `pipenv shell` that internally invokes the virtual environment `activate` command. Now, you would be using the activated virtual environment shell.

Instead of being inside the shell or activating the virtual environment, you can execute any command under the virtual environment by using the command `pipenv run <command as an argument>`, for example:

```
pipenv run python manage.py runserver
```

It's really interesting, isn't it?

After installing all the required packages, the `Pipfile` will look like the following:

File—`Pipfile`:

```
[[source]]

url = "https://pypi.python.org/simple"
verify_ssl = true
name = "pypi"

[dev-packages]


[packages]

django = "*"
pylint = "*"
pillow = "*"
zappa = "*"
django-storages = "*"
"boto3" = "*"
boto = "*"
django-imagekit = "*"


[requires]

python_version = "3.6"
```

Now, we are done with the configuration and installation of the required packages.

Let's move on to the next section, where we will be creating an image gallery application, using Django.

Designing an image gallery application

Once we are done with configuration, then we can start implementing the application. The `ImageGallery` application will be straightforward—a user can create a new photo album record and can upload multiple images at once. Once the photo album is created, we will display all existing album records in list view along with associated images as thumbnail views.

Let's see the implementation phase, as per our requirements.

Design overview

I am going to create an image gallery application based on Django. We are going to use Django admin for the purpose of the UI. Django admin has a very pretty UI/UX design. So we are going to create some models, such as a `PhotoAlbum` model that will have a one-to-many relationship with the `Photo` model.

Then we are simply going to register these models with the Django admin panel. Once we are done with the admin configuration, we will configure the static and media settings to upload the dynamic images to an Amazon S3 bucket and serve these static files via the CloudFront CDN network.

Let's take a close look at the implementation.

Initializing the project

Once you have configured the `pipenv`, you need to enable the virtual environment using the command `pipenv` shell. Assuming that you are in the `pipenv` shell, which is nothing but an activated virtual environment. Once you enable the virtual environment, you have access to already installed packages. Hence, we are going to create the Django project scaffolding by executing the following command:

```
django-admin.py startproject <project_name>
```

The following is a screenshot of the project creation process:

```
(chapter_5-N1x3-kJk)         :~/workspace/book/chapter_5(master)$ django-admin.py startproject imageGalleryProject
(chapter_5-N1x3-kJk)         :~/workspace/book/chapter_5(master)$ ls
imageGalleryProject  Pipfile  Pipfile.lock
(chapter_5-N1x3-kJk)         :~/workspace/book/chapter_5(master)$ cd imageGalleryProject/
(chapter_5-N1x3-kJk)         :~/workspace/book/chapter_5/imageGalleryProject(master)$ ls
imageGalleryProject
(chapter_5-N1x3-kJk)         :~/workspace/book/chapter_5/imageGalleryProject(master)$ python manage.py startapp gallery
(chapter_5-N1x3-kJk)         :~/workspace/book/chapter_5/imageGalleryProject(master)$ ls
gallery  imageGalleryProject
(chapter_5-N1x3-kJk)         :~/workspace/book/chapter_5/imageGalleryProject(master)$ tree

├── gallery
│   ├── admin.py
│   ├── apps.py
│   ├── __init__.py
│   ├── migrations
│   │   └── __init__.py
│   ├── models.py
│   ├── tests.py
│   └── views.py
├── imageGalleryProject
│   ├── __init__.py
│   ├── __pycache__
│   │   ├── __init__.cpython-36.pyc
│   │   └── settings.cpython-36.pyc
│   ├── settings.py
│   ├── urls.py
│   └── wsgi.py

4 directories, 14 files
(chapter_5-N1x3-kJk)         :~/workspace/book/chapter_5/imageGalleryProject(master)$ ▌
```

I have created the project and an app as well. From the previous screenshot, you can see the project and app files.

By default, Django enables the admin panel in the root `urls.py` file. Hence, we do not need to configure it again.

Now let's move to the model creation process in the next section.

Implementing models

We are going to create two models—`PhotoAlbum` and `Photo` model, with a relationship of one-to-many. The following is the code snippet of the `gallery/models.py` file:
File—`gallery/models.py`:

```python
from django.db import models
from django.utils.translation import gettext as _
from imagekit.models import ImageSpecField
from imagekit.processors import ResizeToFill


# Create your models here.


def upload_path(instance, filename):
    return '{}/{}'.format(instance.album.name, filename)
```

```python
class PhotoAlbum(models.Model):
    name = models.CharField(_('album name'), max_length=50)
    created_at = models.DateTimeField(auto_now_add=True, auto_now=False)
    updated_at = models.DateTimeField(auto_now=True)

    class Meta:
        db_table = 'photo_album'
        verbose_name = 'photo album'
        verbose_name_plural = 'photo albums'

    def __str__(self):
        return self.name

class Photo(models.Model):
    album = models.ForeignKey(PhotoAlbum, related_name='photos',
on_delete=models.CASCADE)
    image = models.ImageField(_('image'), upload_to=upload_path)
    image_thumbnail = ImageSpecField(source='image',
                                     processors=[ResizeToFill(100, 50)],
                                     format='JPEG',
                                     options={'quality': 60})
    created_at = models.DateTimeField(auto_now_add=True, auto_now=False)
    updated_at = models.DateTimeField(auto_now=True)

    class Meta:
        db_table = 'photo'
        verbose_name = 'photo'
        verbose_name_plural = 'photos'

    def __str__(self):
        return self.image.name.split('/')[1]
```

As planned, I have created two models, along with their relationship. Here, `PhotoAlbum` is straightforward, as it acts as a parent class. The `Photo` model is more interesting, as we are going to store images through it.

In the `Photo` model, I am using the `django-imagekit` (`https://github.com/matthewwithanm/django-imagekit`) library to create and store a thumbnail image of the original uploaded image. It is quite interesting, as it has many features to allow us to work on an image as needed. My intention is to create a thumbnail of an uploaded image; hence, I configured it accordingly.

Once you are done with model creation, you will need to run `makemigrations` and migrate the command to create the actual database tables. Have a look at the following screenshot to see the process of the `makemigrations` command:

```
(chapter_5-N1x3-kJk) abdul@ULTR-711:~/workspace/book/chapter_5/imageGalleryProject(master)$ python manage.py makemigrations
Migrations for 'gallery':
  gallery/migrations/0001_initial.py
    - Create model PhotoGallery
(chapter_5-N1x3-kJk) abdul@ULTR-711:~/workspace/book/chapter_5/imageGalleryProject(master)$ python manage.py migrate
Operations to perform:
  Apply all migrations: admin, auth, contenttypes, gallery, sessions
Running migrations:
  Applying gallery.0001_initial... OK
(chapter_5-N1x3-kJk) abdul@ULTR-711:~/workspace/book/chapter_5/imageGalleryProject(master)$
```

Once we run the `makemigrations` command, then we are ready to configure these models with the admin panel. Let's move on to the next section on configuring the admin panel.

Integrating with the admin panel

Integrating models with the Django admin panel requires enabling the admin URL configurations in the root `urls.py` file. Let's have a look at the code:

File—`imageGalleryProject/urls.py`:

```python
from django.contrib import admin
from django.urls import path

urlpatterns = [
    path('admin/', admin.site.urls),
]
```

Admin configuration is based on the Django application, so we have to configure the admin under the gallery app. The following is the code snippet of the gallery app's `admin.py` file:

File—`gallery/admin.py`:

```python
from django.contrib import admin
from django.utils.html import mark_safe
from gallery.models import PhotoAlbum, Photo
# Register your models here.

class PhotoAdminInline(admin.TabularInline):
    model = Photo
    extra = 1
    fields = ( 'image', 'image_tag', )
    readonly_fields = ('image_tag',)

    def image_tag(self, instance):
        if instance.image_thumbnail.name:
            return mark_safe('<img src="%s" />' %
instance.image_thumbnail.url)
        return ''
```

```
        image_tag.short_description = 'Image Thumbnail'

class PhotoAlbumAdmin(admin.ModelAdmin):
    inlines = [PhotoAdminInline]


admin.site.register(PhotoAlbum, PhotoAlbumAdmin)
```

Here, we configure the `Photo` model as `TabularInline` so that we can add multiple photos or images under one album. We will have a complete workflow demo after deploying the application on AWS Lambda.

At this point in time, you can run the application and store the images on your local machine. But later on, we want to deploy on AWS Lambda and then store images in an Amazon S3 bucket and serve via the Amazon CloudFront CDN network.

Application demonstration

We already configured the models with the admin panel. Now we are going to run the Django's local server by using the `python manage.py runserver` command. It will start the Django server on `http://locahost:8000` URL.

The following is a screenshot of the application:

As mentioned in the preceding screenshot, we are creating a photo album. We defined the one-to-many relationship and used the `TabularInline` to accept multiple photos while creating the album. Take a look at this screenshot:

The list page will appear once we are done with the adding process. Now, you can select the newly created album to view or edit the existing details. Take a look at this screenshot:

Here, you can check that the previously uploaded images are displaying as thumbnails. We used the `django-imagekit` library for configuring the thumbnail image process.

Now, we will see in next section the required process for configuring the Amazon CloudFront CDN and integrating it with our application.

Configuring the Amazon CloudFront CDN

Amazon CloudFront is one of the more popular services. It provides the feature to serve static files through the CDN network, which helps static contents to be distributed in a very efficient way with lower latency to enhance the performance.

To configure Amazon CloudFront, we create a CloudFront distribution through the AWS user console.

Creating CloudFront distributions

Assuming you have a valid AWS account, you can log in the AWS web console using your credentials. Select the **CloudFront** service from the services dropdown and click on the **Create Distribution** button, as shown in the following screenshot:

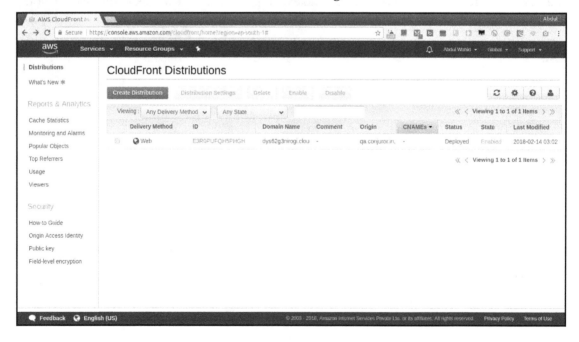

While creating a distribution, Amazon provides two different methods, such as web and RTMP. The web method is used for static content that needs to be served through the CDN network and when all static files are residing in an Amazon S3 bucket. The RTMP method is used to distribute the streaming media files, which allow a user to play the file before it finishes the download.

In our case, we will choose the web method, as we want to distribute the static files. You can select the method as shown in the following screenshot:

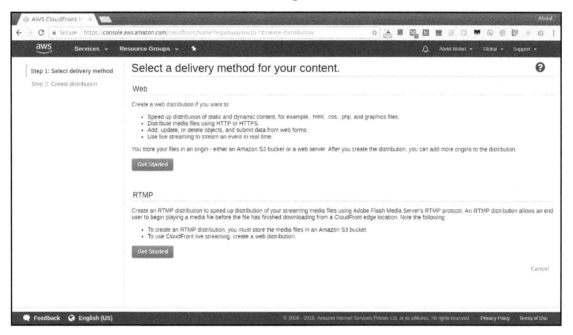

Once you select the web method, the **Create Distribution** form page will open. On this page, we will select the required fields to configure the distribution. Take a look at this screenshot:

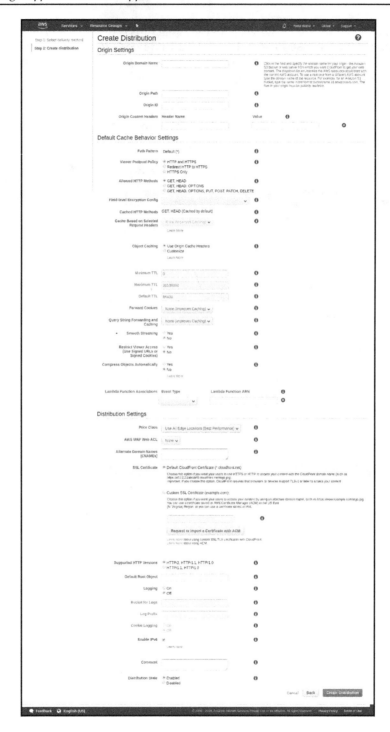

After successful creation of the cloud distribution, we are going to integrate the distribution with our Django application.

Let's move on to the next section, where we will configure the static and media files in the application.

Setting up static and media files

Configuring the static and dynamic files in Django is essential. How we configure and serve static and media files does impact on the overall performance of the application. Hence, configuring the static and media files should be taken care of in an optimized way. Let's have a detailed discussion about it.

Standard configuration

Django has a standard pattern to configure the static and media files. Static and media are two different concerns, where static files refer to fixed content, such as HTML, JS, CSS, and images. Django defines some configuration related to static files in `settings.py` and URL configured in `urls.py`. Media files refer to any files that are handled dynamically by uploading. Django has a very good mechanism to configure and manage static HTML, JS, CSS, and images files.

Normally, the default Django static file configuration assumes that you will have static files along with your code base under a static directory, but, in our case, we want to put all static content under an Amazon S3 bucket and serve it through Amazon CloudFront distribution.

django-storage

We are going to use the `django-storage` (`http://django-storages.readthedocs.io/en/latest/`), a third-party plugin for implementing a custom storage backend. With the help of Django storage, we are going set up the static and media configuration.

The following is the code snippet, which is required to set up the custom storage for static and media files:

File—`gallery/utils.py`:

```
from django.conf import settings
from storages.backends.s3boto import S3BotoStorage
```

```
class StaticStorage(S3BotoStorage):
    location = settings.STATICFILES_LOCATION

    @property
    def connection(self):
        if self._connection is None:
            self._connection = self.connection_class(
                self.access_key, self.secret_key,
                calling_format=self.calling_format, host='s3-ap-
south-1.amazonaws.com')
        return self._connection


class MediaStorage(S3BotoStorage):
    location = settings.MEDIAFILES_LOCATION

    @property
    def connection(self):
        if self._connection is None:
            self._connection = self.connection_class(
                self.access_key, self.secret_key,
                calling_format=self.calling_format, host='s3-ap-
south-1.amazonaws.com')
        return self._connection
```

Now we are going to configure these two custom storage classes in the `settings.py` file as shown here:

File—`imageGalleryProject/settings.py`:

```
AWS_HEADERS = {
    'Expires': 'Thu, 31 Dec 2099 20:00:00 GMT',
    'Cache-Control': 'max-age=94608000',
}

AWS_STORAGE_BUCKET_NAME = 'chapter-5'
AWS_ACCESS_KEY_ID = os.environ.get('AWS_ACCESS_KEY_ID')
AWS_SECRET_ACCESS_KEY = os.environ.get('AWS_SECRET_ACCESS_KEY')
AWS_CLOUDFRONT_DOMAIN = 'dl76lqo8jmttq.cloudfront.net'

MEDIAFILES_LOCATION = 'media'
MEDIA_ROOT = '/%s/' % MEDIAFILES_LOCATION
MEDIA_URL = '/%s/%s/' % (AWS_CLOUDFRONT_DOMAIN, MEDIAFILES_LOCATION)
DEFAULT_FILE_STORAGE = 'gallery.utils.MediaStorage'

STATICFILES_LOCATION = 'static'
STATIC_ROOT = '/%s/' % STATICFILES_LOCATION
STATIC_URL = '/%s/%s/' % (AWS_CLOUDFRONT_DOMAIN, STATICFILES_LOCATION)
```

```
STATICFILES_STORAGE = 'gallery.utils.StaticStorage'
```

These are the settings you will be required to put into `settings.py`, and now its time to configure the `urls.py`. I would recommend that you update the root `urls.py`, as shown here:

File—`imageGalleryProject/urls.py`:

```
from django.conf import settings
from django.conf.urls.static import static

urlpatterns = [
    # ... the rest of your URLconf goes here ...
] + static(settings.STATIC_URL, document_root=settings.STATIC_ROOT)
  + static(settings.MEDIA_URL, document_root=settings.MEDIA_ROOT)
```

Once you configure the URLs, then you are all set. To verify the configuration, you can run the command `collectstatic` to collect all your static files at the configured location:

```
$ python manage.py collectstatic
```

This command will retrieve all the static files belonging to the mentioned `INSTALL_APPS` and upload them to the `STATIC_ROOT`. Now, when you upload any file, it will be uploaded to Amazon S3 and serve via Amazon CloudFront.

It's time to configure Zappa and process the deployment.

Building, testing, and deploying the Django application using Zappa

Zappa configuration is straightforward. The Zappa package is available in the pip repository as well. But we are going to install it with pipenv, which helps us to keep track of the version management. The following is the command you will need to install Zappa:

```
$ pipenv install zappa
```

After the Zappa installation, you will need to initialize Zappa with the command `zappa init`. This command will prompt a shell questioner to configure Zappa with the required, basic information. Let's have a look at the next section, where we will discuss Zappa's basic configuration.

Configuring Zappa

Once you are done with the `zappa init` command, Zappa creates a `zappa_settings.json` file. This file contains the configuration information, which is required to perform the deployment. The following is the code snippet of the `zappa_settings.json` file:

```
{
    "dev": {
        "aws_region": "ap-south-1",
        "django_settings": "imageGalleryProject.settings",
        "profile_name": "default",
        "project_name": "imagegallerypro",
        "runtime": "python3.6",
        "s3_bucket": "chapter-5",
        "remote_env": "s3://important-credentials-bucket/environments.json"
    }
}
```

Here, we defined the configuration as per the requirements. As the key defines each configuration, we can see the usages of it. Consider the following:

- `aws_region`: The AWS region where the Lambda will get uploaded
- `django_settings`: The import path of Django's settings file
- `profile_name`: The AWS CLI configuration profile which is defined in the `~/.aws/credentials` file
- `project_name`: The project name for the uploading Lambda function
- `runtime`: The python runtime interpreter
- `s3_bucket`: Creates an Amazon s3 bucket and uploads the deployment packages
- `remote_env`: Sets the environment variable of all the key-value pairs mentioned in the uploaded JSON file at the Amazon S3 location

With the help of this configuration information, we will proceed with the deployment.

Building and deploying

Once we are done with the configuration, then we can process the deployment. Zappa provides two different commands to perform the deployment, such as `zappa deploy <stage_name>` and `zappa update <stage_name>`. Initially, we will use the `zappa deploy <stage_name>` command, as it is the first time that we are deploying this Lambda application.

If you have already deployed the application and want to redeploy it, then you would use the `zappa update <stage_name>` command. In the previous chapter, we had a detailed discussion about the deployment process of Zappa, so you can refer to this, if you need to.

The following is the screenshot of our deployment process:

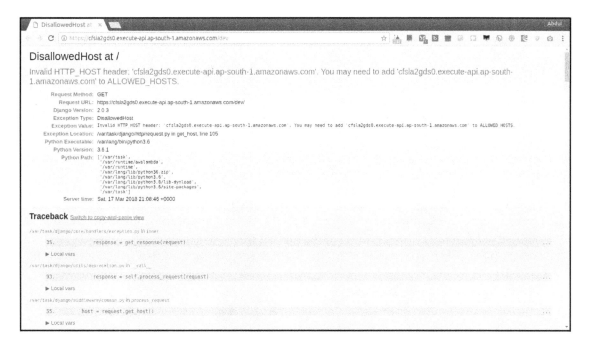

As you can see, after successful deployment, we got the API gateway endpoint URL. Let's check how the deployment happened by visiting the admin panel at the mentioned URL. Take a look at this screenshot:

Oops! We encountered an error. This error says that we have an invalid HTTP_HOST, and this is true because we have not configured it into the list of ALLOWED_HOSTS in the settings.py file, as mentioned here:

```
ALLOWED_HOSTS = ['localhost', 'cfsla2gds0.execute-api.ap-
south-1.amazonaws.com']
```

This would resolve the issue. Now, let's move on to check out the admin panel:

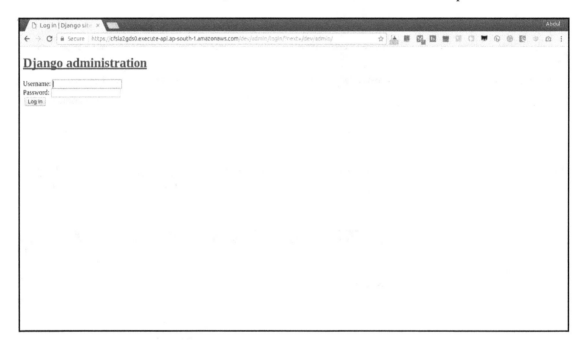

Oops! It seems as though we failed to load the static contents. But we configured the static and media content with Amazon S3 and Amazon CloudFront.

So, to resolve this error, we will need to run the command `python manage.py collectstatic`. This command will upload all the static content to Amazon S3 and it will be available via Amazon CloudFront. Take a look at this screenshot:

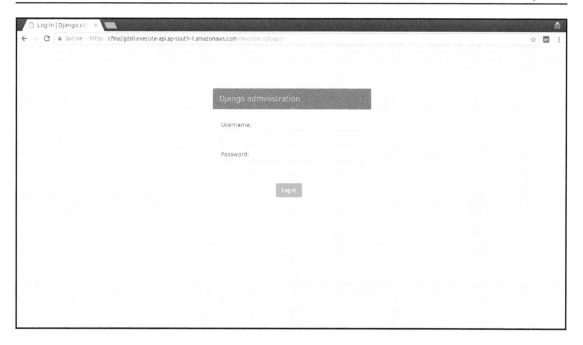

Wow! We resolved the issue, and our application is live and serverless. That was really easy to deploy. I hope you did enjoy the deployment of the Django based application.

Here, we never dealt with any server software, such as Apache or Nginx and other complex configuration. Zappa makes it really easy to deploy your application as serverless.

Now we will see what more we can do with the help of Zappa. Refer our next section for more excitement!

Django management command using Zappa

Zappa provides a feature to perform the Django's `manage` command operations on deployed Lamdba instances, directly from your Terminal console. With the help of `zappa mange <stage_name> <manage-command>`, you can execute and check the status of your Django application.

The following is a screenshot of the execution of this command:

```
(imageGalleryProject-KAW6aJSD) abdul@QULTP-711:~/workspace/book/chapter_5/imageGalleryProject(master)$ zappa manage dev showmigrations admin
[START] RequestId: bcc908da-3bde-11e8-8f67-bb3b239cecde Version: $LATEST
[DEBUG] 2018-04-09T10:14:07.141Z bcc908da-3bde-11e8-8f67-bb3b239cecde Zappa Event: {'manage': 'showmigrations admin'}
admin
 [X] 0001_initial
 [X] 0002_logentry_remove_auto_add
[END] RequestId: bcc908da-3bde-11e8-8f67-bb3b239cecde
[REPORT] RequestId: bcc908da-3bde-11e8-8f67-bb3b239cecde
Duration: 174.89 ms
Billed Duration: 200 ms
Memory Size: 512 MB
Max Memory Used: 81 MB

(imageGalleryProject-KAW6aJSD) abdul@QULTP-711:~/workspace/book/chapter_5/imageGalleryProject(master)$
```

There are some limitations though. It is only for Django's `manage` command to use, hence it's bound to Django projects only.

For passing any arguments, you can use the `manage` command in string format, such as:

```
$ zappa manage dev "migrate --fake-initial"
```

But it will not be useful for those commands that require user input, such as `createsuperuser`. So, in this kind of situation, you can write a Python script in string format and pass it as an argument for `zappa invoke <env> '<raw_script>' --raw`. Take a look at this screenshot:

```
(imageGalleryProject-KAW6aJSD) abdul@QULTP-711:~/workspace/book/chapter_5/imageGalleryProject(master)$ zappa invoke dev "print (1 + 2 + 3)" --raw
Calling invoke for stage dev..
[START] RequestId: 8a119b48-3be1-11e8-92c4-85e7dddb61bb Version: $LATEST
[DEBUG] 2018-04-09T10:34:10.531Z 8a119b48-3be1-11e8-92c4-85e7dddb61bb Zappa Event: {'raw_command': 'print (1 + 2 + 3)'}
6
[END] RequestId: 8a119b48-3be1-11e8-92c4-85e7dddb61bb
[REPORT] RequestId: 8a119b48-3be1-11e8-92c4-85e7dddb61bb
Duration: 20.11 ms
Billed Duration: 100 ms
Memory Size: 512 MB
Max Memory Used: 80 MB

(imageGalleryProject-KAW6aJSD) abdul@QULTP-711:~/workspace/book/chapter_5/imageGalleryProject(master)$
```

That's it.

I hope you enjoyed it. It makes a developer's life easy. We may require these feature as we are dealing with serverless environments.

Summary

We learned how to build a serverless Django application. Zappa makes it very easy to perform the build operation and helps you to make a serverless deployment, which is very handy.

We covered all essential details we needed while implementing the serverless Django application. I explained the code written for this application; I am also sharing the entire code base at our GitHub repository (`https://github.com/PacktPublishing/Building-Serverless-Python-Web-Services-with-Zappa/tree/master/chapter_5/imageGalleryProject`).

I hope you enjoyed this chapter. In the next chapter, we will implement the same application, but as a RESTful API, and see what challenges we come across.

Questions

1. What is Amazon CloudFront?
2. What is pipenv used for?

6
Building a Django REST API with Zappa

In this chapter, we are going to create a RESTful API, using the Django Rest Framework. It will be based on a simple RESTful API with **CRUD** (**create**, **retrieve**, **update**, and **delete**) operations. We can consider the previously developed **ImageGallery** application with REST API extensions. Here, we will create an API for `PhotoAlbum`, where a user can create a new album, along with images through the REST API interface.

The topics we will cover in this chapter include the following:

- Installing and configuring the Django REST Framework
- Designing REST APIs
- Building, testing, and deploying the Django application using Zappa

Technical requirements

Before going further, there are some technical prerequisites to be met. These prerequisites are required to set up and configure the development environment. Following is the list of required software:

- Ubuntu 16.04/Mac/Windows
- Python 3.6
- Pipenv tool
- Django
- Django Rest Framework

- Django Rest Framework JWT
- Django Storages
- Django Imagekit
- Boto3
- Zappa

We are going to install these packages in a virtual environment. In the next section, we will see the detailed information about the installation process.

Installing and configuring the Django REST Framework

We have already covered the virtual environment setup process in detail in the *Setting up a virtual environment* section of `Chapter 5`, *Building a Django Application with Zappa*. You can follow these instructions to configure the pipenv tool and create a new virtual environment for this chapter. Let's move to the next section for installing the required packages using the pipenv tool.

Installing the required packages

We are going to develop the REST API using the Django REST framework, so we need to install the following packages using the `pipenv install <package_name>` command:

- `django`
- `djangorestframework`
- `djangorestframework-jwt`
- `django-storages`
- `django-imagekit`
- `boto3`
- `zappa`

You can install multiple packages at once by mentioning the other packages separated by whitespace, such as `pipenv install <package_one> <package_two> ....`

Once you install these packages, then we are good to proceed with the implementation, and we will have the following mentioned `Pipfile`:
File—`Pipfile`:

```
[[source]]

url = "https://pypi.python.org/simple"
verify_ssl = true
name = "pypi"


[dev-packages]



[packages]

django = "*"
djangorestframework = "*"
django-storages = "*"
django-imagekit = "*"
"boto3" = "*"
zappa = "*"


[requires]

python_version = "3.6"
```

Pipenv maintains the versions along with its git hashes in the `Pipfile.lock` file. So we don't need to worry about it.

We are done with configuring the development environment, and now it's time to implement the REST API. Stay tuned for the next section, where we are going to design the REST API using the Django Rest Framework.

Designing REST APIs

We are going to design the REST API for our ImageGallery application. We developed this application with Django's admin interface. Now we will extend the existing implementation of the ImageGallery application with a RESTful API interface. Before implementing the solution, let's have a look at a brief introduction to the Django REST Framework.

What is the Django Rest Framework?

Django Rest Framework is an open source library that is designed to implement the REST API in an optimistic way. It follows the Django design pattern with different terminologies. You can find the QuickStart tutorials at its documentation site (`http://www.django-rest-framework.org/#quickstart`).

Django Rest Frameworks is powerful and supports ORM and non-ORM data sources. It has built-in support for the Browsable API client (`https://restframework.herokuapp.com/`) and many other features as well.

It is recommended to not use the Web Browsable API interface in the production environment. You can disable it by setting up the render class in `settings.py`.

The following mentioned is the code snippet of `settings.py` file.

File—`settings.py`:

```
REST_FRAMEWORK = {
    'DEFAULT_RENDERER_CLASSES': (
        'rest_framework.renderers.JSONRenderer',
    )
}
```

Integrating the REST Framework

To integrate the Django REST Framework, you can simply install it using the pipenv packing tool, as mentioned in the previous section on setting up the virtual environment. Once you are done with the installation part, you can proceed to add the `rest_framework` in your `INSTALLED_APPS` settings. Take a look at this code:

```
INSTALLED_APPS = (
    ...
    'rest_framework',
)
```

If you want to use the Web Browsable API along with the login and logout view, then you can add the following URL pattern in your root `urls.py` file:

```
urlpatterns = [
    ...
    url(r'^api-auth/', include('rest_framework.urls'))
```

```
]
```

That's it! Now we have successfully integrated the Django REST Framework and we can move on to creating the REST API. Before creating the REST API, we need to implement the authentication and authorization layer so that each of our REST APIs will be secure from unauthorized access.

Let's see how can we make our REST API secure in the next section. Stay tuned.

Implementing authentication and authorization

Authentication and authorization are essential parts to be considered while designing the REST APIs. With the help of these layers, we can prevent unauthorized access to our application. There are many types of implementation patterns are available, but we will use **JWT (JSON Web Token)**. Read more about it at `https://en.wikipedia.org/wiki/JSON_Web_Token`. JWT is really useful for implementing distributed microservices architecture, and it doesn't rely on centralized server databases to verify the authenticity of the token.

There are many Python libraries available to implement the JWT token mechanism. In our case, we would like to use the `django-rest-framework-jwt` library (`https://getblimp.github.io/django-rest-framework-jwt/`), as it provides the support for Django Rest Framework.

I assume that you already have installed this library while setting up the environment in the *Virtual environment* section described earlier. Let's see how should we configure the `django-rest-framework-jwt` library in next section.

Configuring django-rest-framework-jwt

Once you are done with the installation, you need to add some predefined classes related to permission and authentication in `settings.py` as shown in the following code snippet.

File—`settings.py`:

```
REST_FRAMEWORK = {
    'DEFAULT_RENDERER_CLASSES': (
        'rest_framework.renderers.JSONRenderer',
    ),
    'DEFAULT_PERMISSION_CLASSES': (
        'rest_framework.permissions.IsAuthenticated',
    ),
```

```
        'DEFAULT_AUTHENTICATION_CLASSES': (
            'rest_framework_jwt.authentication.JSONWebTokenAuthentication',
            'rest_framework.authentication.SessionAuthentication',
            'rest_framework.authentication.BasicAuthentication',
        ),
    }
```

Now we need to append the URL for obtaining a token, based on user credentials. In the root `urls.py`, we will be appending the following statement:

```
from django.urls import path
from rest_framework_jwt.views import obtain_jwt_token
#...

urlpatterns = [
    '',
    # ...

    path(r'api-token-auth/', obtain_jwt_token),
]
```

The `api-token-auth` API will return a JWT token on successful authentication, for example:

```
$ curl -X POST -d "username=admin&password=password123"
http://localhost:8000/api-token-auth/

{"token":"eyJ0eXAiOiJKV1QiLCJhbGciOiJIUzI1NiJ9.eyJ1c2VyX2lkIjoxLCJ1c2VybmFt
ZSI6ImFiZHVsd2FoaWQiLCJleHAiOjE1MjYwNDUwNjgsImVtYWlsIjoiYWJkdWx3YWhpZDI0QGd
tYWlsLmNvbSJ9.Iw0ZTtdZpsQqrKIkf2VKoWw91txYp9DLkBYMS9OPoCU"}
```

This token can be used to authorize all other protected APIs by adding an authorization header along with the token, as shown here:

```
$ curl -H "Authorization: JWT <your_token>"
http://localhost:8000/protected-url/
```

There are other use cases where you would need to perform many operations on your issued token. For this, you would need to go through the documentation of `django-rest-framework-jwt` (https://getblimp.github.io/django-rest-framework-jwt/).

Now let's start implementing the API for our ImageGallery application.

Implementing serializers

Django Rest Framework designed a serializers module similar to the Django forms module to implement the JSON presentation layer. Serializers are responsible for serializing and deserializing the data; you can see a detailed explanation about data serialization here (`http://www.django-rest-framework.org/tutorial/1-serialization/#creating-a-serializer-class`).

The serializers module has many useful classes, such as `Serializer`, `ModelSerializer`, `HyperlinkedModelSerializer`, and more (`http://www.django-rest-framework.org/api-guide/serializers/`). Each class has similar operations but with extended features. A `Serializer` class is used to design custom data representation similar to Django's form representation, and `ModelSerializer` is used to represent the model class data similar to Django's `ModelFrom` class. `HyperlinkedModelSerializer` extends the representation of `ModelSerializer` with hyperlinked representation and with a primary key to relate the associated data.

We need to create a serializer class, using `ModelSerializer`. Take a look at this code.

File—`gallery/serializers.py`:

```
from rest_framework import serializers
from gallery.models import PhotoAlbum, Photo


class PhotoSerializer(serializers.ModelSerializer):

    class Meta:
        model = Photo
        fields = ('id', 'image', 'created_at', 'updated_at')


class PhotoAlbumSerializer(serializers.ModelSerializer):

    class Meta:
        model = PhotoAlbum
        fields = ('id', 'name', 'photos', 'created_at', 'updated_at')
        depth = 1
```

Here, we created `PhotoSerializer` and `PhotoAlbumSerializer` classes, using the `ModelSerializer` class. These serializers are associated with the model classes; hence, the data representation will be based on model structure.

Let's move on to the next section, where we are going to create views.

Implementing viewsets

Django Rest Framework has a module named viewsets. It follows a similar pattern as the Django default views functionality but extends features to work with the `serializer` class. Read more about the viewsets at `http://www.django-rest-framework.org/api-guide/viewsets/`. The following is the code snippet for viewsets classes related to `Photo` and `PhotoAlbum` models.

File—`gallery/views.py`:

```
from rest_framework import viewsets
from gallery.models import Photo, PhotoAlbum
from gallery.serializers import PhotoSerializer, PhotoAlbumSerializer


class PhotoViewset(viewsets.ModelViewSet):

    queryset = Photo.objects.all()
    serializer_class = PhotoSerializer

    def get_queryset(self, *args, **kwargs):
        if 'album_id' not in self.kwargs:
            raise APIException('required album_id')
        elif 'album_id' in self.kwargs and \
                not
Photo.objects.filter(album__id=self.kwargs['album_id']).exists():
                                        raise NotFound('Album not
found')
        return Photo.objects.filter(album__id=self.kwargs['album_id'])

    def perform_create(self, serializer):
        serializer.save(album_id=int(self.kwargs['album_id']))


class PhotoAlbumViewset(viewsets.ModelViewSet):

    queryset = PhotoAlbum.objects.all()
    serializer_class = PhotoAlbumSerializer
```

You can see here that we have created two different viewsets classes associated with `Photo` and `PhotoAlbum` models. The `PhotoAlbum` model has a one-to-many relationship with the `Photo` model. Hence, we will write a nested API such as `albums/(?P<album_id>[0-9]+)/photos`. In order to return related records of photos based on the `album_id`, we override the `get_queryset` method to filter the `queryset` based on the given `album_id`.

Similarly, we override the `perform_create` method to set the associated `album_id` while creating a new record. We will provide a complete demonstration in the upcoming section.

Let's have a look at URLs configurations, where we configure the nested API pattern.

Configuring the URL routes

Django REST Framework provides a `router` module to configure the standard URL configurations. It automatically adds support for all required URLs related to the mentioned viewsets. Read more about the `routers` here: `http://www.django-rest-framework.org/api-guide/routers/`. The following is the code snippet related to our route configuration.

File—`gallery/urls.py`:

```
from django.urls import path, include
from rest_framework import routers
from gallery.views import PhotoAlbumViewset, PhotoViewset

router = routers.DefaultRouter()
router.register('albums', PhotoAlbumViewset)
router.register('albums/(?P<album_id>[0-9]+)/photos', PhotoViewset)

urlpatterns = [
    path(r'', include(router.urls)),
]
```

Here, we created a default router and registered the viewsets with a URL prefix. The router will automatically determine the viewsets and will generate the required API URLs.

Now you can simply include the previously mentioned URLs patterns in the root configuration. The following is the code snippet of the root level `urls.py` file.

File—`imageGalleryProject/urls.py`:

```
from django.contrib import admin
from django.urls import path, include
from rest_framework_jwt.views import obtain_jwt_token

urlpatterns = [
    path('admin/', admin.site.urls),
    path(r'', include('gallery.urls')),
    path(r'api-token-auth/', obtain_jwt_token),
]
```

Once you include the `gallery.urls` patterns, then it will be available at the application level. We are done with implementation, so now it's time to see the demonstration. Let's move on to the next section, where will explore Zappa configuration, along with execution and deployment process on AWS Lambda.

Building, testing, and deploying Django app using Zappa

Django provides a lightweight deployment web server that runs on the local machine at port `8000`. You can debug and test your application before moving on to the production environment. Read more about it here (`https://docs.djangoproject.com/en/2.0/ref/django-admin/#runserver`).

Let's move on to the next sections, where we are going to explore application demonstration and deployment on AWS Lambda.

Executing in the local environment

With the help of the `runserver` command, you can execute the application in the local web deployment server, with an address such as `http://127.0.0.1:8000`. The following snippet shows the logs after executing the `python manage.py runserver` command:

```
$ python manage.py runserver
Performing system checks...
System check identified no issues (0 silenced).

May 14, 2018 - 10:04:25
Django version 2.0.5, using settings 'imageGalleryProject.settings'
Starting development server at http://127.0.0.1:8000/
Quit the server with CONTROL-C.
```

Now it's time to see the execution of your API. We are going to use Postman, an API client tool, to test the REST API. You can download the Postman app from `https://www.getpostman.com/`. Let's see all the API executions in the next sections.

API authentication

Before accessing the resource APIs, we need to authenticate the user and get a JWT access token. Let's get an access token using the `api-token-auth` API. We are going to use the `curl` command-line tool to executes the API. The following is the `curl` command execution:

```
$ curl -H "Content-Type: application/json" -X POST -d
'{"username":"abdulwahid", "password":"abdul123#"}'
http://localhost:8000/api-token-auth/
{"token":"eyJ0eXAiOiJKV1QiLCJhbGciOiJIUzI1NiJ9.eyJ1c2VyX2lkIjoxLCJ1c2VybmFt
ZSI6ImFiZHVsd2FoaWQiLCJleHAiOjE1Mjk1NjYxOTgsImVtYWlsIjoiYWJkdWx3YWhpZDI0QGd
tYWlsLmNvbSJ9.QypghhspJrNsp-v_XxlZeQFi_Wsujqh27EjlJtOaY_4"}
```

Here, we got the JWT token in response to user authentication. Now we are going to use this token as an authorization header to access other API resources.

GET request on API "/albums/"

This API will list all records from the `PhotoAlbum` model. Let's try to the `/album/` API with `GET` request method using the cRUL command as follows:

```
$ curl -i http://localhost:8000/albums/

HTTP/1.1 401 Unauthorized
Date: Thu, 21 Jun 2018 07:33:07 GMT
Server: WSGIServer/0.2 CPython/3.6.5
Content-Type: application/json
WWW-Authenticate: JWT realm="api"
Allow: GET, POST, HEAD, OPTIONS
X-Frame-Options: SAMEORIGIN
Content-Length: 58
Vary: Cookie

{"detail":"Authentication credentials were not provided."}
```

Here, we got a 401 Unauthorized error from, the server with the message **Authentication credentials were not provided**. This is how we secured all our APIs using the JWT token authentication mechanism.

Now, if we were to just add the authorization header with the access token we got from the authentication API, we would get the records from the server. The following cURL execution shows a successful API access with the authorization header:

```
$ curl -i -H "Authorization: JWT
eyJ0eXAiOiJKV1QiLCJhbGciOiJIUzI1NiJ9.eyJ1c2VyX2lkIjoxLCJ1c2VybmFtZSI6ImFiZH
Vsd2FoaWQiLCJleHAiOjE1Mjk1NjY4NjUsImVtYWlsIjoiYWJkdWx3YWhpZDI0QGdtYWlsLmNvb
SJ9.Dnbwuf3Mu2kcfk8KrbC-ql941fHzK0z_5TgCP15CeaM"
http://localhost:8000/albums/
HTTP/1.1 200 OK
Date: Thu, 21 Jun 2018 07:40:14 GMT
Server: WSGIServer/0.2 CPython/3.6.5
Content-Type: application/json
Allow: GET, POST, HEAD, OPTIONS
X-Frame-Options: SAMEORIGIN
Content-Length: 598

[
    {
        "created_at": "2018-03-17T22:39:08.513389Z",
        "id": 1,
        "name": "Screenshot",
        "photos": [
            {
                "album": 1,
                "created_at": "2018-03-17T22:47:03.775033Z",
                "id": 5,
                "image":
"https://chapter-5.s3-ap-south-1.amazonaws.com/media/Screenshot/AWS_Lambda_
Home_Page.png?X-Amz-Algorithm=AWS4-HMAC-SHA256&X-Amz-
Credential=AKIAIXNW3FK64BZR3DLA%2F20180621%2Fap-
south-1%2Fs3%2Faws4_request&X-Amz-Date=20180621T073958Z&X-Amz-
Expires=3600&X-Amz-SignedHeaders=host&X-Amz-
Signature=721acd5b023e13132f606a3f72bd672bad95a0dcb24572099c4cb49cdc34df71"
,
                "updated_at": "2018-03-17T22:47:18.298215Z"
            }
        ],
        "updated_at": "2018-03-17T22:47:17.328637Z"
    }
]
```

As you can see, we got the data from the "/albums/" API by providing the Authorization header. Here, we can use | python -m json.tool to print the return response in a JSON readable format.

POST request on API "/albums/<album_id>/photos/"

Now we can add more photos to the existing record. The <indexentry content="Django REST API execution, in local environment:POST request on API "/albums//photos/"">following is the log snippet of the cRUL command execution, where we are uploading a image file to existing photo album:

```
$ curl -i -H "Content-Type: multipart/form-data" -H "Authorization: JWT
eyJ0eXAiOiJKV1QiLCJhbGciOiJIUzI1NiJ9.eyJ1c2VyX2lkIjoxLCJ1c2VybmFtZSI6ImFiZH
Vsd2FoaWQiLCJleHAiOjE1Mjk1NzE5ODEsImVtYWlsIjoiYWJkdWx3YWhpZDI0QGdtYWlsLmNvb
SJ9.3CHaV4uI-4xwbzAVdBA4ooHtaCdUrVn97uR_G8MBM0I" -X POST -F
"image=@/home/abdulw/Pictures/serverless.png"
http://localhost:8000/albums/1/photos/

HTTP/1.1 201 Created
Date: Thu, 21 Jun 2018 09:01:44 GMT
Server: WSGIServer/0.2 CPython/3.6.5
Content-Type: application/json
Allow: GET, POST, HEAD, OPTIONS
X-Frame-Options: SAMEORIGIN
Content-Length: 450

{
    "created_at": "2018-06-21T09:02:27.918719Z",
    "id": 7,
    "image":
"https://chapter-5.s3-ap-south-1.amazonaws.com/media/Screenshot/serverless.
png?X-Amz-Algorithm=AWS4-HMAC-SHA256&X-Amz-
Credential=AKIAJA3LNVLKPTEOWH5A%2F20180621%2Fap-
south-1%2Fs3%2Faws4_request&X-Amz-Date=20180621T090228Z&X-Amz-
Expires=3600&X-Amz-SignedHeaders=host&X-Amz-
Signature=4e28ef5daa6e1887344514d9953f17df743e747c32b532cde12b840241fa13f0"
,
    "updated_at": "2018-06-21T09:02:27.918876Z"
}
```

Now, you can see that the image has been uploaded to AWS S3 storage, and we got the CDN link as we already configured AWS S3 and CloudFront. Let's see the list of all records once again:

```
$ curl -H "Authorization: JWT
eyJ0eXAiOiJKV1QiLCJhbGciOiJIUzI1NiJ9.eyJ1c2VyX2lkIjoxLCJ1c2VybmFtZSI6ImFiZH
Vsd2FoaWQiLCJleHAiOjE1Mjk1NzIzNTYsImVtYWlsIjoiYWJkdWx3YWhpZDI0QGdtYWlsLmNvb
SJ9.m2w1THn5Nrpy0dCi8k0bPdeo67OHNYEKO-yTX5Wnuig"
http://localhost:8000/albums/ | python -m json.tool
```

```
[
    {
        "created_at": "2018-03-17T22:39:08.513389Z",
        "id": 1,
        "name": "Screenshot",
        "photos": [
            {
                "album": 1,
                "created_at": "2018-03-17T22:47:03.775033Z",
                "id": 5,
                "image":
"https://chapter-5.s3-ap-south-1.amazonaws.com/media/Screenshot/AWS_Lambda_
Home_Page.png?X-Amz-Algorithm=AWS4-HMAC-SHA256&X-Amz-
Credential=AKIAJA3LNVLKPTEOWH5A%2F20180621%2Fap-
south-1%2Fs3%2Faws4_request&X-Amz-Date=20180621T090753Z&X-Amz-
Expires=3600&X-Amz-SignedHeaders=host&X-Amz-
Signature=832abe952870228c2ae22aaece81c05dc1414a2e9a78394d441674634a6d2bbf"
,
                "updated_at": "2018-03-17T22:47:18.298215Z"
            },
            {
                "album": 1,
                "created_at": "2018-06-21T09:01:44.354167Z",
                "id": 6,
                "image":
"https://chapter-5.s3-ap-south-1.amazonaws.com/media/Screenshot/serverless.
png?X-Amz-Algorithm=AWS4-HMAC-SHA256&X-Amz-
Credential=AKIAJA3LNVLKPTEOWH5A%2F20180621%2Fap-
south-1%2Fs3%2Faws4_request&X-Amz-Date=20180621T090753Z&X-Amz-
Expires=3600&X-Amz-SignedHeaders=host&X-Amz-
Signature=90a00ad79f141c919d8e65474325534461cf837f462cb52a840afb3863b72013"
,
                "updated_at": "2018-06-21T09:01:44.354397Z"
            },
            {
                "album": 1,
                "created_at": "2018-06-21T09:02:27.918719Z",
                "id": 7,
                "image":
"https://chapter-5.s3-ap-south-1.amazonaws.com/media/Screenshot/serverless.
png?X-Amz-Algorithm=AWS4-HMAC-SHA256&X-Amz-
Credential=AKIAJA3LNVLKPTEOWH5A%2F20180621%2Fap-
south-1%2Fs3%2Faws4_request&X-Amz-Date=20180621T090753Z&X-Amz-
Expires=3600&X-Amz-SignedHeaders=host&X-Amz-
Signature=90a00ad79f141c919d8e65474325534461cf837f462cb52a840afb3863b72013"
,
                "updated_at": "2018-06-21T09:02:27.918876Z"
            }
```

```
        ],
        "updated_at": "2018-03-17T22:47:17.328637Z"
    }
]
```

Now our application has been implemented as per our requirements. We can move on to deploy the application over AWS Lambda using Zappa. Now let's move towards the next section to configure Zappa.

Configuring Zappa

Once you are done with the `zappa init` command, then Zappa creates a `zappa_settings.json` file. This file contains the configuration information which is required to perform the deployment. The following is the code snippet of the `zappa_settings.json` file:

```
{
    "dev": {
        "aws_region": "ap-south-1",
        "django_settings": "imageGalleryProject.settings",
        "profile_name": "default",
        "project_name": "imagegallerypro",
        "runtime": "python3.6",
        "s3_bucket": "chapter-5",
        "remote_env": "s3://important-credentials-bucket/environments.json"
    }
}
```

Here, we defined the configuration as per the requirements. As the key defines each configuration, we can see the usages of it:

- `aws_region`: The AWS region where the Lambda will get uploaded.
- `django_settings`: The import path of Django's settings file.
- `profile_name`: The AWS CLI configuration profile which is defined in the `~/.aws/credentials` file.
- `project_name`: The project name for the uploading the Lambda function.
- `runtime`: The Python runtime interpreter.
- `s3_bucket`: Creates an Amazon s3 bucket and uploads the deployment packages.
- `remote_env`: Sets the environment variable of all the key-value pairs mentioned in the uploaded JSON file at the Amazon S3 location.

With the help of this configuration information, we will proceed with the deployment.

Building and deploying

Once we are done with the configuration, then we can process the deployment. Zappa provides two different commands to perform the deployment such as `zappa deploy <stage_name>` and `zappa update <stage_name>`. Initially, we will use the `zappa deploy <stage_name>` command, as it is the first time that we are deploying this Lambda application.

If you have already deployed the application and want to redeploy, then you would use the `zappa update <stage_name>` command. In the previous chapter, we had a detailed discussion about the deployment process of Zappa, so you can refer to it.

The following is a log snippet of our deployment process:

```
$ zappa update dev
(python-dateutil 2.7.3
(/home/abdulw/.local/share/virtualenvs/imageGalleryProject-4c9zDR_T/lib/pyt
hon3.6/site-packages), Requirement.parse('python-dateutil==2.6.1'),
{'zappa'})
Calling update for stage dev..
Downloading and installing dependencies..
 - pillow==5.1.0: Downloading
100%|
```
```
                       | 1.95M/1.95M [00:00<00:00, 7.73MB/s]
 - sqlite==python36: Using precompiled lambda package
Packaging project as zip.
Uploading imagegallerypro-dev-1529573380.zip (20.2MiB)..
100%|
```
```
                       | 21.2M/21.2M [00:06<00:00, 2.14MB/s]
Updating Lambda function code..
Updating Lambda function configuration..
Uploading imagegallerypro-dev-template-1529573545.json (1.6KiB)..
100%|
```
```
                       | 1.65K/1.65K [00:00<00:00, 28.9KB/s]
Deploying API Gateway..
Scheduling..
Unscheduled imagegallerypro-dev-zappa-keep-warm-handler.keep_warm_callback.
```

```
Scheduled imagegallerypro-dev-zappa-keep-warm-handler.keep_warm_callback
with expression rate(4 minutes)!
Your updated Zappa deployment is live!:
https://cfs1a2gds0.execute-api.ap-south-1.amazonaws.com/dev
```

Once you are done with the deployment process, Zappa will generate a hosted URL as mentioned in the preceding log snippet. Hence our application has been deployed successfully and hosted at this URL https://cfs1a2gds0.execute-api.ap-south-1. amazonaws.com/dev.

Let's move to the next section, Where we are going to perform some execution on deployed application.

Executing in the production environment

Once you have deployed the application successfully then you will get the hosted application link. This link is nothing but the link generated by configuring the AWS API gateway with AWS Lambda by Zappa.

Now you can use the application in a production environment. A screenshot of the authentication API is present in the next section.

Authentication API

As we have seen the authentication execution in the local environment, it will be the same but in the production environment as well. The following is the log snippet of the authentication API execution deployed on AWS Lambda:

```
$ curl -H "Content-Type: application/json" -X POST -d
'{"username":"abdulwahid", "password":"abdul123#"}'
https://cfs1a2gds0.execute-api.ap-south-1.amazonaws.com/dev/api-token-auth/
{"token":"eyJ0eXAiOiJKV1QiLCJhbGciOiJIUzI1NiJ9.eyJ1c2VyX2lkIjoxLCJ1c2VybmFt
ZSI6ImFiZHVsd2FoaWQiLCJleHAiOjE1Mjk1NzQyOTMsImVtYWlsIjoiYWJkdWx3YWhpZDI0QGd
tYWlsLmNvbSJ9.pHuHaJpjlESwdQxXMiqGOuy2_lpVW1X26RiB9NN8rhI"}
```

As you can see here, the functionality doesn't impact anything as the application is up and running on the serverless environment. Let's look at another API.

GET request on API /albums/

As you have the access token gained by the authentication API, you are eligible to access all protected APIs. The following is a screenshot of the GET request for the /albums/ API:

```
$ curl -H "Authorization: JWT
eyJ0eXAiOiJKV1QiLCJhbGciOiJIUzI1NiJ9.eyJ1c2VyX21kIjoxLCJ1c2VybmFtZSI6ImFiZH
Vsd2FoYWIiLCJleHAiOjE1Mjk1NzQ4MzgsImVtYWlsIjoiYWJkdWx3YWhwZDI0QGdtYWlsLmNvb
SJ9.55NucqsavdgxcmNNs6_hbJMCw42mWPyylaVvuiP5KwI"
https://cfs1a2gds0.execute-api.ap-south-1.amazonaws.com/dev/albums/ |
python -m json.tool

[
    {
        "created_at": "2018-03-17T22:39:08.513389Z",
        "id": 1,
        "name": "Screenshot",
        "photos": [
            {
                "album": 1,
                "created_at": "2018-03-17T22:47:03.775033Z",
                "id": 5,
                "image":
"https://chapter-5.s3-ap-south-1.amazonaws.com/media/Screenshot/AWS_Lambda_
Home_Page.png?X-Amz-Algorithm=AWS4-HMAC-SHA256&X-Amz-
Credential=AKIAJA3LNVLKPTEOWH5A%2F20180621%2Fap-
south-1%2Fs3%2Faws4_request&X-Amz-Date=20180621T094957Z&X-Amz-
Expires=3600&X-Amz-SignedHeaders=host&X-Amz-
Signature=0377bc8750b115b6bff2cd5acc024c6375f5fedc6de35275ea1392375041adc0"
,
                "updated_at": "2018-03-17T22:47:18.298215Z"
            }
        ],
        "updated_at": "2018-03-17T22:47:17.328637Z"
    }
]
```

That's it. We are done with the deployment of the serverless environment. I hope you it was beneficial to you.

Summary

In this chapter, we learned about developing the REST API in the Django REST Framework. We covered the process of securing the API using the JWT authentication mechanism. Finally, we deployed the application in a serverless environment using Zappa.

In the next chapter, we are going to develop a high-performance API based application using a very lightweight Python framework. We will also explore more Zappa configuration options to set up a caching mechanism. Stay tuned to discover more gems from the Zappa world.

Questions

1. What is Django Rest Framework?
2. What is the use of Django-storage?

7
Building a Falcon Application with Zappa

In this chapter, we are going to implement an application based on the Falcon framework. This application will be related to quotes; you will be able to fetch a quote of the day and generate a random quote. I hope it will be interesting to you. We are going to include a scheduler, which will be responsible for fetching a random quote from a third party API and putting it into our database. We will set this scheduler to be executed once a day. Let's get ready for the ride.

Topics we will cover in this chapter include the following:

- Installing and configuring Falcon
- Designing Falcon APIs
- Building, testing, and deploying the Falcon APIs using Zappa

Technical requirements

Before moving ahead with the development work in this chapter, I would like to recommend fulfilling the prerequisites in order to set up the development environment. The following is the list of technical requirements:

- Ubuntu 16.04/macOS/Windows
- Python 3.6
- Pipenv tool
- Falcon

- Peewee
- Requests
- Gunicorn
- Zappa

In the next section, I have described the complete information for setting up the environment. Let's gear up for it and discover the journey toward serverless.

Installing and configuring Falcon

Configuring the Python application development requires us to set up virtual environments. With the help of a virtual environment, we are going to maintain all required packages. As discussed in Chapter 6, *Building a Django REST API with Zappa*, the pipenv packing tool maintains all installed packages in a virtual environment and keeps track of versions and dependencies. Let's move on to set up the virtual environment using the pipenv tool.

Setting up the virtual environment

Before starting the actual implementation, we will set up the virtual environment using the pipenv tool. The following is the command to create a new virtual environment:

```
$ pipenv --python python3.6
```

Here, I explicitly mentioned the Python version because I use many other Python versions on my system. This command will create a `Pipfile` as shown here:

```
[[source]]

url = "https://pypi.python.org/simple"
verify_ssl = true
name = "pypi"


[dev-packages]

[packages]

[requires]

python_version = "3.6"
```

As you can see, the preceding code has basic information about the environment but doesn't have anything under packages because we have not yet installed any packages. This file maintains a list of all installed packages. The pipenv tool creates a virtual environment at `~/.local/share/virtualenvs/`, and it will create the new environment from the directory when we call the preceding command. Once you execute the command, `Pipfile` will be created, as mentioned previously.

You can execute the `pipenv shell` command to enable the virtual environment. Let's move on to the next section where we will install all the required packages.

Installing required packages

As we mentioned earlier, we are going to create a Falcon-based API application. So, we need to install some packages that we are going to use in our application. The following is the list of packages we will use in the implementation:

- `falcon`
- `zappa`
- `gunicorn`
- `peewee`
- `requests`

You can install these packages using the `pipenv install <package_name>` command.

 You can install multiple packages at once by specifying the other packages separated by whitespace, such as `pipenv install <package_one> <package_two> ....`

Once you have installed all these packages, pipenv will create a file named `Pipfile.lock`, which holds the information about versioning and dependencies. `Pipfile` will get updated.

The following is the code snippet of `Pipfile`:

File—`Pipfile`:

```
[[source]]

url = "https://pypi.python.org/simple"
verify_ssl = true
name = "pypi"
```

```
[dev-packages]

pylint = "*"


[packages]

falcon = "*"
zappa = "*"
gunicorn = "*"
peewee = "*"
requests = "*"


[requires]

python_version = "3.6"
```

Now that we are done with the virtual environment setup, it is time to move on to implementing the application. But before moving on to setting up the environment, let's understand some important packages and their usage.

What is Falcon?

Falcon is a bare-metal Python web API framework. It can be used to build microservices with very fast performance.

It is very flexible and easy to implement. It has a markable benchmark, compared to other frameworks. There are many giant organizations that are using Falcon such as Linkedin, OpenStack, RackSpace, and more. The following is a sample code snippet from Falcon's site:

```python
# sample.py

import falcon

class QuoteResource:
    def on_get(self, req, resp):
        """Handles GET requests"""
        quote = {
            'quote': (
                "I've always been more interested in "
                "the future than in the past."
            ),
            'author': 'Grace Hopper'
```

```
        }

        resp.media = quote

api = falcon.API()
api.add_route('/quote', QuoteResource())
```

It requires gunicorn to execute the API on the localhost server, as shown in the following code block:

```
$ gunicorn sample:api
```

Falcon is really simple, and it's much easier to implement REST APIs in Falcon, as it encourages us to follow REST architectural styles. You can read more about Falcon at: https://falconframework.org/#.

What is Peewee?

Peewee is a simple and small **ORM (Object Relational Mapper)**. It is designed to provide an ORM interface similar to Django or SQLAlchemy. It supports databases such as MySQL, Postgres, and SQLite.

The following is a sample code snippet , from Peewee's GitHub page, for defining model classes:

```
from peewee import *
import datetime


db = SqliteDatabase('my_database.db')

class BaseModel(Model):
    class Meta:
        database = db

class User(BaseModel):
    username = CharField(unique=True)

class Tweet(BaseModel):
    user = ForeignKeyField(User, backref='tweets')
    message = TextField()
    created_date = DateTimeField(default=datetime.datetime.now)
    is_published = BooleanField(default=True)
```

It's really amazing—we got the feasibility of designing the database models in Django fashion with a tiny wrapper. Peewee makes it really great and can be considered for writing small microservices.

Read more about Peewee at: `http://docs.peewee-orm.com/en/latest/`.

Let's move on to the next section, where we will be using Falcon and Peewee practically.

Designing Falcon APIs

We are going to design a REST API based on a quote concept. A quote might be something a famous person said, or it might be a dialog from a movie. We are going to use Mashape's **Random Famous Quotes** API (`https://market.mashape.com/andruxnet/ random-famous-quotes`). Mashape is an API platform and it provides many categories of APIs.

In our case, we will create a single API with the following operations:

- Generate or retrieve a quote for the day
- Generate a random quote

For the first operation, we will need to store a random quote from the Mashape API into our database on a daily basis. Hence, we need to design a task scheduler to execute on a daily basis and to store the quote from the Mashape API into our database so that our API user can get the quote for the day.

For the second operation, we don't need to persist each and every randomly generated quote from the Mashape API. Instead, we return the generated random quote to our API user.

Scaffolding the application

When designing any application, scaffolding is an essential step to consider before implementing the solution. It helps us to manage the code base in an optimistic way. The following is the scaffolding of our application:

Here, we divided the code base into different modules based on functionality. Let's have a look at each module in the upcoming sections.

Designing the model class

A model is an entity that represents the essential fields and structure of the data. Each model class represents a database table. In our case, we need to have a single database table. Hence, we will create a single model class to store the data. The following is the code snippet of models.py.

File—models.py:

```python
import os
import datetime
from shutil import copyfile
from peewee import *


# Copy our working DB to /tmp..
db_name = 'quote_database.db'
src = os.path.abspath(db_name)
dst = "/tmp/{}".format(db_name)
copyfile(src, dst)

db = SqliteDatabase(dst)
```

```
class QuoteModel(Model):

    class Meta:
        database = db

    id = IntegerField(primary_key= True)
    quote = TextField()
    author = CharField()
    category = CharField()
    created_at = DateTimeField(default= datetime.date.today())

db.connect()
db.create_tables([QuoteModel])
```

Here, we defined the `QuoteModel` by extending the `Model` class and defined attributes using the features of the Peewee library. The most essential part here is the database connectivity; as you can see, we used an SQLite database. We created the database file and placed it in the `/tmp` directory so that it would accessible in an AWS Lambda environment.

Once we have defined the database using the `SqliteDatabase` class, we connect the database and create database tables as defined by models.

The `db.create_tabless` method creates tables only if they do not exist.

Now we are ready to use this `Model` class to perform any query operation. But, before creating resources, let's have a look at `mashape.py`, where we integrated the third-party API to get a random quote.

Mashape API integration

Mashape is the largest API marketplace for private and public APIs. There are thousands of API providers and consumers registered. Have a look at the marketplace at `https://market.mashape.com`. We are going to use the Random Famous Quote API (`https://market.mashape.com/andruxnet/random-famous-quotes`). Once you are logged in to the Mashape marketplace, you can explore these APIs in detail. The following code snippet has one of the APIs that we are using to fetch a random quote.

The following is the code snippet of the `mashape.py` file.

File—`mashape.py`:

```
import os
import requests


def fetch_quote():
    response = requests.get(
        os.environ.get('Mashape_API_Endpoint'),
        headers={
            'X-Mashape-Key': os.environ.get('X_Mashape_Key'),
            'Accept': 'application/json'
        }
    )
    if response.status_code == 200:
        return response.json()[0]
    return response.json()
```

Here, we have written a method named `fetch_quote`. This method is responsible for fetching the quote from the Mashape API and returning the quote data in Python dictionary format. We are going to use this method at different places as per our requirements.

Creating API resources

We are going to use Falcon to create a single API with an allowed method as HTTP GET only. This API will have two different operations as we mentioned in the previous sections. The following is the code snippet of `resources.py`.

File—`resources.py`:

```
import os
import datetime
import requests
import falcon

from models import QuoteModel
from mashape import fetch_quote

class QuoteResource:
    def on_get(self, req, resp):
        """Handles GET requests"""
        if req.get_param('type') in ['daily', None]:
            data = QuoteModel.select().where(QuoteModel.created_at ==
datetime.date.today())
```

```
            if data.exists():
                data = data.get()
                resp.media = {'quote': data.quote, 'author': data.author,
'category': data.category}
            else:
                quote = fetch_quote()
                QuoteModel.create(**quote)
                resp.media = quote
        elif req.get_param('type') == 'random':
            resp.media = fetch_quote()
        else:
            raise falcon.HTTPError(falcon.HTTP_400,'Invalid Quote
type','Supported types are \'daily\' or \'random\'.')

api = falcon.API()
api.add_route('/quote', QuoteResource())
```

Here, we created the `QuoteResource` class and implemented the `on_get` method to handle `GET` requests. In order to perform different operations of generating the daily quote and random quote, we defined a query parameter named `type`, for example, `http://<API_URL>?type=daily|random`. Hence, based on the query parameter, we serve the request.

We are done with the implementation. We will look at the execution, scheduling, and deployment in the next section.

Building, testing, and deploying Falcon APIs using Zappa

Irrespective of other frameworks, Falcon requires the `gunicorn` library for execution. Gunicorn is a lightweight Python WSGI HTTP server. Falcon doesn't have any default behavior to server WSGI; instead, Falcon mainly focuses on API architectural styles and performance. Let's move on to executing the API in the local environment.

Local execution using gunicorn

For local execution, we are going to use `gunicorn`. The following is the log of the `gunicorn` execution:

```
$ gunicorn resources:api
[2018-05-18 15:40:57 +0530] [31655] [INFO] Starting gunicorn 19.8.1
```

```
[2018-05-18 15:40:57 +0530] [31655] [INFO] Listening at:
http://127.0.0.1:8000 (31655)
[2018-05-18 15:40:57 +0530] [31655] [INFO] Using worker: sync
[2018-05-18 15:40:57 +0530] [31662] [INFO] Booting worker with pid: 31662
```

We are using the `resources` module and the `api` object for the execution. We created the `api` object using the `resources` module.

API for the daily quote

We implemented the `/quote` API and separated operations based on the query parameters. Let's execute the `/quote?type=daily` API. The following is the log snippet of the daily quote API execution using the cURL command-line tool:

```
$ curl http://localhost:8000/quote?type=daily
{"quote": "I'll get you, my pretty, and your little dog, too!", "author":
"The Wizard of Oz", "category": "Movies"}
```

This API will return a unique quote every day.

API of the random quote

Now, let's execute another operation on the `/quote` API such as `/quote?type=random`. This API will return a random quote on each request. The following is a log of the API execution:

```
$ curl http://localhost:8000/quote?type=random
{"quote": "The only way to get rid of a temptation is to yield to it.",
"author": "Oscar Wilde", "category": "Famous"}
```

This API will return a random quote record on each request.

Configuring Zappa

Once we have installed Zappa while setting up the virtual environment, we are good to configure Zappa with our application. The following are the operations we would execute in order to configure Zappa.

Zappa initialization

The `zappa init` command is the first step to configuring Zappa. This command will start a user-interactive questionnaire to set up Zappa with the required information. I followed the default suggestions except for the function name. The following is the generated code snippet of the Zappa `settings.json` file.

File—`zappa_settings.json`:

```
{
    "dev": {
        "app_function": "resources.api",
        "aws_region": "ap-south-1",
        "profile_name": "default",
        "project_name": "chapter-7",
        "runtime": "python3.6",
        "s3_bucket": "zappa-0edixmwpd",
        "remote_env": "s3://book-configs/chapter-7-config.json"
    }
}
```

Here, we defined the configuration as per the requirements. As the key defines each configuration, we can see the usages of it:

- `aws_region`: The AWS region where the lambda would get uploaded
- `app_function`: The import path of the `api` object from the `resources` module
- `profile_name`: The AWS CLI configuration profile that is defined in the `~/.aws/credentials` file
- `project_name`: The project name for the uploading lambda function.
- `runtime`: The Python runtime interpreter
- `s3_bucket`: Creates an Amazon S3 bucket and uploads the deployment packages
- `remote_env`: Sets the environment variable of all the key-value pairs mentioned in the uploaded JSON file at the Amazon S3 location

With the help of this configuration information, we can proceed with the deployment.

Zappa deployment

Once we are done with the configuration, then we can process the deployment. Zappa provides two different commands to perform the deployment, `zappa deploy <stage_name>` and `zappa update <stage_name>`. Initially, we use the `zappa deploy <stage_name>` command as it is the first time that we are deploying this lambda application.

If you have already deployed the application and want to redeploy it, then you would use the `zappa update <stage_name>` command. In the previous chapter, we had a detailed discussion about the deployment process of Zappa, so you can refer to that for more information.

The following is the log of our deployment process:

```
$ zappa update dev
Important! A new version of Zappa is available!
Upgrade with: pip install zappa --upgrade
Visit the project page on GitHub to see the latest changes:
https://github.com/Miserlou/Zappa
Calling update for stage dev..
Downloading and installing dependencies..
 - sqlite==python36: Using precompiled lambda package
Packaging project as zip.
Uploading chapter-7-dev-1529584381.zip (5.9MiB)..
100%|
                                                          | 6.17M/6.17M [00:03<00:00, 1.08MB/s]
Updating Lambda function code..
Updating Lambda function configuration..
Uploading chapter-7-dev-template-1529584474.json (1.6KiB)..
100%|
                                                          | 1.62K/1.62K [00:00<00:00, 9.09KB/s]
Deploying API Gateway..
Scheduling..
Unscheduled chapter-7-dev-schedulers.set_quote_of_the_day.
Unscheduled chapter-7-dev-zappa-keep-warm-handler.keep_warm_callback.
Scheduled chapter-7-dev-schedulers.set_quote_of_the_day with expression
cron(0 12 * * ? *)!
Scheduled chapter-7-dev-zappa-keep-warm-handler.keep_warm_callback with
expression rate(4 minutes)!
Your updated Zappa deployment is live!:
https://0uqnn5q13a.execute-api.ap-south-1.amazonaws.com/dev
```

Here, I use `zappa update dev` to deploy my existing application. This command will print the deployed URL at the end; we can use it to test the application in the production environment.

Executing in the production environment

Since we deployed our application on AWS Lambda using Zappa, Zappa configures the API Gateway with the proxy to AWS Lambda. Hence, it will have a randomly generated API Gateway link, as mentioned in the previous section.

Now, let's execute our API using the generated link (`https://0uqnn5ql3a.execute-api.ap-south-1.amazonaws.com/dev/quote`).

Daily quote API execution

The execution operation will be similar to the local execution, but it will have a little bit of an impact on the API Gateway, because there are many features available in the AWS API Gateway that can be used to enhance our API performance and optimization.

The following is the log snippet of the daily quote API execution using cURL tool:

```
$ curl
https://0uqnn5ql3a.execute-api.ap-south-1.amazonaws.com/dev/quote?type=dail
y
{"quote": "You've got to ask yourself one question: 'Do I feel lucky?'
Well, do ya, punk?", "author": "Dirty Harry", "category": "Movies"}
```

Our application is live as a serverless application. You can use it without worrying much about the server, as it is capable of serving millions of request per second and Amazon will take care of its scalability and availability. Let's try another API.

Random quote API execution

Let's execute the random quote API. The following is a snippet of the random quote API execution:

```
$ curl -s -w 'Total time taken: %{time_total}\n'
https://0uqnn5ql3a.execute-api.ap-south-1.amazonaws.com/dev/quote?type=rand
om
{"quote": "A friendship founded on business is better than a business
founded on friendship.", "author": "John D. Rockefeller", "category":
"Famous"}
```

```
Total time taken: 1.369
```

You can see that this execution takes 1.369 seconds, because we are explicitly making another request to the Mashape API to fetch the random quote. We can make this execution faster by adding caching support to the API Gateway service.

Enabling caching on the API Gateway

The AWS API Gateway provides a feature to add caching for your API endpoint responses. It will help to reduce the network latency and return cached responses to the user without hitting the AWS Lambda function.

Zappa has the ability to configure caching on the AWS API Gateway; you don't need to configure the caching manually from the AWS web console. The following is the configuration needed to add in the `zappa_settings.json` file to enable caching on the API Gateway.

File—`zappa_settings.json`:

```
{
    "dev": {
        "app_function": "resources.api",
        "aws_region": "ap-south-1",
        "profile_name": "default",
        "project_name": "chapter-7",
        "runtime": "python3.6",
        "s3_bucket": "zappa-0edixmwpd",
        "remote_env": "s3://book-configs/chapter-7-config.json",
        "cache_cluster_enabled": false,
        "cache_cluster_size": 0.5,
        "cache_cluster_ttl": 300,
        "cache_cluster_encrypted": false,
    }
}
```

As mentioned, the caching options in the `zappa_settings.json` file. Let's see its usage:

- `cache_cluster_enabled`: Default is `false`; this option is set to `true` to enable the API Gateway cache cluster.
- `cache_cluster_size`: Default is 0.5 GB; this indicates the cache memory size. If required, we can increase the size as well.
- `cache_cluster_ttl`: Default is 300 seconds; this option is to set the **time-to-live** (**TTL**) for the response caches in memory. It has a maximum limit of 3,600 seconds, and in order to disable it, you can set it to 0 seconds.

- `cache_cluster_encrypted`: Default is `false`; set this option to `true` if you want to encrypt the cached responses data.

This is how you can enable the API Gateway caching mechanism without any manual intervention. Only `GET` request methods should be cached.

> The AWS API Gateway doesn't support the free tier. It's charged on an hourly basis. Read more about API Gateway Pricing at `https://aws.amazon.com/api-gateway/pricing/`.

Event scheduling

AWS Lambda can be configured alongside AWS CloudWatch Events. If you want to execute your Lambda function to be executed on a regular schedule, for example, every five minutes, you can use rate expression or you can configure a `cron` expression to schedule a timed event for the execution.

You can read more about schedule expression at `https://docs.aws.amazon.com/lambda/latest/dg/tutorial-scheduled-events-schedule-expressions.html`.

Configuring the AWS Lambda with a scheduled event requires more manual intervention. You can have a look at the official documentation at `https://docs.aws.amazon.com/lambda/latest/dg/with-scheduled-events.html`.

Zappa provides a very flexible way to configure the schedule events without any manual intervention.

Configuring events using Zappa

Zappa supports both scheduled events and AWS events. Scheduled events are bound to time and date, whereas AWS events are related to any AWS service such as AWS S3 events and more.

We can schedule the Lambda function execution based on any AWS events, as shown in the following code snippet:

```
{
    "production": {
        ...
        "events": [{
            "function": "your_module.process_upload_function",
```

```
            "event_source": {
                "arn": "arn:aws:s3:::my-bucket",
                "events": [
                  "s3:ObjectCreated:*"
                ]
            }
        }],
    ...
    }
}
```

Zappa supports almost all AWS events to execute the AWS lambda function. You can read more about execution in response to AWS events at `https://github.com/Miserlou/Zappa#executing-in-response-to-aws-events`.

Once you add the events configuration, you can execute the following command to schedule the events:

```
$ zappa schedule production
```

In our case, we are going to schedule a time-bounded event to execute a function to fetch a daily quote and store it in the database. Let's see how we can configure our application to schedule a daily event.

Scheduling an event to set the quote of the day

As we already designed our `/quote?type=daily` API to fetch a quote of the day, this API will return the quote if it exists in the database or else fetch it from the Mashape API and store it in the database. This operation is to prevent API failure in case the quote record does not exist in the database.

But we want to make sure that the quote record does exist in the database. For that, we are going to schedule a daily event that will occur at midnight. We will execute a function to perform the `fetch quote` operation.

The following is the Zappa settings snippet with events configuration.

File—`zappa_settings.json`:

```
{
    "dev": {
        "app_function": "resources.api",
        "aws_region": "ap-south-1",
        "profile_name": "default",
        "project_name": "chapter-7",
```

```
"runtime": "python3.6",
"s3_bucket": "zappa-0edixmwpd",
"remote_env": "s3://book-configs/chapter-7-config.json",
"cache_cluster_enabled": false,
"cache_cluster_size": 0.5,
"cache_cluster_ttl": 300,
"cache_cluster_encrypted": false,
"events": [{
    "function": "schedulers.set_quote_of_the_day",
    "expression": "cron(0 12 * * ? *)"
}]
        }
    }
```

Here, we are scheduling a function to be executed is
`schedulers.set_quote_of_the_day` at midnight, set by `cron` expression. The following
is the code snippet of the `schedulers` module.

File—`schedulers.py`:

```
from models import QuoteModel
from mashape import fetch_quote


def set_quote_of_the_day(event, context):
    QuoteModel.create(**fetch_quote())
```

As mentioned in the preceding code snippet, the method named `set_quote_of_the_day`
will be executed by the scheduled event and will perform the operation to fetch the quote
and store it in the database.

Now, in order to enable the scheduled events, let's run the `zappa schedule`
`dev` command. The following is the log of the `schedule` command execution:

```
$ zappa schedule dev
Calling schedule for stage dev..
Scheduling..
Unscheduled chapter-7-dev-zappa-keep-warm-handler.keep_warm_callback.
Unscheduled chapter-7-dev-schedulers.set_quote_of_the_day.
Scheduled chapter-7-dev-schedulers.set_quote_of_the_day with expression
cron(0 12 * * ? *)!
Scheduled chapter-7-dev-zappa-keep-warm-handler.keep_warm_callback with
expression rate(4 minutes)!
```

That's it; we are done with scheduling now. Now, daily, at midnight,
the `set_quote_of_the_day` method will invoke and perform a fetch quote operation.

Summary

In this chapter, we learned to create high-performance APIs based on the Falcon framework. We also learned to configure the API Gateway caching mechanism using Zappa. The most interesting part we covered was scheduling. Now you don't need to worry about any third-party scheduling tools, as Zappa makes it super easy to enable scheduling based on time and AWS events.

I hope you enjoyed this chapter. Now let's dive into the next chapter to explore Zappa's features. We are going to set the custom domain for our application and SSL certificates.

Questions

1. How does Falcon differ from other Python frameworks?
2. What are the benefits of Peewee library over SQLAlchemy?
3. How does scheduling work?

Custom Domain with SSL

8

In this chapter, we are going to configure a custom domain for the quote application developed in the previous chapter. Configuring custom domains is an essential part of moving the application to the production environment because of its serverless nature. This process involves several operations and is different from traditional configuration with Apache or NGINX. We will look at the quote application that is already deployed in the serverless infrastructure.

Topics we will cover in this chapter include:

- Configuring the custom domain with AWS Route53
- Generating SSL certificates using the Amazon Certificate Manager
- Integrating the custom domain using Zappa

Technical requirements

There are some prerequisites to meet before you start this chapter. We are going to work with some AWS services and a real domain name. Therefore, you will need the following:

- Ubuntu 16.04/Windows/macOS
- Pipenv tool
- Zappa and other Python dev packages
- Registered domain
- AWS account

We are going to use some Python packages, which are mentioned in later sections. Apart from the development environment, you will need to have your own registered domain and permission to update its default nameservers. Let's move to the next section, where we will be exploring the domain nameserver configuration with AWS Route 53.

Configuring custom domain with AWS Route 53

Creating a custom domain for our application requires owning a domain. Domain names can be purchased from a domain registrar. In our case, I purchased a domain name called `abdulwahid.info` from **GoDaddy** (`https://in.godaddy.com/`), the **domain name system** (**DNS**) service provider.

Every domain serves over the internet through nameservers managed by the DNS service provider. There are many service providers that offer services to manage and host a website from their end. We are going to user the AWS Route 53 service.

What is AWS Route 53?

AWS Route 53 is a scalable cloud DNS web service. Route 53 is really effective at configuring the domain with any AWS services. It connects with infrastructure running on AWS as well as outside of AWS. Route 53 provides a variety of routings, such as latency base routing, Geo DNS, geoproximity, and weighted round robin. All these routings can be combined to provide low-latency bandwidth. Route 53 provides a domain name registration service as well. If we register a domain on AWS Route 53, then we don't need to manage the DNS configuration. All DNS configurations would automatically use AWS services.

But we didn't register our domain on Route 53, so we need to replace the default GoDaddy nameservers with Route 53. In the next section, we'll discuss how to change the nameservers.

Changing nameservers to Route 53

We are going to move control for the existing domain to Route 53. This process requires changing the default nameservers of the domain `abdulwhaid.info` to the new nameservers created by Route 53.

With reference to the AWS official documentation (`https://docs.aws.amazon.com/Route53/latest/DeveloperGuide/CreatingHostedZone.html`) about creating a hosted zone for configuring Route 53 with an existing domain on a different registrar, perform the following steps:

1. Sign into the AWS Console and open the Route 53 console at `https://console.aws.amazon.com/route53/`.
2. If you are new to Route 53, choose **Get Started Now** under **DNS Management.**
3. If you are already using Route 53, then choose **Hosted zones** in the left navigation pane, as shown in the following screenshot:

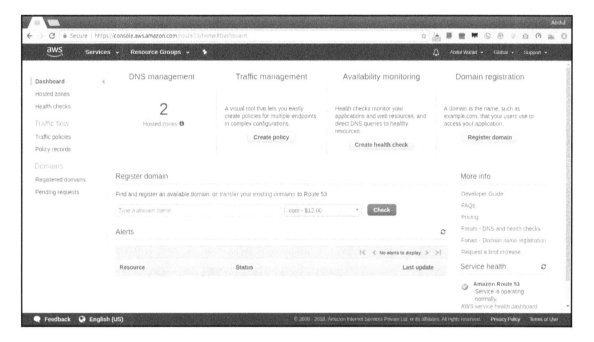

4. Now, from the hosted zones page, click on **Create Hosted Zone** with the the domain `abdulwahid.info`, as shown in the following screenshot:

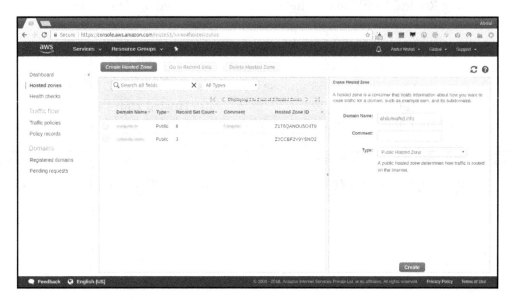

5. Once you have created the hosted zone for the domain `abdulwahid.info`, Route 53 will create two records, **Nameservers (NS)** and **Start Of Authority (SOA)**, as shown in the following screenshot:

6. Now, we need to use the NS records and replace the default NS record generated at the domain registrar (that is, GoDaddy), where we created the domain `abdulwahid.info`. The following is the screenshot of the default NS records:

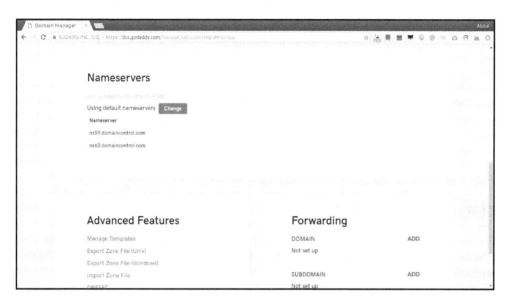

7. Change the default NS to **Custom** and enter the NS records generated at Route 53, as shown in the following screenshot:

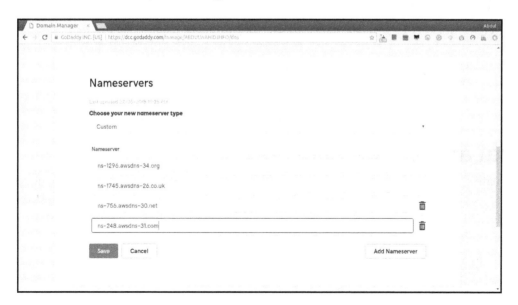

8. Click on **Save**, and we are done. Now it will take some time to process by the domain registrar. You will get a confirmation email from the domain registrar.

 Route 53 manage the route traffic using hosted zones for a specific domain. A hosted zone is like a container that holds information about the domain and knows how to route the traffic on the internet.

Once you get the confirmation email, then the domain `abdulwahid.info` will be managed by Route 53. Let's move to the next section to learn more about the SSL certificate configuration using AWS Certificate Manager.

Generating SSL certificates using AWS Certificate Manager

SSL provides security for your web server and application users. With the help of SSL, you can prevent hacker attacks on your data that's communicated between your web server and browser. Before implementing the SSL security into our application, let's understand some basic methodologies about SSL.

What is SSL?

SSL (**Secure Sockets Layer**) is a standard security protocol used to secure the communication between a web server and browser by encrypting the data. SSL will make sure the data transmitted from browsers to your web server is encrypted. In order to create an SSL connection, we require to generate SSL certificates and configure our web server to serve under the SSL layer. The next section will discuss SSL certificates.

What are SSL certificates?

For creating an SSL connection, we need an SSL certificate. SSL certificates can be generated from the **Certificate Authority** (**CA**). Before generating the certificate, we need to provide information about our website and business details. Based on this information, two cryptographic keys will be generated: a public and a private key.

Now using the public key and business details, we need to process a **Certificate Signing Request** (**CSR**) with the CA. Once the CA has authorized our details successfully, it will issue an SSL certificate that matches our private key.

Now, we are ready to configure the SSL certificate with our application. This is process is a traditional way of generating an SSL certificate. But we are going to use Amazon Certificate Manager to generate an SSL certificate.

Generating SSL certificate using Amazon Certificate Manager (ACM)

There are several ways of generating an SSL certificate. The following are some of the ways you can acquire an SSL/TSL certificate for your application:

- You can buy an SSL certificate from the SSL Certificate Authority.
- You can generate a free SSL/TSL certificate on your own by using **Let's Encrypt** (https://letsencrypt.org/). Let's Encrypt is an open Certificate Authority that provides free SSL/TSL certificates.
- You can generate an SSL using **AWS Certificate Manager** (**ACM**). We are going to use ACM to generate an SSL certificate for our application.

ACM is a service that manages and creates SSL/TSL certificates for AWS-based services and applications. An ACM certificate works with multiple domain names and subdomains. You can also use ACM to create a wildcard SSL.

ACM is strictly linked with **AWS Certificate Manager Private Certificate Authority** (**ACM PCA**). ACM PCA is responsible for validating the domain authority and issuing the certificate.

Now, we are going to generate an ACM certificate for our domain and subdomain. Follow these steps to create an ACM certificate:

 Please note, API Gateway supports ACM certificates from one region only. Hence, we are going to use the **US East** region. You can read more about this at https://github.com/Miserlou/Zappa/pull/1142.

1. Sign into the AWS Console and open the ACM console at https://ap-south-1. console.aws.amazon.com/acm.

2. If you are new to AWS ACM, then click on **Get Started** under **Provision certificates**, or if you are already using AWS ACM, then choose **Request a certificate**, as shown in the following screenshot:

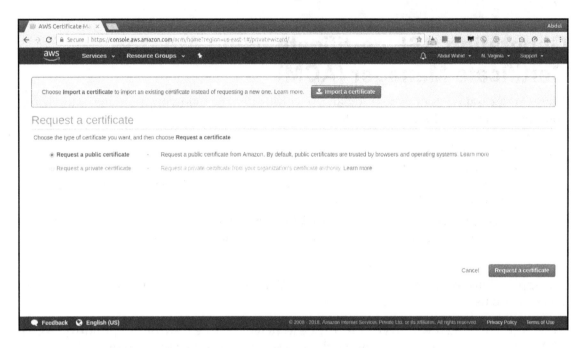

Here, we are going to choose **Request a public certificate**.

You can read more about public certificate at `https://docs.aws.amazon.com/acm/latest/userguide/gs-acm-request-public.html`.

3. On the next page, you need to give the details of your domain names. We are going to request a wildcard certificate against our domain using an asterisk (*) as a subdomain name. Hence, this certificate can be used to protect multiple sites under the same domain. The following is the screenshot for adding the domain name:

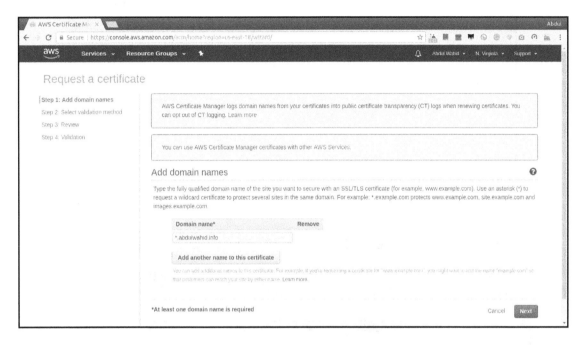

4. On the next page, you need to choose a validation method. There are two types of methods available, as follows:

- **DNS validation:** This method requires permission to modify the DNS records for the domains in your certificate, so that it can directly validate with the record set.
- **Email validation:** This method can be used if you do not have permission to modify the DNS records. Hence, you can validate the domain with registered emails recorded with the domain registrar.

We are going to use the DNS validation method. This is because we own the DNS access in the Route 53 hosted zone because of the mapped nameserver at the domain registrar. DNS validation is straightforward. Have a look at the following screenshot:

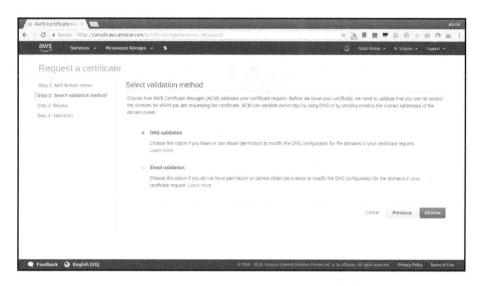

5. Now, we are ready to go. Clicking on Review will display the selected configurations, as shown in the following screenshot:

6. Once you have clicked on **Confirm and request** from the **Review** page, you need to complete the validation process. The following screenshot states that the validation status is pending, so we need to perform the validation by expanding the domain section:

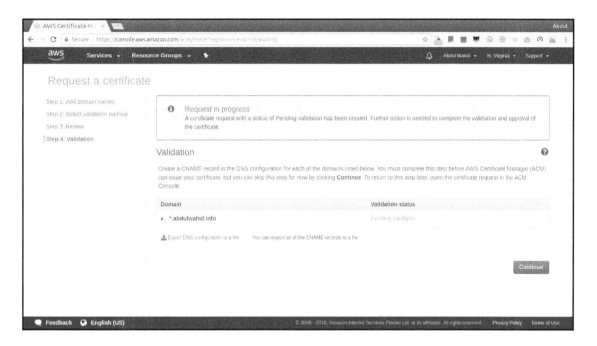

7. Once you expand the domain section, you will see some instructions to complete the validation process. We chose the DNS validation method. Therefore, this method needs to add a **CNAME** record to the DNS configuration. As per the following screenshot, you can perform the action to update the DNS configuration with the given **CNAME** by clicking on the **Create record in Route 53** button:

8. Once you have clicked on **Create record in Route 53**, it will raise a confirmation popup with the **CNAME** record, as shown in the following screenshot:

9. Once you click on the **Create** button, it automatically updates the DNS configuration in Route 53 with the given **CNAME** record. You will see the success message, as shown in the following screenshot:

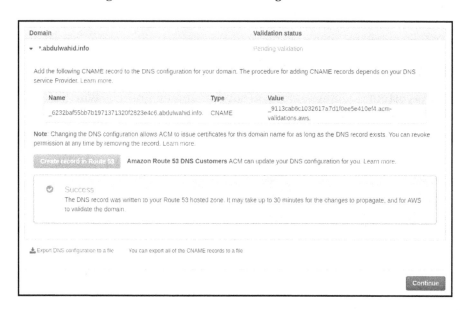

10. Click on **Continue**, and we are done. You will be redirected to the certificates dashboard page, as shown in the following screenshot:

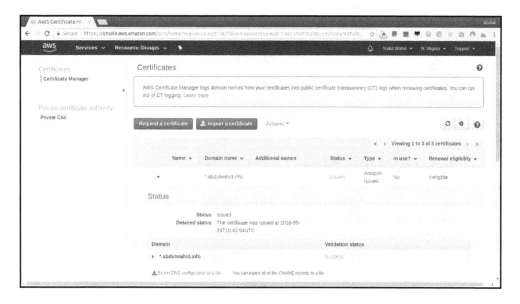

ACM CA has successfully issued an SSL certificate against your domain. As you can see, the status in green states **Issued**. Now, it's time to configure the domain and certificate with our application. In the next section, we are going to configure a subdomain with the issued SSL certificate with our quote API application.

Integrating custom domain using Zappa

Zappa supports custom domain names and subdomain integrations with SSL certificates. We have discussed the sources of SSL/TSL certificate generation in the previous sections. Zappa can deploy domains with the following CAs:

- Your own purchased SSL from the Certificate Authority provider
- Let's Encrypt
- AWS

You can read more details about the deployment of the domain with the aforementioned CAs at: `https://github.com/Miserlou/Zappa#ssl-certification`.

We are going to use the AWS Certificate Authority SSL certificate. We have already generated the ACM certificate in the last section. It's now time to integrate the ACM certificate with a subdomain for our application.

Let's move to the next section, where we are going to configure our quote API application with a subdomain and ACM certificate.

Deploying to a domain with ACM certificate

As we have already issued the ACM certificate, now let's configure our application to the desired domain and perform the deployment process. Zappa provides a `domain` attribute to configure the domain name for the application and `certificate_arn` for the ACM certificate. You need to configure these two attributes in `zappa_settings.json`.

Before that, we need to get the value of `certificate_arn`, as it is the **ARN** (**Amazon Resource Name**) generated by ACM for the domain for which we had issued the certificate. You can get the value of the ARN from the ACM dashboard by expanding the domain section, as shown in the following screenshot:

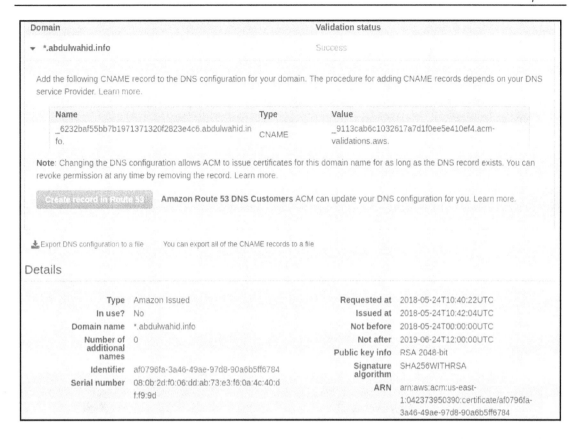

You can see the ARN at the bottom right of the screen. Now, copy the value of the ARN attribute and put it in the `zappa_settings.json` as a value for `certificate_arn`, as shown in the following code snippet from the `zappa_settings.json`.

File—`zappa_settings.json`:

```
{
    "dev": {
        "app_function": "resources.api",
        "aws_region": "ap-south-1",
        "profile_name": "default",
        "project_name": "chapter-8",
        "runtime": "python3.6",
        "s3_bucket": "zappa-0edixmwpd",
        "remote_env": "s3://book-configs/chapter-7-config.json",
        "cache_cluster_enabled": false,
        "cache_cluster_size": 0.5,
        "cache_cluster_ttl": 300,
        "cache_cluster_encrypted": false,
```

```
        "events": [{
            "function": "schedulers.set_quote_of_the_day",
            "expression": "cron(0 12 * * ? *)"
        }],
        "domain": "quote.abdulwahid.info",
        "certificate_arn":"arn:aws:acm:us-
east-1:042373950390:certificate/af0796fa-3a46-49ae-97d8-90a6b5ff6784"
    }
}
```

Here, we configure the domain as `quote.abdulwahid.info` and set `certificate_arn`. Now, let's deploy the application using the `zappa deploy <stage_name>` command, as we are deploying the application for the first time. Have a look at the following code:

```
$ zappa deploy dev
Important! A new version of Zappa is available!
Upgrade with: pip install zappa --upgrade
Visit the project page on GitHub to see the latest changes:
https://github.com/Miserlou/Zappa
Calling deploy for stage dev..
Downloading and installing dependencies..
 - sqlite==python36: Using precompiled lambda package
Packaging project as zip.
Uploading chapter-7-dev-1529679507.zip (5.9MiB)..
100%|███████████████████████████████████████████████████
████████████████████████████████████████████████████████
████████████████████████████████████████████████████████
██████████████| 6.17M/6.17M [00:02<00:00, 2.27MB/s]
Scheduling..
Scheduled chapter-7-dev-schedulers.set_quote_of_the_day with expression
cron(0 12 * * ? *)!
Scheduled chapter-7-dev-zappa-keep-warm-handler.keep_warm_callback with
expression rate(4 minutes)!
Uploading chapter-7-dev-template-1529679513.json (1.6KiB)..
100%|███████████████████████████████████████████████████
████████████████████████████████████████████████████████
████████████████████████████████████████████████████████
████████████| 1.62K/1.62K [00:00<00:00, 4.76KB/s]
Waiting for stack chapter-7-dev to create (this can take a bit)..
100%|███████████████████████████████████████████████████
████████████████████████████████████████████████████████
████████████████████████████████████████████████████████
████████████████████| 4/4 [00:09<00:00, 2.66s/res]
Deploying API Gateway..
Deployment complete!:
https://5phr2bp4id.execute-api.ap-south-1.amazonaws.com/dev
```

As you can see, the application was deployed on the randomly generated API endpoint.

But in order to configure the application, we need to associate the API Gateway with the ACM certificate using the `zappa certify` command, as shown in the following log snippet:

```
$ zappa certify
Calling certify for stage dev..
Are you sure you want to certify? [y/n] y
Certifying domain quote.abdulwahid.info..
Created a new domain name with supplied certificate. Please note that it
can take up to 40 minutes for this domain to be created and propagated
through AWS, but it requires no further work on your part.
Certificate updated!
```

Once you run the `zappa certify` command, it will create and associate the API Gateway with the configured certificate.

Now, let's update the deployment once again, using the `zappa update <stage_name>` command, as shown in the following code.

```
$ zappa update dev
Important! A new version of Zappa is available!
Upgrade with: pip install zappa --upgrade
Visit the project page on GitHub to see the latest changes:
https://github.com/Miserlou/Zappa
Calling update for stage dev..
Downloading and installing dependencies..
 - sqlite==python36: Using precompiled lambda package
Packaging project as zip.
Uploading chapter-7-dev-1529679710.zip (5.9MiB)..
100%|███████████████████████████████████████████████████████
█████████████████████████████████████████████████████████████
███████████████████████████████| 6.17M/6.17M [00:03<00:00, 863KB/s]
Updating Lambda function code..
Updating Lambda function configuration..
Uploading chapter-7-dev-template-1529679717.json (1.6KiB)..
100%|███████████████████████████████████████████████████████
█████████████████████████████████████████████████████████████
█████████████████████| 1.62K/1.62K [00:00<00:00, 6.97KB/s]
Deploying API Gateway..
Scheduling..
Unscheduled chapter-7-dev-schedulers.set_quote_of_the_day.
Unscheduled chapter-7-dev-zappa-keep-warm-handler.keep_warm_callback.
Scheduled chapter-7-dev-schedulers.set_quote_of_the_day with expression
cron(0 12 * * ? *)!
Scheduled chapter-7-dev-zappa-keep-warm-handler.keep_warm_callback with
```

```
expression rate(4 minutes)!
Your updated Zappa deployment is live!: https://quote.abdulwahid.info
(https://5phr2bp4id.execute-api.ap-south-1.amazonaws.com/dev)
```

That's it. As you can see, our application is live on `https://quote.abdulwahid.info`.
Now, let's have a look at the execution in the next section.

Application execution with the configured domain

We have deployed and configured our quote API application on a serverless infrastructure.
Let's see the API execution using the Postman API client.

Daily quote API

We designed this API (`https://quote.abdulwahid.info/quote?type=daily`) to
return a quote on a daily basis. Our configured scheduler will update the schedule UTC
time every day. Have a look at the following cURL log snippet:

```
$ curl https://quote.abdulwahid.info/quote?type=daily
{"quote": "Many wealthy people are little more than janitors of their
possessions.", "author": "Frank Lloyd Wright", "category": "Famous"}
```

Random quote API

The random quote API (`https://quote.abdulwahid.info/quote?type=random`) will
return a random quote on every request. Have a look at the following cURL log snippet:

```
$ curl https://quote.abdulwahid.info/quote?type=random
{"quote": "My mother thanks you. My father thanks you. My sister thanks
you. And I thank you.", "author": "Yankee Doodle Dandy", "category":
"Movies"}
```

That's it. We have successfully deployed our application over a serverless architecture. We
also configured the custom domain with our application. This will be live for testing
purposes.

Summary

In this chapter, we learned about creating a custom domain and configuring the domain with Route 53. Using Route 53, we managed the domain DNS configurations. To generate the SSL certificate, we used ACM, which is easy and straightforward to use. Later, we configured Zappa with a domain using the ARN of the generated ACM certificate. I hope this chapter helps you understand the mechanism of configuring a custom domain for your application.

Now we are going to learn more about scheduling a task and the asynchronous execution of a method on AWS Lambda. We are going to enhance the quote API application further with a mobile subscription model. Let's gear up for the next chapter to dive into the world of asynchronous using AWS Lambda.

Questions

1. What is AWS Route 53?
2. What do we mean by domain nameservers?
3. How does ACM secure the hosted API on AWS Lambda?

Asynchronous Task Execution on AWS Lambda

9

In this chapter, we are going to cover asynchronous task execution on AWS Lambda. AWS Lambda makes autoscaling and asynchronous execution very easy to achieve. Zappa can help us to configure tasks so that they are executed in an asynchronous manner on AWS Lambda. Zappa implements features to manage responses for asynchronous tasks.

The topics we will cover in this chapter include the following:

- Asynchronous execution
- AWS Lambda asynchronous invocation using Zappa
- Configuring the Quote API application with asynchronous features
- Deploying and executing the Quote API using Zappa

Technical requirements

Before starting this chapter, make sure you fulfill the prerequisites for working with the application. Here are the technical requirements you need to meet:

- Ubuntu 16.04/Windows/macOS
- Python3.6
- Pipenv tool
- Falcon framework
- Zappa
- Registered domain
- AWS account

This chapter enhances the application developed in Chapter 8, *Custom Domain with SSL*. Hence, some of the requirements can be used from previously configured prerequisites. Let's move ahead to learn more about asynchronous execution in AWS Lambda.

Asynchronous execution

Asynchronous execution plays an essential role in developing high-performance and optimized applications. AWS Lambda supports asynchronous execution. There are different approaches to executing AWS Lambda functions in asynchronous mode.

Understanding asynchronous execution

Asynchronous execution is the process of executing specific blocks of code without blocking user intervention. To understand it better, consider the jQuery Ajax mechanism for sending asynchronous requests to the server, which does so without blocking the user and capturing the success response or error response in a callback method. Have a look at the following diagram to get a better understanding:

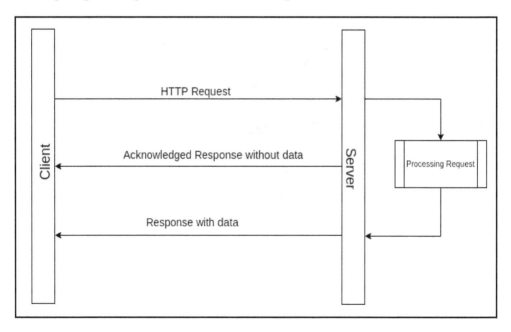

Now, as you can see, once the server gets an asynchronous request from the client, the server returns an acknowledged response immediately. Once the request processing is done, either a success or failure response will be returned; otherwise, nothing will be returned.

Whether a response is returned from the asynchronous method depends on the requirements. We may or may not need to have a response returned. If we do wish to return a response, then there should be a mechanism to handle or capture the response at the client side.

In a similar fashion, AWS Lambda functions can be executed in an asynchronous manner, where we would not be blocking user intervention to wait for the return response. There are some use cases where we are required to capture the response of an AWS Lambda function executed asynchronously. We will discuss capturing responses in the coming sections.

Let's see how AWS Lambda executes asynchronously.

Asynchronous AWS Lambda execution using Boto3

An AWS Lambda function is nothing but a function (a block of code) in the cloud. A function can be invoked synchronously or asynchronously. To achieve asynchronous execution in any programming language, we execute functions in a separate thread or process. In Python, for instance, there are various libraries available for achieving asynchronous execution. Similarly, AWS Lambda supports asynchronous execution very well.

Let's take a look at the following code snippet:

```
client = boto3.client('lambda')
response = client.invoke(
    FunctionName='string',
    InvocationType='Event'|'RequestResponse'|'DryRun',
    LogType='None'|'Tail',
    ClientContext='string',
    Payload=b'bytes'|file,
    Qualifier='string'
)
```

We can invoke the AWS Lambda function using the Boto3 library. The preceding code is the syntax of the `invoke` method of the Lambda client. You can read more about the `invoke` method's mechanism at Boto3's official documentation here: `http://boto3.` `readthedocs.io/en/latest/reference/services/lambda.html#Lambda.Client.invoke`.

 Boto3 is a well-organized and well-maintained AWS SDK for Python. It helps developers to interact with AWS services using Python. Zappa also uses Boto3 in order to interact with AWS services.

Let's briefly elaborate on `InvocationType`, which is used to decide whether to execute the function in either synchronous mode or asynchronous mode. If you want to invoke an existing AWS Lambda function in synchronous mode, then you can choose `InvocationType` as `RequestResponse`, and for asynchronous mode, you can choose `InvocationType` as `Event`.

The following code is an example of asynchronous execution of a Lambda function:

```
client = boto3.client('lambda')
response = client.invoke(
    FunctionName='MyFunction',
    InvocationType='Event'
)
```

That's it. This would invoke the Lambda function in asynchronous mode. With the help of Boto3, you can perform execution of AWS Lambda functions asynchronously. Now let's see how we can perform asynchronous execution using Zappa.

AWS Lambda asynchronous invocation using Zappa

An AWS Lambda function is nothing but a function deployed at an AWS Lambda container. Hence, executing it is just a matter of invoking a function. There are various methods of invocation provided by AWS. How you go about integrating and configuring the invocation to achieve asynchronous execution is entirely up to you. We have seen in the previous section how to go about asynchronous execution using the Boto3 SDK. Now, we are going to explore the various ways of invocation that are provided by Zappa.

Asynchronous AWS Lambda invocation using the task decorator

Zappa provides a super-easy way to configure your Lambda execution in asynchronous mode. Zappa has an implementation of asynchronous execution using a decorator method called `zappa.async.task`. This decorator can be used with any function we want to execute in asynchronous mode. The following is an example from Zappa's official GitHub page (`https://github.com/Miserlou/Zappa#asynchronous-task-execution`):

```python
from flask import Flask
from zappa.async import task
app = Flask(__name__)

@task
def make_pie():
    """ This takes a long time! """
    ingredients = get_ingredients()
    pie = bake(ingredients)
    deliver(pie)

@app.route('/api/order/pie')
def order_pie():
    """ This returns immediately! """
    make_pie()
    return "Your pie is being made!"
```

As you can see, we used the `task` decorator on the `make_pie` method. Now, when you call the API, it will return the response immediately and execute the `make_pie` method in asynchronous mode. Executing `make_pie` asynchronously is nothing more than instantiating the AWS Lambda instance with the context of the `make_pie` method execution. This is how you can execute a function asynchronously. Now, another challenge is collecting the response from an asynchronously executed function. We will discuss this in an upcoming section.

Amazon SNS as the task source

Amazon Simple Notification Service (SNS) is a managed pub/sub messaging service. It supports various protocols, such as HTTP, HTTPS, email, email-JSON, Amazon SQS, applications, AWS Lambda, and SMS. We can create topics and subscribes via any of these protocols, though we can use AWS SNS and perform a pub/sub operation through its web console.

We have already invoked AWS Lambda via API Gateway, which is how all our implemented APIs are working. In a similar fashion, we can subscribe our AWS Lambda with Amazon SNS with a specific topic. Now, whenever any message is published on that topic, it will invoke the subscribed AWS Lambda as well.

Zappa provides an easy way of configuring Amazon SNS with AWS Lambda. With the help of the `zappa.async.task_sns` decorator, we can configure a method for execution that will be invoked by an Amazon SNS event. The following is the sample code snippet to understand the `task_sns` decorator binding:

```python
from zappa.asycn import task_sns

@task_sns
def method_to_invoke_from_sns_event():
    pass
```

You also need to update the following settings in the `zappa_settings.json` file:

```json
{
  "dev": {
    ..
      "async_source": "sns",
      "async_resources": true,
    ..
  }
}
```

When you call the `zappa schedule` command, it will automatically create and subscribe to SNS. Any message publication over an SNS topic creates a unique message ID as well. Hence, you can track the message response in CloudWatch Logs using the generated message ID.

This feature enables you to use the Lambda invocation to perform an operation based on the SNS event. You may use it to develop a **One-Time Password** (**OTP**) generation application, for instance, where you wouldn't be required to persist the OTP data. Instead, it would be published to a specific topic, and subscribers would get that information. Finally, AWS Lambda and mobile numbers can be subscriptions of an AWS SNS topic. This would invoke the AWS Lambda method and with the published message context over an SNS topic.

Let's look at the direct invocation method in the next section.

Direct invocation

Zappa provides another mechanism for performing the direct invocation of a Lambda function. Previously, we have been using the `task` and `task_sns` decorators, but now we are going to use the `zappa.async.run` method to perform the direct invocation.

The following is a sample code snippet of the `zappa.async.run` method being used:

```
from zappa.async import run

# Invoking a method in async mode using Lambda
run(method_name_to_invoke, args, kwargs)

# Invoking a method in async mode using SNS
run(method_name_to_invoke, args, kwargs, service="sns")
```

This feature would help you to configure the `async` invocation dynamically based on your requirements. Decorator task methods are fixed from compilation, but this method statement can be called, conditionally, at runtime.

Remote invocation

By default, Zappa performs the direct invocation of a method at the current Lambda instance. But, if you wish to perform the Lambda invocation as a separate Lambda function on a different region, then you can update your task decorator, as shown in the following code snippet:

```
@task(remote_aws_lambda_function_name='subscribe-mobile-prod',
remote_aws_region='us-east-1')
def subscribe_mobile_number(*args, **kwargs):
    """ This may take a long time! """
    validate(kwargs.get("mobile"))
    add_subscription(mobile=kwargs.get("mobile"))
```

We are using the `task` decorator, but with additional arguments, such as `remote_aws_lambda_function_name` and `remote_aws_region`. These arguments state to execute the particular Lambda function in a specific region. This is how you can perform a **remote invocation**.

Let's enhance the Quote API application with these different types of invocation to achieve asynchronous execution.

Configuring the Quote API application with async features

In the last chapter, we created a Quote API and configured a custom domain. Now we are going to enhance and optimize the existing application. There will be some new features that we are going to add to the application in order to demonstrate the different types of invocations.

We are going to use the existing code base as a different project, so it would be good to copy the existing code base in a new directory; in our case, we will copy the Chapter08 code base as Chapter09; however, you will be required to update the zappa_settings.json file. In the upcoming section, we will be covering the Zappa settings changes.

SMS subscription with Amazon SNS for the daily quote

We are going to add the new feature of the SMS subscription for receiving quotes on a daily basis. This would require us to configure Amazon SNS using the Boto3 library. Boto3 is a complete Python SDK library that enables us to interact with AWS services programmatically. Let's move on and configure Amazon SNS in the next section.

Configuring Amazon SNS using Boto3

You need to have met the prerequisites and followed the installation instructions detailed in the previous chapter, where we configured the environment with Boto3 and other required libraries. Assuming that you have configured the environment, I will now move ahead to explore the configuration.

Let's have a look at the following code snippet:

```
client = boto3.client('sns',
          aws_access_key_id= os.environ['aws_access_key_id'],
          aws_secret_access_key= os.environ['aws_secret_access_key'],
          region_name= 'us-east-1')
```

As you can see, we are creating a client object of Amazon SNS using Boto3. We need to have access key credentials in order to get access programmatically.

This is an essential step when connecting with Amazon SNS. Once you have successfully created the `client` object, you can perform various actions, such as creating a topic, subscribing a service with a protocol, and publishing the message on the topic.

Let's move toward the actual implementation of the SMS subscription using Amazon SNS.

Implementing the SMS subscription functionality

For implementing the subscription functionality, we require to validate the mobile number. Hence we are going to implement the OTP verification functionality before subscribing any mobile number. We require to have a database table to persist the data for OTP generated codes along with mobile number. The following is the code snippet of `models.py` class with along with `OTPModel` class:

```python
import os
import datetime
from shutil import copyfile
from peewee import *


# Copy our working DB to /tmp..
db_name = 'quote_database.db'
src = os.path.abspath(db_name)
dst = "/tmp/{}".format(db_name)
copyfile(src, dst)

db = SqliteDatabase(dst)


class QuoteModel(Model):

    class Meta:
        database = db

    id = IntegerField(primary_key= True)
    quote = TextField()
    author = CharField()
    category = CharField()
    created_at = DateTimeField(default= datetime.date.today())


class OTPModel(Model):

    class Meta:
        database = db
```

```
        id = IntegerField(primary_key= True)
        mobile_number = CharField()
        otp = IntegerField()
        is_verified = BooleanField(default=False)
        created_at = DateTimeField(default= datetime.date.today())


    db.connect()
    db.create_tables([QuoteModel, OTPModel])
```

In order to have complete SMS subscription functionality, we are going to create the core class of SMS subscriptions, which will be named `QuoteSubscription`. This class will have all the required functionality for subscribing/unsubscribing a particular mobile number for getting a daily quote message. The following is the code snippet for the `QuoteSubscription` class.

File—`sns.py`:

```
import os
import re
import boto3


class QuoteSubscription:

    def __init__(self):
        """
        Class constructor to initialize the boto3 configuration with Amazon
SNS.
        """
        self.client = boto3.client(
            'sns',
            aws_access_key_id=os.environ['aws_access_key_id'],
            aws_secret_access_key=os.environ['aws_secret_access_key'],
            region_name='us-east-1')
        topic = self.client.create_topic(Name="DailyQuoteSubscription")
        self.topic_arn = topic['TopicArn']


    def subscribe(self, mobile):
        """
        This method is used to subscribe a mobile number to the Amazon SNS
topic.
        Required parameters:
            :param mobile: A mobile number along with country code.
            Syntax - <country_code><mobile_number>
            Example - 919028XXXXXX
```

```
        """
        assert(bool(re.match("^(\+\d{1,3}?)?\d{10}$", mobile))), 'Invalid
mobile number'
        self.client.subscribe(
            TopicArn=self.topic_arn,
            Protocol='sms',
            Endpoint=mobile,
        )


    def unsubscribe(self, mobile):
        """
        This method is used to unsubscribe a mobile number from the Amazon
SNS topic.
        Required parameters:
            :param mobile: A mobile number along with country code.
            Syntax - <country_code><mobile_number>
            Example - 919028XXXXXX
        """
        assert(bool(re.match("^(\+\d{1,3}?)?\d{10}$", mobile))), 'Invalid
mobile number'
        try:
            subscriptions =
self.client.list_subscriptions_by_topic(TopicArn=self.topic_arn)
            subscription = list(filter(lambda x: x['Endpoint']==mobile,
subscriptions['Subscriptions']))[0]
            self.client.unsubscribe(
                SubscriptionArn= subscription['SubscriptionArn']
            )
        except IndexError:
            raise ValueError('Mobile {} is not subscribed.'.format(mobile))


    def publish(self, message):
        """
        This method is used to publish a quote message on Amazon SNS topic.
        Required parameters:
            :param message: string formated data.
        """
        self.client.publish(Message=message, TopicArn=self.topic_arn)


    def send_sms(self, mobile_number, message):
        """
        This method is used to send a SMS to a mobile number.
        Required parameters:
            :param mobile_number: string formated data.
            :param message: string formated data.
```

```
        """
        self.client.publish(
            PhoneNumber=mobile_number,
            Message=message
        )
```

This class has a method for performing the subscription functionality for a mobile number. In order to demonstrate asynchronous executions, we are going to write some functions explicitly, which will be using `QuoteSubscription` features.

Let's create a file called `async.py` with the following code snippet:

```python
import random
from zappa.async import task
from sns import QuoteSubscription
from models import OTPModel


@task
def async_subscribe(mobile_number):
    quote_subscription = QuoteSubscription()
    quote_subscription.subscribe(mobile=mobile_number)


@task
def async_unsubscribe(mobile_number):
    quote_subscription = QuoteSubscription()
    quote_subscription.unsubscribe(mobile=mobile_number)


@task
def async_publish(message):
    quote_subscription = QuoteSubscription()
    quote_subscription.publish(message=message)


@task
def async_send_otp(mobile_number):
    otp = None
    quote_subscription = QuoteSubscription()
    data = OTPModel.select().where(OTPModel.mobile_number == mobile_number,
OTPModel.is_verified == False)
    if data.exists():
        data = data.get()
        otp = data.otp
    else:
        otp = random.randint(1000,9999)
        OTPModel.create(**{'mobile_number': mobile_number, 'otp': otp})
```

```
    message = "One Time Password (OTP) is {} to verify the Daily Quote
subscription.".format(otp)
    quote_subscription.send_sms(mobile_number=mobile_number,
message=message)
```

As you can see, we defined these methods and added the @task decorator. On the local environment, it would execute in normal methods, but on an AWS Lambda context, it would execute in asynchronous mode.

Let's move to the resources API implementation. We are going to modify the existing resources a little bit. There will be some new APIs related to SMS subscription.

File—resources.py:

```python
import os
import re
import datetime
import requests
import falcon
import boto3

from models import QuoteModel, OTPModel
from mashape import fetch_quote
from async import async_subscribe, async_unsubscribe, async_send_otp


class DailyQuoteResource:
    def on_get(self, req, resp):
        """Handles GET requests"""
        try:
            data = QuoteModel.select().where(QuoteModel.created_at ==
datetime.date.today())
            if data.exists():
                data = data.get()
                resp.media = {'quote': data.quote, 'author': data.author,
'category': data.category}
            else:
                quote = fetch_quote()
                QuoteModel.create(**quote)
                resp.media = quote
        except Exception as e:
            raise falcon.HTTPError(falcon.HTTP_500, str(e))


class SubscribeQuoteResource:
    def on_get(self, req, resp):
        """Handles GET requests"""
        try:
```

```
            mobile_number = '+{}'.format(req.get_param('mobile'))
            otp = req.get_param('otp')
            otp_data = OTPModel.select().where(OTPModel.mobile_number ==
mobile_number, OTPModel.otp == otp, OTPModel.is_verified == False)
            if mobile_number and otp_data.exists():
                otp_data = otp_data.get()
                otp_data.is_verified = True
                otp_data.save()
                async_subscribe(mobile_number)
                resp.media = {"message": "Congratulations!!! You have
successfully subscribed for daily famous quote."}
            elif mobile_number and not otp_data.exists():
                async_send_otp(mobile_number)
                resp.media = {"message": "An OTP verification has been sent
on mobile {0}. To complete the subscription, Use OTP with this URL pattern
https://quote-api.abdulwahid.info/subscribe?mobile={0}&otp=xxxx.".format(mo
bile_number)}
            else:
                raise falcon.HTTPError(falcon.HTTP_500, 'Require a valid
mobile number as a query parameter. e.g
https://<API_ENDPOINT>/subscribe?mobile=XXXXXXX')
        except Exception as e:
            raise falcon.HTTPError(falcon.HTTP_500, str(e))


class UnSubscribeQuoteResource:
    def on_get(self, req, resp):
        """Handles GET requests"""
        try:
            mobile_number = '+{}'.format(req.get_param('mobile'))
            if mobile_number:
                async_unsubscribe(mobile_number)
                resp.media = {"message": "You have successfully
unsubscribed from daily famous quote. See you again."}
        except Exception as e:
            raise falcon.HTTPError(falcon.HTTP_500, str(e))


api = falcon.API()
api.add_route('/daily', DailyQuoteResource())
api.add_route('/subscribe', SubscribeQuoteResource())
api.add_route('/unsubscribe', UnSubscribeQuoteResource())
```

Here we created some API using the resources classes as mentioned in the preceding code snippet. Each resource class represents a single API endpoint. So we have created three API endpoints and each have its own workflow execution and usage.

Let's explore usages of each API endpoints as following:

- `/daily`: This API endpoint is intended to return the daily quote data.
- `/subscribe`: This API endpoint is designed to subscribe any mobile number for daily quote SMS. It implements a OTP verification before subscribing any mobile number. Hence it follows a URL pattern for performing the subscription operation. It requires two steps for subscribing such as generating the OTP for subscription and then verifying the OTP to confirm the subscription. For generating the OTP for subscription, you need to use the API with the `mobile` query parameter such as `http://localhost:8000/subscribe?mobile=919028XXXX` and for subscription confirmation you need to use this API with `mobile` and `otp` parameters such as `http://localhost:8000/subscribe?mobile=919028790411&otp=XXXX`.
- `/unsubscribe`: This API endpoint is designed to unsubscribe the existing subscribed mobile number.

 API query parameters has defined pattern, Hence you need to use these pattern for a valid parameter. For mobile parameter, you should send the mobile mobile number in this format `<country_code><mobile_number>`. For `opt` parameter, you should send 4 digits integer numbers.

As mentioned in the preceding code snippet, the `SubscribeQuoteResource` and `UnSubscribeQuoteResource` classes are using async methods to perform the mobile number subscription and unsubscription operations. This would all be executed in asynchronous mode on AWS Lamda.

Now let's move ahead to deploy the application, and then we will go through its execution.

Deploying and executing the Quote API using Zappa

Deployment is an essential part of any web application. We are blessed with Zappa and AWS Lambda, which provide us with the essence of being serverless. As we are enhancing the Quote API application created in the previous chapter, there will some modifications as per our current requirements.

In the coming sections, we will be discussing some changes in Zappa settings.

Setting up the virtual environment

As discussed before, we are using the `Chapter08` code base. There is some modification required in the `zappa_settings.json` file, such as the `project_name` needing to be changed to `Chapter09`, as shown in the following snippet:

```
{
...
"project_name": "chapter-9"
...
}
```

Once you've changed `project_name`, you need to configure the virtual environment with `pipenv`, by using the `pipenv install` command. This will create a new virtual environment with a changed `project_name`.

We are using the Boto3 library to interact with Amazon SNS. Hence, we will need to install Boto3 as well, by using the `pipenv install boto3` command.

Setting up environment variables

Apart from the virtual environment, we need to configure some environment variables. We are using the Mashape API (a third-party API marketplace) and the Boto3 library. Hence, we are going to configure the environment variables with the Mashape API key and our AWS access credentials.

Zappa provides several mechanisms for the configuration of environment variables. We are going to use `"remote_env"`. This approach requires the uploading of a JSON file on an S3 bucket.

The following is the code snippet of the configured JSON file:

```
{
    "Mashape_API_Endpoint" : "https://XXXXXXXXXXXXXX",
    "X_Mashape_Key": "XXXXXXXXXXXXXXXXXXXXXXXXXX",
    "aws_access_key_id" : "XXXXXXXXXXXXX",
    "aws_secret_access_key" :"XXXXXXXXXXXXXXXXXXXXXXXXXXXXx"
}
```

Once you've uploaded this file to the S3 bucket, you can then use the S3 path of this file as a value to `"remote_env"`, as shown in the following code snippet:

```
{
...
"remote_env": "s3://book-configs/chapter-9-config.json",
...
}
```

Zappa will automatically set environment variables based on this JSON file.

 AWS and other API credentials are confidential and sensitive data; hence, you must avoid committing that data in public Git repositories. With the help of `remove_env`, you can set the credentials as environment variables on AWS Lambda and keep it all secure on S3.

Adding a custom domain with SSL

It's time to configure a specific domain for the enhanced version of the Quote API application. Zappa provides a keyword named `domain` to be set with your domain name in a file setting.

The following is the code snippet for configuring the domain:

```
{
    ...
    "domain": "quote-api.abdulwahid.info",
    ...
}
```

Once you configure the domain, you need to certify it with an SSL certificate. We already generated the wildcard SSL certificate using the **Amazon Certificate Manager** (**ACM**). Hence, we will be using that same ACM ARN, as shown in the following code:

```
{
    ...
    "domain": "quote-api.abdulwahid.info",
    "certificate_arn":"arn:aws:acm:us-
east-1:042373950390:certificate/af0796fa-3a46-49ae-97d8-90a6b5ff6784"
    ...
}
```

Now you need to run the `zappa certify` command in order to create the subdomain and configure the certificate. Have a look at following log snippet:

```
$ zappa certify
Calling certify for stage dev..
Are you sure you want to certify? [y/n] y
Certifying domain quote-api.abdulwahid.info..
Created a new domain name with supplied certificate. Please note that it
can take up to 40 minutes for this domain to be created and propagated
through AWS, but it requires no further work on your part.
Certificate updated!
```

As shown in the preceding log snippet, it can take up to 40 minutes for this domain to be created and propagated through AWS, but it requires no further work on your part.

Let's move to the next section, where we will be configuring an event for publishing a quote SMS to all mobile subscribers.

Scheduling an event to publish an SMS

We are going to send a quote SMS on a daily basis to all SMS subscribers. SMS subscription features have been implemented using Amazon SNS with the QuoteSubscription class. We will give a detailed explanation about the subscription workflow in the upcoming section. But before we perform the subscription execution, we should have a configured and scheduled event that will publish a quote on the SNS topic.

We have already created the SNS topic in the QuoteSubscription constructor. Also, we have written an `async` method, `async_publish`, in the `async.py` file. Now we are going to use this method for sending a quote message asynchronously.

In order to keep a modularized code base, we have created a `schedulers.py` file to keep all scheduling methods in one place.

Let's see the code snippet for `schedulers.py`:

```python
from models import QuoteModel
from mashape import fetch_quote
from sns import QuoteSubscription
from async import async_publish


def set_quote_of_the_day(event, context):
    QuoteModel.create(**fetch_quote())


def publish_quote_of_the_day(event, context):
    quote = fetch_quote()
    async_publish(message=quote['quote'])
```

As we've already created a schedule method, `set_quote_of_the_day`, in the last chapter, we now have to create a method called `publish_quote_of_the_day`, which is responsible for publishing the quote message on the Amazon SNS topic.

Let's configure the Zappa settings in order to schedule the event. The following is a code snippet of the `zappa_settings.json` file:

```json
{
    ...
    "events": [
        ...,
        {
        "function": "schedulers.publish_quote_of_the_day",
        "expression": "cron(0 12 * * ? *)"
        }],
    ...
}
```

We configured the scheduling method to be invoked using the `cron` expression for every day at 2: 00 AM **UTC** time (**Coordinated Universal Time**), which will be 7:30 AM **IST** (**Indian Standard Time**). Hence, all subscribers in India will receive the SMS in the morning. You can schedule the `cron` expression as per your requirements.

When we create the instance of the `QuoteSubscription` class, it creates an SNS topic, as shown in the following screenshot:

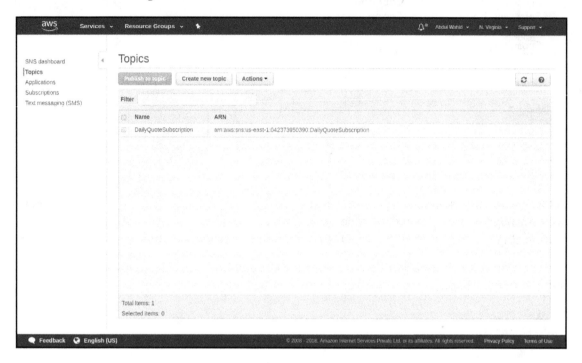

Do not Disturb (**DND**) may be enabled on your mobile. DND works on promotional SMS. So, in that case, you can change the default message type in the **Text messaging preferences** section, as shown in the following screenshot:

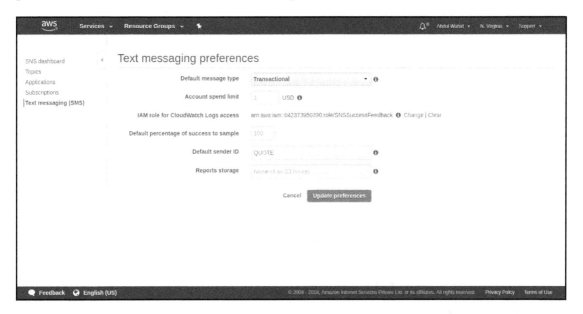

The following code snippet is the final `zappa_settings.json` file:

```
{
    "dev": {
        "app_function": "resources.api",
        "aws_region": "ap-south-1",
        "profile_name": "default",
        "project_name": "chapter-9",
        "runtime": "python3.6",
        "s3_bucket": "zappa-0edixmwpd",
        "remote_env": "s3://book-configs/chapter-9-config.json",
        "cache_cluster_enabled": false,
        "cache_cluster_size": 0.5,
        "cache_cluster_ttl": 300,
        "cache_cluster_encrypted": false,
        "events": [{
            "function": "schedulers.set_quote_of_the_day",
            "expression": "cron(0 12 * * ? *)"
        },
        {
          "function": "schedulers.publish_quote_of_the_day",
          "expression": "cron(0 2 * * ? *)"
```

```
      }],
      "domain": "quote-api.abdulwahid.info",
      "certificate_arn":"arn:aws:acm:us-
east-1:042373950390:certificate/af0796fa-3a46-49ae-97d8-90a6b5ff6784"
    }
  }
```

That's it, we are done with configuring the domain with the Quote API application! Now we are going to use the configured domain to access the API.

Deployment

Zappa deployment requires the `zappa_settings.json` file, which generates the `zappa init` command. But we already have the `zappa_setttings.json` file, so we don't need to run this command again.

If you are deploying the application for the first time, you would need to use `zappa deploy <stage_name>`, and if the application is already deployed, then you would need to use `zappa update <stage_name>`.

The following is a log snippet of the `zappa update` command:

```
$ zappa update dev
Important! A new version of Zappa is available!
Upgrade with: pip install zappa --upgrade
Visit the project page on GitHub to see the latest changes:
https://github.com/Miserlou/Zappa
Calling update for stage dev..
Downloading and installing dependencies..
 - sqlite==python36: Using precompiled lambda package
Packaging project as zip.
Uploading chapter-9-dev-1528709561.zip (5.9MiB)..
100%|████████████████████████████████████████
████████████████████████████████████████████
██████████| 6.17M/6.17M [00:02<00:00, 2.21MB/s]
Updating Lambda function code..
Updating Lambda function configuration..
Uploading chapter-9-dev-template-1528709612.json (1.6KiB)..
100%|████████████████████████████████████████
████████████████████████████████████████████
██████████| 1.62K/1.62K [00:00<00:00, 17.0KB/s]
Deploying API Gateway..
Scheduling..
```

```
Unscheduled chapter-9-dev-schedulers.set_quote_of_the_day.
Unscheduled chapter-9-dev-zappa-keep-warm-handler.keep_warm_callback.
Scheduled chapter-9-dev-schedulers.set_quote_of_the_day with expression
cron(0 12 * * ? *)!
Scheduled chapter-9-dev-zappa-keep-warm-handler.keep_warm_callback with
expression rate(4 minutes)!
Your updated Zappa deployment is live!: https://quote-api.abdulwahid.info
(https://5ldrsesbc4.execute-api.ap-south-1.amazonaws.com/dev)
```

Wow! We deployed the Quote API application successfully! Now you see that the configured domain is up and runing with the Quote API application.

Let's move to the next section, where we will see the execution of the Quote API application.

Quote API execution

We are going to use the `curl` command-line tool (`https://curl.haxx.se/`). It makes interaction with any HTTP/HTTPS links from the command line very easy indeed. (Developers tend to use it more while writing Shell scripts, though.) Let's see the execution of each API.

The daily quote API

This API will return quote data as a JSON-formatted response. As we've already scheduled an event to store the quote record into a SQLite database, we will now return the quote based on today's date. When called repeatedly on the same day, it will return the same quote; but once the day has changed, then another quote would be needed. The following is a log snippet of the `curl` command execution:

```
$ curl https://quote-api.abdulwahid.info/daily
{"quote": "May the Force be with you.", "author": "Star Wars", "category":
"Movies"}
```

Daily quote SMS subscription

We have integrated Amazon SNS to implement the SMS subscription feature. We designed the API `/subscribe?mobile=<mobile_number>&otp=<otp_code>` to create a subscription for getting daily quote messages on registered mobiles.

The following is a log snippet showing the execution of the subscription API:

```
$ curl https://quote-api.abdulwahid.info/subscribe?mobile=919028XXXXXX
{"message": "An OTP verification has been sent on mobile +919028XXXXXX. To
complete the subscription, Use OTP with this URL pattern
https://quote-api.abdulwahid.info/subscribe?mobile=+919028XXXXXX&otp=XXXX."
}


$ curl
https://quote-api.abdulwahid.info/subscribe?mobile=919028XXXXXX&otp=XXXX
{"message": "Congratulations!!! You have successfully subscribed for daily
famous quote."}
```

That's it! We've already scheduled an event to publish the daily quote message to the relevant SNS topic, which will broadcast to all subscriptions. As a result, subscribers will now receive a quote SMS on a daily basis. Once you hit this API, it creates an SNS subscription. The following is a screenshot of the Amazon SNS web console:

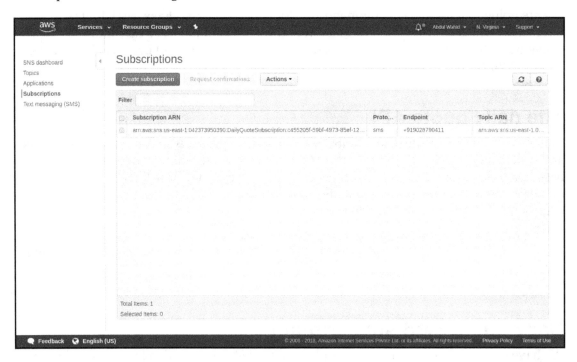

You can see one subscription record has been created. Now on every message that is publish, this subscription will receive the published message.

Daily quote SMS unsubscription

The unsubscription API will be responsible for removing any subscribed mobile numbers. This API has a similar workflow to the /subscribe API, using something very close to /subscribe?mobile=<mobile_number>.

See the following log snippet of the /unsubscribe API being executed:

```
$ curl https://quote-api.abdulwahid.info/unsubscribe?mobile=919028XXXXxx
{"message": "You have successfully unsubscribed from daily famous quote.
See you again."}
```

This removes the related subscription from Amazon SNS subscriptions. The following is a screenshot of the Amazon SNS web console following execution of the unsubscription API:

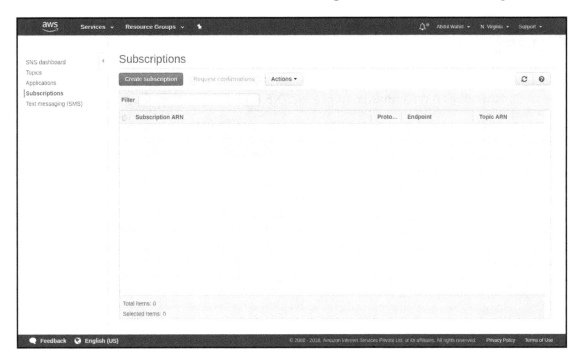

You can see that the subscription that was there has now been removed, and so we've achieve the SMS subscription/unsubscription alongside an asynchronous execution mechanism.

Summary

In this chapter, we learned about the asynchronous workflow and its usage. We also explored in detail the asynchronous invocation of AWS Lambda functions using Zappa. In order to demonstrate asynchronous Lambda funtion execution, we implemented the Quote API application along with an SMS subscription feature. I hope you enjoyed this chapter and that it was really beneficial to you!

Now we are going to see some advanced Zappa configurations in order to utilize the power of Zappa's automation process for maintaining application deployment. Let's get ready for the next chapter and move your journey toward a new adventure.

Questions

1. What is AWS SNS?
2. How does AWS Lambda invoke an SNS topic?

10
Advanced Zappa Settings

In this chapter, we are going to explore various settings and configurations provided by Zappa. This really helps you to deploy your application in an efficient way. Hence, there are various settings to configure your application. These settings are related to some AWS services and their features and functionality. We are going to explore these settings by applying them to our existing Quote API application that we developed in `Chapter 9`, *Asynchronous Task Execution on AWS Lambda*.

In this chapter, we are going to cover the following topics:

- Keeping the server warm
- Enabling CORS
- Handling a larger project
- Enabling bash compilation
- Caching unhandled exceptions

Technical requirements

There are some prerequisites to meet before moving ahead. The following requirements need to be fulfilled in order to meet the prerequisites:

- Ubuntu 16.04/Windows/macOS
- Python 3.6
- Pipenv tool
- Zappa
- Falcon API
- Python packages
- Registered domain
- AWS account

Some previously configured prerequisites can be used from Chapter 9, *Asynchronous Task Execution on AWS Lambda*. This means that you can continue with your configured domain and AWS service. You may need to update the Zappa setting file for this chapter.

Let's move ahead and explore additional settings uses with the Quote API application.

Keeping the server warm

Zappa enables a feature that keeps AWS Lambda in a warm state. AWS Lambda has a cold start because of containerization, and so Lambda requires that you set up the environment in order to execute functions. Whenever AWS Lambda receives a request, it instantiates the Lambda function along with its required environment and finally destroys the instance after fulfilling the request.

That's how AWS Lambda works. Hence, Zappa implements this mechanism using the AWS CloudWatch event schedule feature in order to keep the instantiated Lambda instance in a warm state. Keeping Lambda in the warm state is nothing but triggering the CloudWatch event as a ping request every four minutes to prevent the destruction of the Lambda instance.

This feature is enabled by default, but if you want to disable this feature, then you can set the keep_warm flag to false in the Zappa settings JSON file.

The following code snippet is used to disable the keep warm feature:

```
{
    "dev": {
        ...
        "keep_warm": true/false
        ...
    }
}
```

In our case, we want to keep the default setting as it is so that our application will always be in a warm state. Let's move on to the next section, where we will explore other useful settings.

Enabling CORS

Cross-Origin Resource Sharing (**CORS**) is an essential part of serving the API over the same domain or a different hosted domain. The AWS API Gateway provides a feature to enable CORS functionality. Once you have configured an API resource on an API Gateway, you must enable CORS using the API Gateway web console. Enabling CORS over API Gateway resources requires that you set the `OPTION` method with some response headers, such as the following:

- Access-Control-Allow-Methods
- Access-Control-Allow-Headers
- Access-Control-Allow-Origin

You can take a look at the manual process of configuring CORS in the API Gateway in AWS's official documentation (`https://docs.aws.amazon.com/apigateway/latest/developerguide/how-to-cors.html`).

Zappa automates the process of configuring CORS with API Gateway resources by using a setting attribute called `cors`, as mentioned in the following code snippet:

```
{
    "dev": {
        ...
        "cors": true/false
        ...
    }
}
```

Zappa sets the default value of `cors` as `false`. If you want to enable CORS for your API resources, then you can set it `true`. It also supports adding response headers.

> `"cors": true` doesn't work well with `"binary_support": true`. Hence, you can disable the API Gateway-level CORS, or you can add application-level CORS functionality.

As mentioned previously, you can also use application-level CORS. There are many libraries available for integrating CORS, and some frameworks have good libraries such as `django-cors-headers` (`https://github.com/ottoyiu/django-cors-headers`) and Flask-CORS (`https://github.com/corydolphin/flask-cors`).

That's all for configuring the CORS feature. I would prefer to enable CORS at the application level as you would have better control in handling it.

Handling larger projects

In this section, we are going to discuss the process of handling large-sized projects over AWS Lamda. AWS Lambda, by default, supports different code entry types. Now, we are going to discuss this feature in more detail, as we will show you how we can process this through the AWS Lambda console and using the Zappa library.

Handling larger projects using the AWS Lambda console

AWS Lambda supports three different code entry types—**Edit code inline**, **Upload a ZIP file**, and **Upload a file from Amazon S3**, as mentioned in the following screenshot of the AWS Lambda function web console:

This entry type allows a user to put their code base in AWS Lambda. Let's elaborate:

- **Edit code inline**: Using this entry type, you can put code directly through AWS Lambda's web console, as mentioned in the preceding screenshot. With the help of its online editor, you can write and perform code execution. This can be considered for a small code base.
- **Upload a ZIP file**: AWS Lambda supports uploading a .zip file of your code base. We discussed the build packaging of the code base in Chapter 1, *Amazon Web Services for Serverless*. This feature has a limitation regarding the file size as it only supports files that are 50 MB in size for uploading, but it has another option for large-sized projects.

- **Upload a file from Amazon S3**: This feature allows a user to upload the build package to Amazon S3 storage, irrespective of size. This means that you can refer to the uploaded build package on Amazon S3 with its S3 link.

Handling larger projects using Zappa

Zappa does consider the build package size while processing for deployment. Zappa only supports two code entry types, which are **Upload a .ZIP file directly on AWS Lambda** and **Upload a .ZIP file on Amazon S3**.

By default, Zappa uploads the build package on AWS Lambda, but in the case of deploying a large-sized project, Zappa provides a `"slim_handler"` attribute to set in Zappa's settings file, as mentioned in the following code snippet of the `zappa_settings.json` file:

```
{
    "dev": {
            ...
            "slim_handler": true/false
            ...
    }
}
```

Set `"slim_handler"` to `true` in case the project size is more than 50 MB. Once you set this attribute, Zappa will automatically upload the build package to the Amazon S3 bucket and will configure the AWS Lambda handler function to consider the build package from Amazon S3 bucket.

Enabling bash tab compilation

Bash tab compilation is a feature in the command-line environment. This will display a list of autocomplete suggestions by pressing the *Tab* key. Zappa has many commands, and if you register the `Zappa` module with the Python `argcomplete` module, the `zappa` command will support the tab compilation feature.

In order to acquire this feature, you need to install the `argcomplete` (`https://github.com/kislyuk/argcomplete`) module, either on your system or in the virtual environment:

- System-level installation:

```
$ sudo apt update
$ sudo apt install python-argcomplete
```

- Virtual environment installation:

```
$ pip install argcomplete
```

Once you configure the module, then you need to activate Python's `argcomplete` module at a global level. The following is the command to activate the global Python `argcomplete` module:

```
$ activate-global-python-argcomplete
```

In order to register the `Zappa` module with `argcomplete`, you need to add the following line in your `~/.bashrc` file:

```
eval "$(register-python-argcomplete zappa)"
```

Source it again for immediate effect in the current context of Terminal by executing the following command:

```
$ source ~/.bashrc
```

Now, once you register the `Zappa` module with `argcomplete`, Zappa commands will be available in the compilation. The following is a screenshot of Zappa command compilation:

```
abdulw@ULTP-711:~/workspace/book/Chapter09(master)$ zappa
certify      --help      package     status      unschedule
--color      init        rollback    tail        update
deploy       invoke      schedule    template    -v
-h           manage      shell       undeploy    --version
```

This is how you can use `argcomplete` for Zappa commands. However, it would be helpful to be more productive in the deployment process. Let's move on to the next section, where we will discuss catching unhandled exceptions.

Catching unhandled exceptions

Zappa provides a feature to capture unhandled exceptions. This will allow you to process the unhandled exception to raise an alert notification via email, SNS, or other sources. It depends on your requirements, but you can choose any sources to raise a notification. This will be really helpful so that you can track anything that's broken down in any deployed environment.

For example, if we wanted to send bulk email notifications to all developers and QA engineers for any deployed environment, Zappa provides an easy way to configure the mechanism of catching the unhandled exception. With the help of the `exception_handler` attribute, you can bind an exception handler method from which you can process the exception to send bulk email notifications.

The following is a code snippet of the Zappa settings file:

```
{
    "dev": {
        ...
        "exception_handler": "your_module.unhandled_exceptions",
    },
    ...
}
```

Here, the exception handler is a method that's defined in a module. So, let's modify our existing project from `Chapter 9`, *Asynchronous Task Execution on AWS Lambda,* to add the exception handler.

We already configured AWS SNS for notification. Hence, I am going to send the unhandled exception to email via AWS SNS. The following is the code snippet of the `unhandled_exception` method that we created in the Quote API application of `Chapter 9`, *Asynchronous Task Execution on AWS Lambda.*

File—`notify.py`:

```
import os
import boto3


def unhandled_exceptions(e, event, context):
    client = boto3.client('sns',
aws_access_key_id=os.environ['aws_access_key_id'],
aws_secret_access_key=os.environ['aws_secret_access_key'],
                          region_name='us-east-1')
    topic = client.create_topic(Name="UnhandledException")
    client.publish(Message={'exception': e, 'event': event},
TopicArn=topic['TopicArn'])
    return True # Prevent invocation retry
```

Here, we are publishing the exception and event data to a subscribed email in the `"UnhandledException"` topic.

We can enhance the subscriptions to manage the list of email subscriptions of developers and QA engineers. This is how this feature is really helpful in tracing unhandled exceptions. We hope that this is beneficial for managing your deployments.

Summary

In this chapter, we learned about some additional features of Zappa. These features allow us to manage DevOps operations in a very efficient way. We also explored handling large-sized projects, implementing CORS, and managing unhandled exceptions. I hope you enjoyed this chapter and that you become hands-on with these features in your application.

Questions

1. What is the use of keeping AWS Lambda in a warm state?
2. What is CORS?
3. What is the deployment flow for large-sized projects?

11
Securing Serverless Applications with Zappa

this chapter, we are going to learn about securing Python-based applications that are deployed on AWS Lambda. In the previous chapters, we learned about developing an application and deploying it on a serverless infrastructure using Zappa. Zappa also supports several mechanisms that enable you to implement a security layer for your application. Securing an application from unauthorized access is an essential process for any web application, but it would be more interesting to be able to secure a web application on a serverless infrastructure.

Therefore, we will be developing an API-based application and will demonstrate some mechanisms to secure it from unauthorized access. Let's move on and explore detailed information about setting up the development environment.

In this chapter, we will cover the following topics:

- Implementing a random quote API
- Enabling secure endpoints on the API Gateway
- Tracing AWS Lambda failures with dead letter queues
- Analyzing Zappa applications with AWS X-Ray
- Securing your Zappa application using AWS VPC

Technical requirements

In this chapter, we are going to cover more AWS features in order to enhance the security layer using Zappa. Before diving into this chapter, make sure that you have fulfilled the following prerequisites:

- Ubuntu 16.04/macOS/Windows
- Python 3.6
- Pipenv tool
- AWS account
- Gunicorn
- Zappa
- Other Python packages

Once you have enabled the development environment, we can move on and develop a simple Falcon-based API for generating a random quote on request. In further sections, we will be securing this API with different mechanisms and approaches using Zappa.

Implementing a random quote API

In this section, we are going to create a RESTful API that generates a random quote. This will include the Falcon-based API implementation with Mashape API integration, like we did in `Chapter 9`, *Asynchronous Task Execution on AWS Lambda*. This time, we are not going to integrate a database as we don't want to persist any information. This will be a simple HTTP `GET` request to our API and then we will return a JSON response with a randomly generated quote using the Mashape API. Let's look at the prerequisites in the next section.

Prerequisites

I hope you have met the previously mentioned technical requirements and set up the development environment using the pipenv tool. Now, you need to sign up at the **Mashape** API marketplace (`https://market.mashape.com/`), where we will be using the **Random Famous Quote** API (`https://market.mashape.com/andruxnet/random-famous-quotes`). Once you acquire the credentials to use this API, then we need to configure it in our application.

We are going to use Zappa's `remote_env` feature to share these credentials as environment variables from the AWS S3 file, hence why you need to upload a JSON file on AWS S3.

File—`book-config/chapter-11-config.json`:

```
{
    "Mashape_API_Endpoint" :
"https://andruxnet-random-famous-quotes.p.mashape.com/",
    "X_Mashape_Key": "XXXXXXXXXXXXXXXXXXXXXXXXXXXXX"
}
```

Once you upload this file to S3 storage, you can use the `remove_env` feature in your `zappa_settings.json` file. The following is an example of `zappa_settings.json` with `remote_env` configuration:

```
{
    "dev": {
        ...
        "remote_env": "s3://book-configs/chapter-11-config.json"
        ...
    }
}
```

We will be adding this setting once we initialize Zappa for deployment. As of now, you can set up these credentials as environment variables manually, like we are doing here:

```
$ export
Mashape_API_Endpoint=https://andruxnet-random-famous-quotes.p.mashape.com/
$ export X_Mashape_Key=XXXXXXXXXXXXXXXXXXX
```

Now, let's move to the next section, where we are going to implement the RESTful API for generating random quote data.

Developing the random quote API

Since we have discussed the Mashape API configuration, let's write a code snippet to implement functionality for fetching the random quote data. Have a look at the following code snippet:

File—`mashape.py`:

```
import os
import requests
```

```
def fetch_quote():
    response = requests.get(
        os.environ.get('Mashape_API_Endpoint'),
        headers={
            'X-Mashape-Key': os.environ.get('X_Mashape_Key'),
            'Accept': 'application/json'
        }
    )
    if response.status_code == 200:
        return response.json()[0]
    return response.json()
```

As you can see, we wrote a method named `fetch_quote`, which is responsible for fetching the random quote data from the Mashape API. We are going to use this method for further implementation.

Now, let's write a resource API for our users, who will be using our API to get a random quote. The following is a code snippet of the resource API.

File—`resource.py`:

```
import falcon
from mashape import fetch_quote


class RandomQuoteResource:
    def on_get(self, req, resp):
        """Handles GET requests"""
        try:
            resp.media = fetch_quote()
        except Exception as e:
            raise falcon.HTTPError(falcon.HTTP_500, str(e))


api = falcon.API()
api.add_route('/', RandomQuoteResource())
```

Here, we implemented a RESTful API using the Falcon framework. This API is mapped with the root URL, that is, `"/"`. We used the `on_get` method to only accept the HTTP GET request; other requests will be denied access. Once a user initiates a GET request, this API will return the random quote data.

You can execute this API on your local environment by running this API on the localhost using `gunicorn`:

```
$ gunicorn resources:api
[2018-07-11 13:59:28 +0530] [3562] [INFO] Starting gunicorn 19.9.0
```

```
[2018-07-11 13:59:28 +0530] [3562] [INFO] Listening at:
http://127.0.0.1:8000 (3562)
[2018-07-11 13:59:28 +0530] [3562] [INFO] Using worker: sync
[2018-07-11 13:59:28 +0530] [3565] [INFO] Booting worker with pid: 3565
```

Once you run the `gunicorn resources:api` command, then the API will be available on the localhost with `8000` port. Let's execute the API using the `curl` command:

```
$ curl http://localhost:8000
{"quote": "Whenever I climb I am followed by a dog called 'Ego'.",
"author": "Friedrich Nietzsche", "category": "Famous"}
```

That's it. We are done with the implementation. Now, it's time to deploy the application on AWS Lambda using Zappa. Let's move on to the next section, where we will discuss the deployment process further.

Deploying with Zappa

To configure Zappa, you should run the `zappa init` command and follow the auto-generated questionnaire. I followed the default suggested settings, and so the following is the auto-generated `zappa_settings.json` file.

File—`zappa_settings.json`:

```
{
    "dev": {
        "app_function": "resources.api",
        "profile_name": "default",
        "project_name": "chapter11",
        "runtime": "python3.6",
        "s3_bucket": "zappa-ss0sm7k4r"
    }
}
```

That's it. Now, with the help of this configuration, you can perform the deployment as mentioned in the following log snippet:

```
$ zappa deploy dev
Calling deploy for stage dev..
Creating chapter11-dev-ZappaLambdaExecutionRole IAM Role..
Creating zappa-permissions policy on chapter11-dev-ZappaLambdaExecutionRole
IAM Role.
Downloading and installing dependencies..
 - sqlite==python36: Using precompiled lambda package
Packaging project as zip.
```

```
Uploading chapter11-dev-1531293742.zip (5.6MiB)..
100%|
██████████████████████████████████████████████████
██████████████████████████████████████████████████
████████████| 5.92M/5.92M [00:02<00:00, 1.16MB/s]
Scheduling..
Scheduled chapter11-dev-zappa-keep-warm-handler.keep_warm_callback with
expression rate(4 minutes)!
Uploading chapter11-dev-template-1531293760.json (1.6KiB)..
100%|
██████████████████████████████████████████████████
██████████████████████████████████████████████████
████████████| 1.62K/1.62K [00:00<00:00, 2.32KB/s]
Waiting for stack chapter11-dev to create (this can take a bit)..
100%|
██████████████████████████████████████████████████
██████████████████████████████████████████████████
███████████████████| 4/4 [00:09<00:00, 2.67s/res]
Deploying API Gateway..
Scheduling..
Unscheduled chapter11-dev-zappa-keep-warm-handler.keep_warm_callback.
Scheduled chapter11-dev-zappa-keep-warm-handler.keep_warm_callback with
expression rate(4 minutes)!
Your updated Zappa deployment is live!:
https://u1pao12esc.execute-api.ap-south-1.amazonaws.com/dev
```

Before going any further, let's integrate a custom domain against this application. We learned about creating an SSL certificate using ACM and configuring a custom domain in Chapter 8, *Custom Domain with SSL*. Hence, we will use the previously created wild SSL certificate. It would be very easy to create a new custom domain just from Zappa settings.

We are going to add the following settings in the `zappa_settings.json` file.

File—`zappa_settings.json`:

```
{
    "dev": {
        "app_function": "resources.api",
        "profile_name": "default",
        "project_name": "chapter11",
        "runtime": "python3.6",
        "s3_bucket": "zappa-ss0sm7k4r",
        "remote_env": "s3://book-configs/chapter-11-config.json",
        "domain": "random-quote.abdulwahid.info",
        "certificate_arn":"arn:aws:acm:us-
east-1:042373950390:certificate/af0796fa-3a46-49ae-97d8-90a6b5ff6784"
    }
}
```

Here, we updated the Zappa settings and added remote environments. Now, let's update the deployment using the `zappa update dev` command. The following is the log snippet of the `zappa update` command:

```
$ zappa update dev
Calling update for stage dev..
Downloading and installing dependencies..
 - sqlite==python36: Using precompiled lambda package
Packaging project as zip.
Uploading chapter11-dev-1531294072.zip (5.6MiB)..
100%|

                        | 5.92M/5.92M [00:02<00:00, 2.19MB/s]
Updating Lambda function code..
Updating Lambda function configuration..
Uploading chapter11-dev-template-1531294078.json (1.6KiB)..
100%|

                        | 1.62K/1.62K [00:00<00:00, 8.55KB/s]
Deploying API Gateway..
Scheduling..
Unscheduled chapter11-dev-zappa-keep-warm-handler.keep_warm_callback.
Scheduled chapter11-dev-zappa-keep-warm-handler.keep_warm_callback with
expression rate(4 minutes)!
Your updated Zappa deployment is live!:
https://random-quote.abdulwahid.info
(https://u1pao12esc.execute-api.ap-south-1.amazonaws.com/dev)
```

Now, the application is updated on AWS Lambda, but we still need to perform the domain certification task to make the domain live. With the help of the `zappa certify` command, we can achieve this.

The following is the log snippet of the `zappa certify` command:

```
$ zappa certify dev
Calling certify for stage dev..
Are you sure you want to certify? [y/n] y
Certifying domain random-quote.abdulwahid.info..
Created a new domain name with supplied certificate. Please note that it
can take up to 40 minutes for this domain to be created and propagated
through AWS, but it requires no further work on your part.
Certificate updated!
```

As mentioned in the preceding logs, our application is live with the given custom domain (`https://random-quote.abdulwahid.info`), but it can take up to 40 minutes to create the domain and propagate it through AWS, though it does not require any further work from your end. Let's move on to the next section, where we will execute the deployed application.

Executing the API

Once the application is live, you can check the API's execution using the cURL tool. The following is the log snippet of the API's execution:

```
$ curl https://random-quote.abdulwahid.info
{"quote": "The significant problems we face cannot be solved at the same
level of thinking we were at when we created them.", "author": "Albert
Einstein", "category": "Famous"}
```

That's all for being serverless. Now, we need to explore some essential steps for securing our application from unauthorized access. Let's move on to the following sections, where we will discuss and implement some solutions to secure the application.

Enabling secure endpoints on API Gateway

Securing API access is an essential criterion. You can limit and restrict the access for your customers who are going to consume the API. Amazon API Gateway does support several mechanisms to secure, limit, and restrict API uses. This will help to maintain the API usages as per your customer base. The following are three types of implementations that are supported by API Gateway:

- API key
- IAM policy
- API Gateway Lambda authorizer

Let's look at each implementation in more detail.

Enabling the API Key

As we described in `Chapter 1`, *Amazon Web Services for Serverless*, regarding Zappa's deployment workflow, where Zappa configures the API Gateway to invoke the AWS Lambda with a proxy pass mechanism, this creates an API on the API Gateway interface. Each API supports various stages. In our case, we have created a `dev` stage while deploying the application. Therefore, the following screenshot shows the state of the API Gateway console:

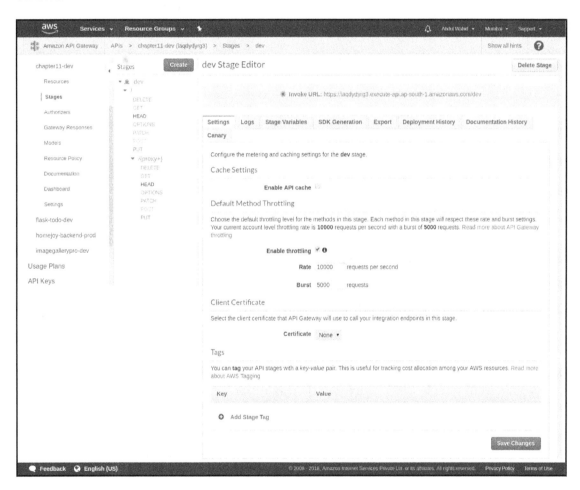

API Gateway supports API keys mechanisms, where you can create an API key along with a usage plan. With the help of this API key, you can restrict access for your customers. Any customer can access the API if they set the `x-api-key` header with the API key value. The API key can be mapped against any API or stage.

The following screenshot shows you the manual process of creating an API key:

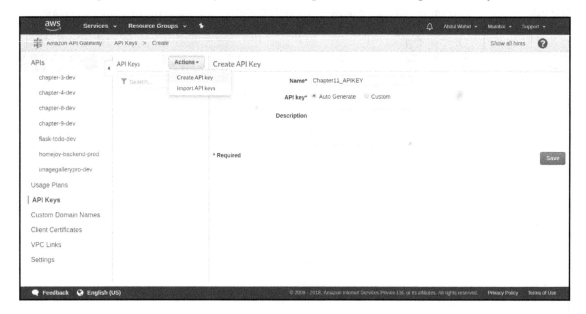

The manual process of creating the API Key can be eliminated using Zappa. That's where Zappa plays an important role, as it will automate the entire process just by configuring the Zappa settings.

Zappa provides the `api_key_required` attribute with a Boolean value. `api_key_required` is set to `false` by default, but if you want to generate the API key, then you need to set it to `true`. Once you set this attribute to `true`, then you are required to redeploy the application.

> The `api_key_required` settings don't work with the `zappa update` command; it only works with the `zappa deploy` command. Therefore, you need to undeploy the application and remove `CNAME` of your deployed custom domain from Route 53 and then remove the Custom domain from the API Gateway console. Once you remove these, then you can deploy the application once again.

The following is a code snippet from the `zappa_settings.json` file with the `"api_key_required"` attribute.

File—`zappa_settings.json`:

```
{
    "dev": {
        "app_function": "resources.api",
        "profile_name": "default",
        "project_name": "chapter11",
        "runtime": "python3.6",
        "s3_bucket": "zappa-ss0sm7k4r",
        "remote_env": "s3://book-configs/chapter-11-config.json",
        "domain": "random-quote.abdulwahid.info",
        "certificate_arn":"arn:aws:acm:us-
east-1:042373950390:certificate/af0796fa-3a46-49ae-97d8-90a6b5ff6784",
        "api_key_required": true
    }
}
```

Now, you can perform the fresh deployment again using the `zappa deploy` command, as mentioned in the following log snippet:

```
$ zappa deploy dev
Calling deploy for stage dev..
Downloading and installing dependencies..
 - sqlite==python36: Using precompiled lambda package
Packaging project as zip.
Uploading chapter11-dev-1531334904.zip (5.6MiB)..
100%|                                                    |
                                                         |
                                                         |
           | 5.92M/5.92M [00:12<00:00, 360KB/s]
Scheduling..
Scheduled chapter11-dev-zappa-keep-warm-handler.keep_warm_callback with
expression rate(4 minutes)!
Uploading chapter11-dev-template-1531334920.json (1.6KiB)..
100%|                                                    |
                                                         |
                                                         |
           | 1.61K/1.61K [00:00<00:00, 10.4KB/s]
Waiting for stack chapter11-dev to create (this can take a bit)..
100%|                                                    |
                                                         |
                                                         |
           | 4/4 [00:09<00:00, 4.69s/res]
Deploying API Gateway..
Created a new x-api-key: zp0snz9tik
```

```
Deployment complete!:
https://laqdydyrg3.execute-api.ap-south-1.amazonaws.com/dev
```

 Note that Zappa will generate the new `x-api-key` and return the API key ID, as mentioned in the preceding log snippet.

Once you are done with the deployment, you will be able to see the auto-generated API key in the API Gateway console, as shown here:

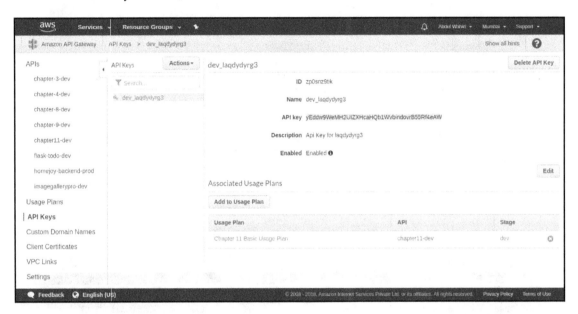

As shown in the preceding screenshot, you can use the API key value in Zappa settings to associate the Zappa deployed API with this key so that the API application needs you to have this value in the `x-api-key` header.

The next step is to associate the API key with a usage plan by clicking on `Add to Usage Plan` in the **Associated Usage Plans** section that's shown in the preceding screenshot. The API key can be associated with multiple usage plans. These°ᴮ₎ plans enable you to define a good structure usage plan for your customers as per your business model. The following is a screenshot of **Chapter 11 Basic Usage Plan** and its basic usage plan:

As you can see in the preceding screenshot, the usage plan enables you to define the throttling limit and timely bounded API request quota for each API key. Once you have defined the plan, then you can associate it with any deployed API and their respective stages, as mentioned in the following screenshot:

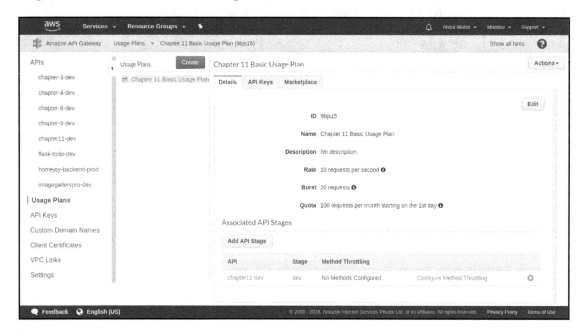

We linked the **Chapter 11 Basic Usage Plan** dev API with the dev stage to this plan. This is how you can set up a business plan of your API for your customers and share the API Key to provide authorized access.

Now, let's use the API key value that's in the preceding API key screenshot in the zappa_settings.json file with the "api_key" attribute. The following is the updated zappa_settings.json file.

File—zappa_settings.json:

```json
{
    "dev": {
        "app_function": "resources.api",
        "profile_name": "default",
        "project_name": "chapter11",
        "runtime": "python3.6",
        "s3_bucket": "zappa-ss0sm7k4r",
        "remote_env": "s3://book-configs/chapter-11-config.json",
        "domain": "random-quote.abdulwahid.info",
```

```
        "certificate_arn":"arn:aws:acm:us-
east-1:042373950390:certificate/af0796fa-3a46-49ae-97d8-90a6b5ff6784",
        "api_key_required": true,
"api_key":"yEddw9WeMH2UIZXHcaHQb1WvbindovrB55Rf4eAW"
    }
}
```

That's it. Let's update the deployment once again using the `zappa update` command, as shown in the following mentioned log snippet:

```
$ zappa update dev
Calling update for stage dev..
Downloading and installing dependencies..
 - sqlite==python36: Using precompiled lambda package
Packaging project as zip.
Uploading chapter11-dev-1531337694.zip (5.6MiB)..
100%|                                                    | 5.92M/5.92M [00:16<00:00,
261KB/s]
Updating Lambda function code..
Updating Lambda function configuration..
Uploading chapter11-dev-template-1531337713.json (1.6KiB)..
100%|                                                    | 1.61K/1.61K [00:00<00:00,
8.50KB/s]
Deploying API Gateway..
Scheduling..
Unscheduled chapter11-dev-zappa-keep-warm-handler.keep_warm_callback.
Scheduled chapter11-dev-zappa-keep-warm-handler.keep_warm_callback with
expression rate(4 minutes)!
Your updated Zappa deployment is live!:
https://random-quote.abdulwahid.info
(https://laqdydyrg3.execute-api.ap-south-1.amazonaws.com/dev)
```

We are done with enabling the API key authentication. Let's move on to the next section to see the API's execution.

Executing the API with the API key header

We enabled the API key's authentication, and so the API key is mandatory with the `x-api-key` header. If a request hits the API without the `x-api-key` header, then it would be denied access with the forbidden response. If a user provides the valid API key value in the `x-api-key` header, then it would be allowed to access the API resource.

API execution without the `x-api-key` header is as follows:

```
$ curl https://random-quote.abdulwahid.info/
{"message":"Forbidden"}
```

API execution with the `x-api-key` header is as follows:

```
$ curl --header "x-api-key: yEddw9WeMH2UIZXHcaHQb1WvbindovrB55Rf4eAW"
https://random-quote.abdulwahid.info/
{"quote": "Problems worthy of attack prove their worth by fighting back.",
"author": "Paul Erdos", "category": "Famous"}
```

We are done with the API key authentication integration. Let's move on to the next section, where we will be exploring another option of authentication using the IAM policy.

IAM policy

Amazon API Gateway supports IAM-based V4 signing request authentication. The API Gateway requires a user to authenticate the request by signing the request. Signing a request is a complete flow of creating a digital signature using the cryptographic function. You can read more about the Signing Request process at the following links:

https://docs.aws.amazon.com/apigateway/api-reference/signing-requests/

Zappa enables this feature by setting the `"iam_authorization"` attribute to `true` in Zappa's settings. This attribute is set to `false` by default. Therefore, you can explicitly set it to true in order enable the IAM-based authentication. This feature enables you to access the API resources based on the IAM policy. You can control this access via the IAM policy (https://docs.aws.amazon.com/apigateway/latest/developerguide/api-gateway-iam-policy-examples.html).

For demonstration purposes, I am going to create a different stage and custom domain for the same application. The following is a snippet of Zappa's settings.

File—`zappa_settings.json`:

```
{
    "dev": {
        "app_function": "resources.api",
        "profile_name": "default",
        "project_name": "chapter11",
        "runtime": "python3.6",
        "s3_bucket": "zappa-ss0sm7k4r",
        "remote_env": "s3://book-configs/chapter-11-config.json",
        "domain": "random-quote.abdulwahid.info",
```

```
            "certificate_arn":"arn:aws:acm:us-
    east-1:042373950390:certificate/af0796fa-3a46-49ae-97d8-90a6b5ff6784",
            "api_key_required": true,
            "api_key":"yEddw9WeMH2UIZXHcaHQb1WvbindovrB55Rf4eAW"
        },
        "dev_iam": {
            "app_function": "resources.api",
            "profile_name": "default",
            "project_name": "chapter11",
            "runtime": "python3.6",
            "s3_bucket": "zappa-ss0sm7k4r",
            "remote_env": "s3://book-configs/chapter-11-config.json",
            "domain": "random-quote-iam.abdulwahid.info",
            "certificate_arn":"arn:aws:acm:us-
    east-1:042373950390:certificate/af0796fa-3a46-49ae-97d8-90a6b5ff6784",
            "iam_authorization": true
        }
    }
```

Here, we created a different stage with `iam_authentication`. This flag will enable IAM-based authentication. Now, again, you need to perform deploy, update, and certify operations to make this stage live with the following domain.

Once it is live, then any unsigned request will be denied access with the 403 status code, as mentioned in the following log snippet of the `curl` execution:

```
$ curl -s -w "\nStatus Code:%{http_code}"
https://random-quote-iam.abdulwahid.info
{"message":"Missing Authentication Token"}
Status Code:403
```

Now, you are required to sign the request to access the deployed resource. Signing a request requires that you follow some processes, as mentioned here: `https://docs.aws.amazon.com/apigateway/api-reference/signing-requests/`. There are also many third-party libraries available to generate the required headers for signing the request. We are going to use the `requests-aws-sign` (`https://github.com/jmenga/requests-aws-sign`) library to access the API resource with a signed request.

The following is a code snippet of signing a request to access the API resource.

File—`aws_sign_request_test.py`:

```
import os
import requests
from requests_aws_sign import AWSV4Sign
from boto3 import session
```

```
# You must provide a credentials object as per
http://boto3.readthedocs.io/en/latest/guide/configuration.html#configuring-
credentials
# This example attempts to get credentials based upon the local environment
# e.g. Environment Variables, assume role profiles, EC2 Instance IAM
profiles
session = session.Session(
    aws_access_key_id=os.environ['aws_access_key_id'],
    aws_secret_access_key=os.environ['aws_secret_access_key'])
credentials = session.get_credentials()

# You must provide an AWS region
region = session.region_name or 'ap-south-1'

# You must provide the AWS service. E.g. 'es' for Elasticsearch, 's3' for
S3, etc.
service = 'execute-api'

url = "https://random-quote-iam.abdulwahid.info/"
auth=AWSV4Sign(credentials, region, service)
response = requests.get(url, auth=auth)

print (response.content)
```

That's it! Now, you can see the output of the preceding script, as shown in the following code:

```
$ python aws_sign_request_test.py
b'{"quote": "Many wealthy people are little more than janitors of their
possessions.", "author": "Frank Lloyd Wright", "category": "Famous"}'
```

Finally, we got API access with a signed request. This way, you can secure your serverless API application with IAM authentication. Let's move on to the next section, where we are going to explore another way of securing the serverless API application.

API Gateway Lambda authorizer

The Amazon API Gateway Lambda authorizer is a simple AWS Lambda function that acts as an authorizer to control access to API Gateway resources. This is because the Lambda authorizer will be responsible for verifying requests via the bearer token form authorization header and returning a valid IAM policy. You can write your custom Lambda authorizer with different authentication strategies based on **JWT (JSON Web Token)**, OAuth, or SAML.

You can add the authorizer from the API Gateway console, as mentioned in the official AWS documentation (`https://docs.aws.amazon.com/apigateway/latest/developerguide/apigateway-use-lambda-authorizer.html`), or you can create the Lambda authorizer from a Lambda blueprint named `api-gateway-authorizer-python` (`https://github.com/awslabs/aws-apigateway-lambda-authorizer-blueprints/blob/master/blueprints/python/api-gateway-authorizer-python.py`) and then associate this Lambda function as an authorizer to your API resource from the API Gateway console.

Once you have configured the authorizer, the API Gateway expects a request along with a bearer token or parameters in the authorization header. It denies the request in the case of a missing authorization header. If a client sends a request with a bearer token in the authorization header to your API resource, then the API Gateway extracts the bearer token and other params from the request header and supplies them as event parameters to the Lambda authorizer function. The Lambda authorizer verifies the token with existing AWS IAM policies or the AWS Cognito users pool and then returns the IAM policies to authorize the request. The API Gateway maintains a session for subrequests by caching the return policy with the request token over a period of pre-configured **TTL** (**time-to-live**) from 300 to 3,600 seconds, the default being 300 seconds.

Zappa supports an easier way to configure the Lambda authorizer. You can define the authorizer attribute in the Zappa settings as follows:

```
{
    "dev" : {
        ...
        "authorizer": {
            "function": "your_module.your_auth_function",
            "arn":
"arn:aws:lambda:<region>:<account_id>:function:<function_name>",
            "result_ttl": 300,
            "token_header": "Authorization", // Optional. Default
    'Authorization'. The name of a custom authorization header containing the
    token that clients submit as part of their requests.
            "validation_expression": "^Bearer \\w+$", // Optional. A
    validation expression for the incoming token, specify a regular expression.
        }
        ...
    }
}
```

We can define the preceding attributes. Each attribute has its own specific usage in order to define a custom Lambda authorizer. Let's explore these attributes in more detail:

- `function`: This will be your own local function to execute token validation. Zappa will automatically create and map this function as an authorizer for your API in the API Gateway.
- `arn`: This will be the `arn` of your existing Lambda function to verify the token. If you choose the blueprint Lambda authorizer function, `api-gateway-authorizer-python` (`https://github.com/awslabs/aws-apigateway-lambda-authorizer-blueprints/blob/master/blueprints/python/api-gateway-authorizer-python.py`), then you can put in the `arn` of your Lambda function that was created by the blueprint.
- `result_ttl`: This is an optional attribute. It enables the **time-to-live** (TTL) period to cache the authorizer result via the API Gateway. By default, it is set to 300 seconds and you can set it to a maximum of 3,600 seconds.
- `token_header`: This is an optional attribute. It is used to set the name of the custom authorization header. It contains the token as part of a submitted request by the client.
- `validation_expression`: This is an optional attribute. It is used to set the validation expression of the token in the authorization header. By default, it supports the `"^Bearer \\w+$"` expression to validate the token expression.

This is how you can create a custom Lambda authorizer for your serverless API. This enables you to create a centralized authentication for all your distributed API microservices that are deployed by Zappa.

Now, let's move ahead to the next section, where we will be exploring the tracing mechanism of AWS failure.

Tracing AWS Lambda failure with dead letter queues

Dead letter queues (DLQ) is a defined mechanism by Amazon to trace the failure of AWS Lambda functions executing asynchronously. AWS Lambda invokes asynchronous mode and retires it twice in case of failure before the event is discarded. DLQ is used to proceed this failure event to an Amazon SQS queue or Amazon SNS topic.

Manual DLQ configuration

DLQ can be configured by setting `TargetArn` (that is, the SQS queue ARN or SNS topic ARN) on the Lambda function's `DeadLetterConfig` parameter, as mentioned here:

```
{
    "Code": {
        "ZipFile": blob,
        "S3Bucket": "string",
        "S3Key": "string",
        "S3ObjectVersion": "string"
    },
    "Description": "string",
    "FunctionName": "string",
    "Handler": "string",
    "MemorySize": number,
    "Role": "string",
    "Runtime": "string",
    "Timeout": number
    "Publish": bool,
    "DeadLetterConfig": {
        "TargetArn": "string"
    }
}
```

Automating DLQ configuration with Zappa

In order to automate this process, Zappa enables this feature by setting up the SQS queue/SNS topic ARN value to `dead_letter_arn`. We created an SNS topic in Chapter 9, *Asynchronous Task Execution on AWS Lambda,* which was named `UnhandledException`. So, let's use the existing SNS topic, which is already subscribed with my email. DQL will only trigger if an asynchronous Lambda function invocation fails and retires. Then, DQL will process the failure exception as a message to the configured SNS topic and we will receive the processed exception data on an subscribed email.

Now, the following code snippet is for the updated Zappa settings.

File—`zappa_settings.json`:

```
{
    "dev": {
        "app_function": "resources.api",
        "profile_name": "default",
        "project_name": "chapter11",
        "runtime": "python3.6",
```

```
        "s3_bucket": "zappa-ss0sm7k4r",
        "remote_env": "s3://book-configs/chapter-11-config.json",
        "domain": "random-quote.abdulwahid.info",
        "certificate_arn":"arn:aws:acm:us-
east-1:042373950390:certificate/af0796fa-3a46-49ae-97d8-90a6b5ff6784",
        "api_key_required": true,
        "api_key":"yEddw9WeMH2UIZXHcaHQb1WvbindovrB55Rf4eAW",
        "dead_letter_arn": "arn:aws:sns:ap-
south-1:042373950390:UnhandledException"
    },
    "dev_iam": {
        "app_function": "resources.api",
        "profile_name": "default",
        "project_name": "chapter11",
        "runtime": "python3.6",
        "s3_bucket": "zappa-ss0sm7k4r",
        "remote_env": "s3://book-configs/chapter-11-config.json",
        "domain": "random-quote-iam.abdulwahid.info",
        "certificate_arn":"arn:aws:acm:us-
east-1:042373950390:certificate/af0796fa-3a46-49ae-97d8-90a6b5ff6784",
        "iam_authorization": true
    }
}
```

Here, I updated the `dead_letter_arn` attribute for the `dev` stage only. Hence, this feature will be available for the `dev` stage. Now, we are all set with DLQ with our `dev` stage Lambda function. Once you are done with this configuration, you are required to perform the deployment using the `zappa deploy` command. That's it! Now, we should have an asynchronous Lambda function mechanism in our code that raises an exception at runtime.

 Please note that for Lambda function-specific changes, you are required to redeploy your function using the `zappa deploy` command. The `zappa update` command will not work here as it is responsible for updating the existing code base, not Lambda configurations.

Raising exceptions in the asynchronous Lambda function

In order to raise an exception in the asynchronous Lambda invocation, we need to have a mechanism to instantiate an asynchronous Lambda function. Let's write a resource API and call an asynchronous task, which will raise an exception.

The following is the updated code of `resources.py`:

```
import falcon
from zappa.async import task
from mashape import fetch_quote


class RandomQuoteResource:
    def on_get(self, req, resp):
        """Handles GET requests"""
        try:
            resp.media = fetch_quote()
        except Exception as e:
            raise falcon.HTTPError(falcon.HTTP_500, str(e))


@task
def async_task():
    raise ValueError("Async Failure Exception")


class AsyncTaskResource:
    def on_get(self, req, resp):
        """Handles GET requests"""
        try:
            async_task()
            resp.media = 'Called async task'
        except Exception as e:
            raise falcon.HTTPError(falcon.HTTP_500, strsk(e))

api = falcon.API()
api.add_route('/', RandomQuoteResource())
api.add_route('/async-failure', AsyncTaskResource())
```

Here, we created an `AsyncTaskResource` as a resource class for the `"/async-failure"` route. This route is defined with the HTTP GET request using the `on_get` method in the `AsyncTaskResource` class. We also created the `async_task` method as an asynchronous method using the task decorator. We have already seen the implementation of asynchronous tasks using Zappa in Chapter 9, *Asynchronous Task Execution on AWS Lambda*. The task decorator will asynchronously execute the method in a separate Lambda instance.

From `async_task`, we are raising a `ValueError` exception. This will result in the asynchronous Lambda execution's failure and will raise the DLQ event on subsequent failure. DLQ will process the exception data to our configured SNS topic ARN. Finally, we will get the exception information in our email.

Let's execute the previously created API. The following is the log snippet of the `async-failure` API:

```
$ curl -H "x-api-key: yEddw9WeMH2UIZXHcaHQb1WvbindovrB55Rf4eAW"
https://random-quote.abdulwahid.info/async-failure
"Called async task"
```

We requested the `/async-failure` API, which responded immediately and instantiated the task in an asynchronous Lambda function. As we explicitly raised an exception in the `async_task` method, this will invoke the DLQ and process the exception information by publishing to the SNS topic. The following is a screenshot of the email notification received from the **AWS Notification Message**:

This way, we can trace the unknown failure. This feature will help us improve the application's quality and reduce the failure rate. Let's move on to the next section, where we are going to explore analyzing the Zappa application using AWS X-Ray.

Analyzing the Zappa application with AWS X-Ray

AWS X-Ray is an analytics service provided by Amazon Web Services. It helps developers to perform analysis on the application behavior and working flow. With the help of X-Ray, developers can understand the application's performance and trace the root cause in order to improve optimization.

AWS X-Ray can be enabled on any compute AWS services. Once you have enabled X-Ray, it starts to generate data segments based on application interaction. For example, if you make an HTTP request to your application, then X-Ray will generate data about the host, request, response, computed time, and errors. Based on these segments of data, X-Ray generates a service graph.

The service graph provides a visualized pattern for the developers to understand the application workflow and helps to determine its performance. Apart from the request and response data generation, X-Ray also generates records for your application interaction with AWS resource, microservices, databases, and HTTP Web API calls.

X-Ray manual integration with AWS Lambda

The AWS Lambda console has a privilege in that it can configure the Lambda function with AWS X-Ray. Hence, any interaction with AWS Lambda will be recorded by AWS X-Ray. You can enable X-Ray on your Lambda function by configuring the function from its console page, as shown in the following screenshot:

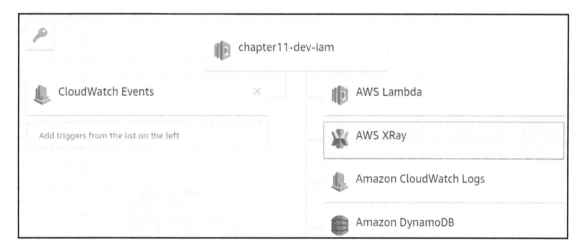

Regarding the AWS Lambda console workflow, you are required to select **AWS XRay**. Then, you can configure its associated settings from the bottom panel of the main section, as shown in the following screenshot:

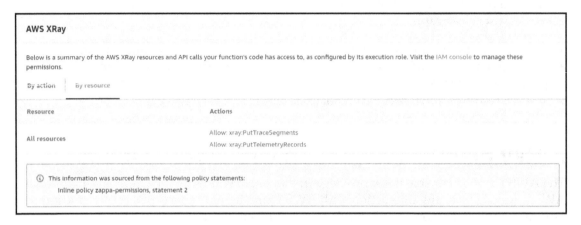

Once you choose the X-Ray, the default execution role permissions will attach to your Lambda function. This way, AWS X-Ray will record the trace to your Lambda function API executions.

Zappa configuration to enable AWS X-Ray support

Zappa is always here to avoid manual interactions in order to configure your Lambda function. Hence, Zappa provides an easy way to configure the AWS X-Ray with your Lambda function. You just need to set `"xray_tracing"` to `true` in your Zappa settings. This will automatically enable the X-Ray tracing support for your Lambda function.

Let's create another stage of our existing API application. This stage will have a basic configuration without authentication and a custom domain, since we just want to demonstrate the X-Ray workflow. The following is the new stage configuration with X-Ray support.

File—`zappa_settings.json`:

```
{
    ...
    "dev_xray": {
        "app_function": "resources.api",
        "profile_name": "default",
```

```
        "project_name": "chapter11",
        "runtime": "python3.6",
        "s3_bucket": "zappa-ss0sm7k4r",
        "remote_env": "s3://book-configs/chapter-11-config.json",
        "xray_tracing": true
    }
}
```

As mentioned previously, we've added a new stage named `"dev_xray"` with basic configuration and AWS X-Ray tracing support. Now, let's deploy this stage using the `zappa deploy` command.

The following is a code snippet of Zappa's `deploy` command:

```
$ zappa deploy dev_xray
Calling deploy for stage dev_xray..
Creating chapter11-dev-xray-ZappaLambdaExecutionRole IAM Role..
Creating zappa-permissions policy on chapter11-dev-xray-
ZappaLambdaExecutionRole IAM Role.
Downloading and installing dependencies..
 - lazy-object-proxy==1.3.1: Using locally cached manylinux wheel
 - sqlite==python36: Using precompiled lambda package
Packaging project as zip.
Uploading chapter11-dev-xray-1531691356.zip (8.2MiB)..
100%|███████████████████████████████████████████████
███████████████████████████████████████████████
██████████████████████████| 8.65M/8.65M [00:19<00:00,
460KB/s]
Scheduling..
Scheduled chapter11-dev-xray-zappa-keep-warm-handler.keep_warm_callback
with expression rate(4 minutes)!
Uploading chapter11-dev-xray-template-1531691381.json (1.6KiB)..
100%|███████████████████████████████████████████████
███████████████████████████████████████████████
███████████████████████████| 1.64K/1.64K [00:00<00:00,
9.68KB/s]
Waiting for stack chapter11-dev-xray to create (this can take a bit)..
100%|███████████████████████████████████████████████
███████████████████████████████████████████████
█████████████████████| 4/4 [00:09<00:00,
4.70s/res]
Deploying API Gateway..
Deployment complete!:
https://r0wagu3zh3.execute-api.ap-south-1.amazonaws.com/dev_xray
```

That's it! Now, our Random Quote API is up and running with different stages. Once the application is deployed, Zappa generates a random API Gateway link, as mentioned in the preceding log snippet. Now, you can just hit the API using the curl tool.

The following is the log snippet of the API's execution:

```
$ curl https://r0wagu3zh3.execute-api.ap-south-1.amazonaws.com/dev_xray
{"quote": "A lie gets halfway around the world before the truth has a
chance to get its pants on.", "author": "Sir Winston Churchill",
"category": "Famous"}
```

We have integrated the AWS X-Ray, and so all our application's interactions will be recorded as tracing segments by AWS X-Ray. The following is a screenshot of AWS X-Ray's service map:

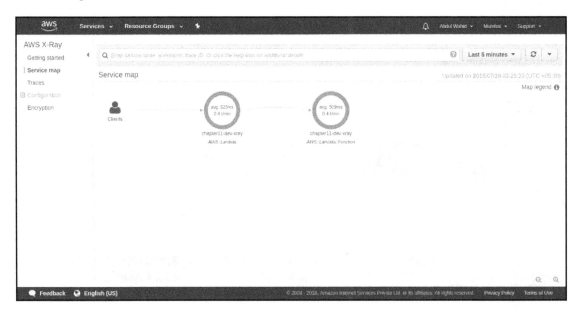

Here, you can see the tracing details of your application. These details are available as per the time frame on its console. AWS X-Ray supports the client SDK library, which enables the developer to persist these traces as per their requirements. AWS X-Ray's client SDK has many implementations with languages and language-specific frameworks. You can read more about AWS X-Ray and its Python-based SDK library at the following links:

```
https://docs.aws.amazon.com/xray/latest/devguide/aws-xray.html
```

```
https://github.com/aws/aws-xray-sdk-python
```

Let's move on to the next section, where we will be exploring AWS VPC integration with your AWS Lambda function.

Securing your Zappa application using AWS VPC

AWS **Virtual Private Cloud** (**VPC**) is an isolated virtual network service dedicated to AWS resources. It's similar to a traditional network mechanism in your own data center. AWS VPC enables you to secure your AWS resources from unauthorized access. AWS provides a default VPC for each region. The default VPC helps you configure all of your AWS resources.

AWS VPC is dedicated to your AWS account and enables an isolated layer. You can configure your AWS resources with the AWS VPC. Once you enable the VPC for your AWS resources, then you can specify the following components as per your requirements, such as IP address range, subnets, security groups, route tables, and others. These components are used to set up the networking policy and strategies.

Manual configuration of VPC

AWS Lambda has the privilege of configuring the VPC. The following is a screenshot of the AWS Lambda configuration:

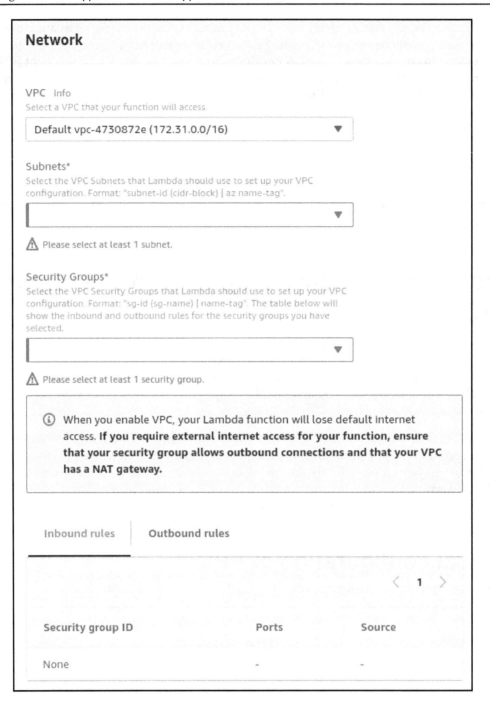

As shown in the preceding screenshot, we have selected a default VPC. We need to configure other components, such as subnets and security groups, that are mandatory. Subnets is a range of IP addresses in the VPC. You should use a public subnet for any resource which requires internet access. The private subnet is used for any resource that doesn't require that you connect to the internet.

Security groups, on the other hand, define the inbound and outbound rules for authorizing any protocol access.

AWS VPC has a complete implementation of the secure network layer. To understand each and every aspect of the VPC concept, you should read its official documentation (https://docs.aws.amazon.com/AmazonVPC/latest/UserGuide/VPC_Introduction.html). We will be focusing on Zappa configuration to enable VPC in an automated way. Let's move on to the next section, where we will be configuring Zappa with VPC.

VPC configuration using Zappa

Zappa has an optimized way of automating the VPC with the deployed application. All you need to provide is the vpc_config attribute with subnet and security groups IDs, as mentioned here:

```
{
    . . .
    "vpc_config": {
        "SubnetIds": [ "subnet-12345678" ],
        "SecurityGroupIds": [ "sg-12345678" ]
    },
    . . .
}
```

I mentioned the default VPC in the previous section. You can get the default subnet IDs from the VPC dashboard page, as shown in the following screenshot:

You can get the security group IDs by selecting **Security Groups** from the left panel, as shown in the following screenshot:

Now, we are going to create another deployment stage with VPC configuration. You need to put the subnet IDs and security group IDs from the preceding screenshots and configure them using Zappa settings, as shown in the following code snippet.

File—`zappa_settings.json`:

```
{
    ...,
    "dev_vpc": {
        "app_function": "resources.api",
        "profile_name": "default",
        "project_name": "chapter11",
        "runtime": "python3.6",
        "s3_bucket": "zappa-ss0sm7k4r",
        "remote_env": "s3://book-configs/chapter-11-config.json",
        "vpc_config": {
            "SubnetIds": [ "subnet-1b10a072", "subnet-6303f22e" ],
            "SecurityGroupIds": [ "sg-892c4be0" ]
        }
    }
}
```

AWS VPC is an isolated network, hence any service running inside the VPC network will not have access to the public internet. In case, you require to have access for public internet for any resources then you must have at least two subnets. With following settings in VPC dashboard:

- For `subnet-a`:
  Select the NAT Gateway section and create a NAT Gateway.
  Select the Internet Gateway section and create an Internet Gateway.
  From the route table section, create a route named as `route-a` pointing the Internet Gateway to `0.0.0.0/0`.

- For `subnet-b`:
  Configure your Lambda function with this subnet.
  From the route table section, create a route named as `route-b` pointing the NAT that belongs to `subnet-a` to `0.0.0.0/0`.

Now, let's create the deployment for the `dev_vpc` stage using the `zappa deploy` command. The following is the log snippet of the `zappa deploy` command:

```
$ zappa deploy dev_vpc
Important! A new version of Zappa is available!
Upgrade with: pip install zappa --upgrade
Visit the project page on GitHub to see the latest changes:
https://github.com/Miserlou/Zappa
```

```
Calling deploy for stage dev_vpc..
Downloading and installing dependencies..
 - lazy-object-proxy==1.3.1: Downloading
100%|
```

```
| 56.0K/56.0K [00:00<00:00, 4.88MB/s]
 - sqlite==python36: Using precompiled lambda package
Packaging project as zip.
Uploading chapter11-dev-vpc-1532712120.zip (8.2MiB)..
100%|
```

```
| 8.65M/8.65M [00:03<00:00, 2.56MB/s]
Scheduling..
Scheduled chapter11-dev-vpc-zappa-keep-warm-handler.keep_warm_callback with
expression rate(4 minutes)!
Uploading chapter11-dev-vpc-template-1532712136.json (1.6KiB)..
100%|
```

```
| 1.64K/1.64K [00:00<00:00, 40.8KB/s]
Waiting for stack chapter11-dev-vpc to create (this can take a bit)..
100%|
```

```
| 4/4 [00:09<00:00, 2.38s/res]
Deploying API Gateway..
Deployment complete!:
https://6odti0061c.execute-api.ap-south-1.amazonaws.com/dev_vpc
```

That's it. Now, our application has been configured with AWS VPC successfully.

Summary

In this chapter, we learned about different security mechanisms and demonstrated their implementation with a small API-based application. AWS has a very good security architecture, but it involves manual interaction processes, whereas Zappa automates these processes and prevents manual interaction. We also covered tracing, analytics, and the notification process of optimizing the application's workflow.

In the next chapter, we are going to explore Zappa development, along with Docker containerization. Stay tuned so that you can sharpen a new skill set.

Questions

1. What is an API Gateway authorizer?
2. What is AWS Lambda DQL?
3. Why is AWS VPC important?

12
Zappa with Docker

In this chapter, we are going to learn about developing a serverless application with an AWS Lambda environment or operating system context, instead of your local development environment. We will be focusing on the problems that arise in different environmental contexts and looking at efficient solutions to these problems.

The topics that we will cover in this chapter include the following:

- Understanding Docker
- Problem statement
- API development with a custom tool dependency
- Building, testing, and deploying with Docker

Technical requirements

Before moving ahead, let's configure some prerequisites, such as the tools and packages that we will require, in order to get the development environment set up. Here is a list of the software and packages that you will need:

- Ubuntu 16.04/macOS/Windows
- Docker
- Python 3.6
- Pipenv tool
- Falcon
- Falcon-multipart
- Gunicorn
- catdoc
- Zappa

Here, we've mentioned the operating system along with other required tools and packages. Choose any of these operating systems and install Docker as per the instructions detailed on its official site (`https://docs.docker.com/`). We will see detailed information about installing Python-specific packages in the upcoming API development section. Let's move to the next section, where we will understand the concept of Docker.

Understanding Docker

Docker is a platform for developing and deploying applications with containers. Docker creates these containers based on Docker images, and a Docker image includes the basic and required components similar to Linux. A Docker container is nothing more than an instance of a Docker image.

A Docker container has many features for supporting and running any application. A Docker container is lightweight, flexible, portable, scalable, and stackable. You can create a container for any service, such as Python or MySQL. Docker enables you to share data by networking with the host machine. With the help of Docker containers, you can create an isolated environment for your application.

You can create your own Docker image with stacked services and configurations. For example, you might use an Ubuntu image-based container and then install the MySQL service before configuring the container accordingly. Then we can build a new image along with the configured service. Finally, we can push the image on a Docker hub repository (`https://hub.docker.com/`), and it depends on our repository privileges as to whether we keep it private or make it public.

You can read more in detail and understand the concept of Docker technology at its official site, `https://docs.docker.com/get-started/#docker-concepts`. We are going to focus on developing an application with an environment-dependent package and deploying over AWS Lambda. Let's move to the next section, where we are going to discuss a real situation for maintaining the AWS Lambda environment at the development level.

Problem statement

Though Zappa takes care of your installed Python packages and deploys them on your Lambda using precompiled Lambda packages (`https://github.com/Miserlou/lambda-packages`) and wheels from your virtual environment, these packages may differ based on the operating system environment. So, there might be a situation where you may require an operating system-specific tool or a custom package for implementing a solution. This kind of package context may vary based on the operating system environment. Hence, it may not work on an AWS Lambda environment.

To overcome the different environmental context issues and maintain installed packages based on the AWS Lambda environment, we need to have a similar environment context for development. Hence, we need a Docker image that has a similar context and environment to AWS Lambda. Finally, **LambCI** (`https://github.com/lambci`) developed a **Docker-Lambda** (`https://github.com/lambci/docker-lambda`) image, which has an identical context to that of AWS Lambda, including system libraries, file structure, users and permissions, environment variables, and other contextual information.

Proposed solution

Keeping this in mind, we are going to develop an API application that will have an OS-level tool dependency. Hence, we will be developing a Falcon-based API to upload a Microsoft Office 2003 file with the `.doc` extension. Once we upload the file, we will retrieve and parse the text data from this file and return in a JSON format. **catdoc** (`http://www.wagner.pp.ru/~vitus/software/catdoc/`) is a command utility for printing text data, like a built-in Linux cat tool. The following code log snippet demonstrates the `catdoc` command execution:

```
$ catdoc sample-doc-file.doc
This is a sample text for demo.
```

Now, this `catdoc` command is installed at the OS level. But in our API, we are going execute this command programmatically to parse and fetch the printed text data from `stdout`. Our API can be used as a parser service, to fetch the text data from the Microsoft Office 2003 format file.

Case study for this solution

I chose this problem because there are few Python libraries available for parsing files of the Doc format. I was developing an application in my organization where I needed to parse all types of text files, such as .pdf, .txt, .docx, and .doc. So, I was met with this situation where I had to use an OS-dependent command-line tool to fetch the text data programmatically. I developed a solution, and it was working perfectly on my local Ubuntu machine; but when I then tried to deploy the application, catdoc was not there in the Lambda environment, and it was a huge problem for me.

I spent days and nights trying to resolve this issue, as I was in the situation of either having to implement it as per the requirements or give up the serverless implementation with Zappa. Giving up on Zappa was not possible for me, as I had fallen in love with Zappa and developed many projects using it.

Fortunately, I was not alone in the Zappa world. I am in touch with the Zappa community and met with Mr João Neves—a true gentleman—who helped me to resolve the issue, and finally, I resolved it in a very efficient way. It was a big victory for Zappa in my organization. I would like a standing ovation to be given for the Zappa community, and especially Mr João Neves.

Let's reveal the actual implementation of the API in the next section.

API development with a custom tool dependency

Our first aim is to develop an API that supports file upload. This API can simply support only a single file upload, with a validation check of the file extension. We are going to perform the operation on an MS Office document file with .doc only. Hence, this API will only allow .doc extension files.

Prerequisites

As mentioned in the *Technical requirements* section for this chapter, we need to configure pipenv with Python version 3.6. We use the following command to initialize the pipenv environment with Python 3.6:

```
$ pipenv --python python3.6
```

Now, install the following packages using the `pipenv install` command:

- `falcon`
- `flacon-multipart`
- `gunicorn`
- `zappa`

Once we've installed these packages, `pipenv` will create a `Pipfile`, as follows:

```
[[source]]

url = "https://pypi.python.org/simple"
verify_ssl = true
name = "pypi"


[dev-packages]


[packages]

falcon = "*"
falcon-multipart = "*"
gunicorn = "*"
zappa = "*"


[requires]

python_version = "3.6"
```

That's it, we are done with the installation! Now we can either enter into the shell of the virtual environment using the `pipenv shell` command, or we can run any command inside the virtual environment using the `pipenv run` command. Let's move ahead to implement the API.

Implementing the /doc-parser API

The API implementation will be straightforward. As per our requirements, we are going to accept only one parameter for uploading the file. Hence, this API will accept only an HTTP POST request method. The following is a code snippet of the /doc-parser API:

```python
import falcon
from falcon_multipart.middleware import MultipartMiddleware
from parser import doc_to_text


class DocParserResource:
    def on_post(self, req, resp):
        """Handles POST requests"""
        try:
            file_object = req.get_param('file')

            # file validation
            if file_object.type != 'application/msword' or
file_object.filename.split('.')[-1] != 'doc':
                raise ValueError('Please provide a valid MS Office 93 -2003
document file.')

            # calling _doc_to_text method from parser.py
            text = doc_to_text(file_object)
            quote = {
                'text': text,
                'file': file_object.filename
            }
            resp.media = quote
        except Exception as e:
            raise falcon.HTTPError(falcon.HTTP_500, str(e))

api = falcon.API(middleware=[MultipartMiddleware()])
api.add_route('/doc-parser', DocParserResource())
```

Here we created an API resource with only the HTTP POST request. This API will accept a file attribute as a multipart data. Once the file is uploaded, we validate the file type and extension. If the file is application/msword and the file extension is ".doc", then we can proceed; otherwise, we return an error.

If the uploaded file is valid, then we will proceed to parse the text data from the file and return the data in JSON format as a response. To parse the file, we have written the doc_to_text method in parser.py.

Let's explore the `doc_to_text` method and understand its workflow. The following is a code snippet of `parser.py`:

```
import os

def doc_to_text(file_object):
    data = ''
    # save file in tmp
    filepath = os.path.join('/tmp', file_object.filename)
    with open(filepath, 'wb') as tmp_file:
        while True:
            chunk = file_object.file.read(4096)
            tmp_file.write(chunk)
            if not chunk:
                break

    # Parse and return text data
    with os.popen('catdoc -a {0}'.format(filepath), 'r') as proc:
        data = proc.read()
    return data
```

As you can see here, we are performing two different tasks. Firstly, we are storing the uploaded file in `/tmp directory`, and secondly, we are parsing the text by running the `catdoc` command programmatically using the `os.popen` command. With the help of the `os.popen` command, we read the `stdout of catdoc` command. There are many options available with the `catdoc` command. I'm using `catdoc -a <doc-file>` to read ASCII characters only. You can explore `catdoc` with the help of the `man catdoc` command.

Let's move on to the next section, where we are going to execute this API.

Executing in the local environment

API execution requires a file upload process. So, I would recommend using a REST API client. In our case, I am using the Advanced REST client. The following screenshot is of the API upload process:

That's it. Our API is working as expected. We now have the text data in JSON format, along with the filename. Now let's move to the next section, where we are going to explore the build process on AWS Lambda using Zappa. We will also explore how the dependency tool raises exceptions, and how the Docker mechanism helps to resolve the issue.

Building, testing, and deploying with Docker

To make a build for the deployment, we need to initialize Zappa using `zappa init`. This command generates an interactive questionnaire to configure the application. Once you configure Zappa, it will generate the `zappa_settings.json` file. The following is a code snippet of the `zappa_settings.json` file:

```json
{
    "dev": {
        "app_function": "resources.api",
        "aws_region": "ap-south-1",
        "profile_name": "default",
        "project_name": "chapter12",
        "runtime": "python3.6",
        "s3_bucket": "zappa-xl0doooe4"
    }
}
```

Let's move ahead to make a build using Zappa without considering the Docker environment.

Building without Docker

Here we are going to consider the default generated `zappa_settings`. Now deploy the application using the `Zappa deploy` command. The following is a log snippet of the `zappa deploy <stage_name>` command:

```
$ zappa deploy dev
Calling deploy for stage dev..
Creating chapter12-dev-ZappaLambdaExecutionRole IAM Role..
Creating zappa-permissions policy on chapter12-dev-ZappaLambdaExecutionRole
IAM Role.
Downloading and installing dependencies..
 - sqlite==python36: Using precompiled lambda package
Packaging project as zip.
Uploading chapter12-dev-1531957045.zip (5.7MiB)..
100%|███████████████████████████████████████████████████
████████████████████████████████████████| 5.93M/5.93M
[00:12<00:00, 372KB/s]
Scheduling..
Scheduled chapter12-dev-zappa-keep-warm-handler.keep_warm_callback with
expression rate(4 minutes)!
Uploading chapter12-dev-template-1531957066.json (1.6KiB)..
100%|███████████████████████████████████████████████████
████████████████████████████████████████| 1.62K/1.62K [00:00<00:00,
3.40KB/s]
Waiting for stack chapter12-dev to create (this can take a bit)..
100%|███████████████████████████████████████████████████
████████████████████████████████| 4/4 [00:09<00:00,
2.66s/res]
Deploying API Gateway..
Deployment complete!: https://rbupm44rza.execute-api.ap-south-1.amazonaws.
com/dev
```

Now that we've deployed the application, let's test the API execution. The following is a screenshot of the API execution using the Advanced REST client:

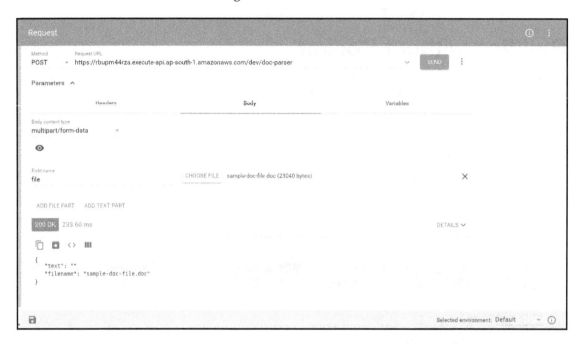

Here we tried to upload the same file but didn't get the content. Even the return response is **OK**. Let's figure this out. What is the cause of this problem? You can tail the Zappa logs using `zappa logs <stage_name>`.

The following is a log snippet of the `zappa logs` command:

```
[1532008716236] /bin/sh: catdoc: command not found
[1532008716237] [INFO] 2018-07-19T13:58:36.237Z
d4b00497-8b5b-11e8-8381-9510b412860f 103.19.39.2 - - [19/Jul/2018:13:58:36
+0000] "POST /doc-parser HTTP/1.1" 200 47 "" "" 0/68.15899999999999
```

Here you can see we got an error, which states that the `catdoc` command cannot be found. That's true and as expected, because `catdoc` is not available in the AWS Lambda environment, and there is no way to install this dependency on AWS Lambda. But why did we not get an exception for it? Well, it's a system-level error, as we used the `os.popen` method to execute the `catdoc` command. Hence, Python does not catch these errors. That's the reason we didn't get an exception.

Well, what about the problem? We are hopeless, as we can't do anything on AWS Lambda, and we cannot change the AWS Lambda environment!

Wait! There is someone who blessed you with a solution—LambCI. LambCI has released a Docker image (`https://github.com/lambci/docker-lambda`) that is a mirror image of the AWS Lambda environment. Now you can use this to solve the problem. Let's move to the next section, where we are going to configure the Docker environment along with the required dependencies.

Configuring Docker with Zappa

With the help of the LambCI Docker image, we will get an AWS Lambda-compatible environment. But, still, we are required to have build dependencies related to the `catdoc` utility. Now, we can use this Docker image with the `build-python3.6` tag to create a Docker container.

The following is a code snippet showing the creation of a Docker container:

```
$ sudo docker run --name doc-parser -v "$PWD":/var/task -v
~/.aws/:/root/.aws/ -e AWS_PROFILE=default -p "8000:8000" -it
lambci/lambda:build-python3.6 bash
```

As you can see in the preceding code snippet, we are using the `docker run` command along with some options. These options are used to configure the container and set up the container environment. Let's have a look at these options:

- `run`: This command is used to create and start the container based on the given image tag. In our case, we are using `"lambci/lambda:build-python3.6"`.
- `--name`: This option is used to create the Docker container's name.
- `-v`: This option is used to mount the directory from the host machine to the Docker container. For multiple directories, we need to repeat this option, as we are mounting the current directory as well the AWS CLI directory for AWS access credentials.
- `-e`: This option is used to set the environment variable into the Docker container. For multiple environment variables, you need to repeat this option.
- `-p`: This option is used to expose and map the Docker container port with the host machine. We are mapping to port `8000` so that we can test the application on the local environment.
- `-it`: This option is used to start the Docker container in interactive mode, where we can interact with the Docker container.

There is also the `bash` command to be executed. This command will land us on the Docker container's Terminal Bash screen. Once you run the command, it will start the Docker container and attach the controller with the Bash screen.

Have a look at the following log snippet of the options just mentioned, and check the mounted files:

```
$ sudo docker run --name doc-parser -v "$PWD":/var/task -v
~/.aws/:/root/.aws/ -e AWS_PROFILE=default -p "8000:8000" -it
lambci/lambda:build-python3.6 bash
bash-4.2# ls
parser.py Pipfile Pipfile.lock __pycache__ resources.py sample-doc-file.doc
zappa_settings.json
bash-4.2# pwd
/var/task
```

As you can see, all files from our current directory have been mounted as per the volume mapping. Now this container has a context similar to that of AWS Lambda. Hence, we can configure any source code of any library or tool.

We are now going to look at the `catdoc` configuration. As mentioned on the catdoc website (`http://www.wagner.pp.ru/~vitus/software/catdoc/`), you can download the source code and compile it through your system. We are going to download the `catdoc` source code inside the container by using the `wget` tool.

Before that, we need to install the `wget` tool in our container, as shown in the following code snippet:

```
bash-4.2# yum install wget
Resolving Dependencies
--> Running transaction check
---> Package wget.x86_64 0:1.18-3.27.amzn1 will be installed
--> Finished Dependency Resolution

Dependencies Resolved

================================================================================
================================================================================
====================
 Package Arch Version Repository Size
================================================================================
================================================================================
====================
Installing:
 wget x86_64 1.18-3.27.amzn1 amzn-updates 981 k
```

```
Transaction Summary
================================================================================
================================================================================
====================
Install 1 Package

Total download size: 981 k
Installed size: 2.4 M
Is this ok [y/d/N]: y
Downloading packages:
wget-1.18-3.27.amzn1.x86_64.rpm | 981 kB 00:00:01
Running transaction check
Running transaction test
Transaction test succeeded
Running transaction
  Installing : wget-1.18-3.27.amzn1.x86_64 1/1
  Verifying : wget-1.18-3.27.amzn1.x86_64 1/1

Installed:
  wget.x86_64 0:1.18-3.27.amzn1

Complete!
```

Once you've installed the `wget` tool, download the `catdoc` source code inside a folder. In our case, we are going to download it inside a `lib` folder. You can create the `lib` and `usr` directories as follows:

```
bash-4.2# mkdir lib
bash-4.2# mkdir usr
bash-4.2# ls
lib parser.py Pipfile Pipfile.lock __pycache__ resources.py sample-doc-
file.doc usr zappa_settings.json
bash-4.2#
```

 The `lib` and `usr` directories are used by the compiled source code of any library, hence these directories are required to maintain the binaries of compiled source code for execution.

Now it's time to install the `catdoc` library from its source code. You need to follow these steps in order to configure the library:

1. Download the `catdoc` source code, as shown in the following code:

```
bash-4.2# wget http://ftp.wagner.pp.ru/pub/catdoc/catdoc-0.95.tar.gz -O
lib/catdoc-0.95.tar.gz
--2018-07-19 23:00:39--
```

```
http://ftp.wagner.pp.ru/pub/catdoc/catdoc-0.95.tar.gz
Resolving ftp.wagner.pp.ru (ftp.wagner.pp.ru)... 78.46.190.96,
2a01:4f8:c17:2e5b::2
Connecting to ftp.wagner.pp.ru (ftp.wagner.pp.ru)|78.46.190.96|:80...
connected.
HTTP request sent, awaiting response... 200 OK
Length: 217779 (213K) [application/x-gzip]
Saving to: 'lib/catdoc-0.95.tar.gz'

lib/catdoc-0.95.tar.gz
100%[================================================================
================>] 212.67K  --.-KB/s    in 0.07s

2018-07-19 23:00:40 (2.93 MB/s) - 'lib/catdoc-0.95.tar.gz' saved
[217779/217779]

bash-4.2#
```

2. Now extract the compressed file using the `tar` command-line utility:

```
bash-4.2# cd lib/
bash-4.2# ls
catdoc-0.95.tar.gz
bash-4.2# tar -xf catdoc-0.95.tar.gz
bash-4.2# ls
catdoc-0.95 catdoc-0.95.tar.gz
```

3. Next, go into the `catdoc` source directory and configure it with a prefix to keep the binary at the application level, as shown in the following snippet:

```
bash-4.2# ls
catdoc-0.95 catdoc-0.95.tar.gz
bash-4.2# cd catdoc-0.95
bash-4.2# ls
acconfig.h CODING.STD configure COPYING INSTALL install-sh missing NEWS src
charsets compat configure.in doc INSTALL.dos Makefile.in mkinstalldirs
README TODO
bash-4.2# ./configure --prefix=/var/task/usr/
```

4. Now run the `make` and `make install` commands, as follows:

```
bash-4.2# make
...
...
...
bash-4.2# make install
```

5. Now you will find that the `catdoc` binary is available at the `/var/task/usr/` directory, as shown in the following code:

```
bash-4.2# ls /var/task/usr/bin/
catdoc catppt wordview xls2csv
bash-4.2# cd /var/task/
bash-4.2# ls
lib parser.py Pipfile Pipfile.lock __pycache__ resources.py sample-doc-file.doc usr zappa_settings.json
```

6. Change the following line in the `parser.py`, where we are just changing the command path:

```python
import os


def doc_to_text(file_object):
    data = ''
    # save file in tmp
    filepath = os.path.join('/tmp', file_object.filename)
    with open(filepath, 'wb') as tmp_file:
        while True:
            chunk = file_object.file.read(4096)
            tmp_file.write(chunk)
            if not chunk:
                break

    # Parse and return text data
    with os.popen('./usr/bin/catdoc -a {0}'.format(filepath), 'r') as proc:
        data = proc.read()
    return data
```

That's it! We've now added the `catdoc` dependency in our application. This dependency has been configured in the Docker container, whereas our Docker container and the AWS Lambda environment have the same OS context. Hence, the configured dependency is going to work on AWS Lambda as well.

Let's move ahead to deploy the application from the container itself. Before initializing the deployment, we need to install all required Python packages using `pipenv`:

1. The following log snippet shows the `pipenv install` command:

```
bash-4.2# pipenv install
Creating a virtualenv for this project...
Pipfile: /var/task/Pipfile
Using /var/lang/bin/python3.6m (3.6.1) to create virtualenv...
Running virtualenv with interpreter /var/lang/bin/python3.6m
```

```
Using base prefix '/var/lang'
New python executable in /root/.local/share/virtualenvs/task-
rlWbeMzF/bin/python3.6m
Also creating executable in /root/.local/share/virtualenvs/task-
rlWbeMzF/bin/python
Installing setuptools, pip, wheel...done.
Setting project for task-rlWbeMzF to /var/task

Virtualenv location: /root/.local/share/virtualenvs/task-rlWbeMzF
Installing dependencies from Pipfile.lock (5f0d9b)...
Ignoring futures: markers 'python_version < "3"' don't match your
environment
Looking in indexes: https://pypi.python.org/simple
████████████████████████████████████████  37/37 — 00:00:45
To activate this project's virtualenv, run pipenv shell.
Alternativaly, run a command inside the virtualenv with pipenv run.
bash-4.2#
```

2. Now, activate the virtual environment using the `pipenv shell` command, as follows:

```
bash-4.2# pipenv shell
Please ensure that the SHELL environment variable is set before activating
shell.
bash-4.2#
```

Oops! We got an error while activating the virtual environment! Let's fix it and then activate the virtual environment once again:

```
bash-4.2# export SHELL=/bin/bash pipenv shell
bash-4.2# pipenv shell
Spawning environment shell (/bin/bash). Use 'exit' to leave.
 . /root/.local/share/virtualenvs/task-rlWbeMzF/bin/activate
bash-4.2# . /root/.local/share/virtualenvs/task-rlWbeMzF/bin/activate
(task-rlWbeMzF) bash-4.2#
```

We set the SHELL environment variable and then re-run the Zappa `shell` command. Therefore, a virtual environment has been activated. Now, let's continue.

Zappa requires an enabled virtual environment, as it builds the deployment package based on the installed packages in the virtual environment.

3. Perform the deployment using either the `zappa deploy` command or the `zappa update` command. We've already deployed the application, which is why we are going to go with `zappa update`:

```
(task-rlWbeMzF) bash-4.2# zappa update dev
(python-dateutil 2.7.3 (/var/runtime), Requirement.parse('python-
dateutil<2.7.0,>=2.6.1'), {'zappa'})
Calling update for stage dev..
Downloading and installing dependencies..
 - sqlite==python36: Using precompiled lambda package
Packaging project as zip.
Uploading chapter12-dev-1532044423.zip (6.5MiB)..
100%|
          | 6.78M/6.78M [00:14<00:00, 286KB/s]
Updating Lambda function code..
Updating Lambda function configuration..
Uploading chapter12-dev-template-1532044458.json (1.6KiB)..
100%|
          | 1.62K/1.62K [00:00<00:00, 5.20KB/s]
Deploying API Gateway..
Scheduling..
Unscheduled chapter12-dev-zappa-keep-warm-handler.keep_warm_callback.
Scheduled chapter12-dev-zappa-keep-warm-handler.keep_warm_callback with
expression rate(4 minutes)!
Your updated Zappa deployment is live!:
https://rbupm44rza.execute-api.ap-south-1.amazonaws.com/dev
```

4. Now we are done with deployment. Let's move to the next section and explore the API execution.

Executing the API on AWS Lambda

You can use any REST client to debug and execute the API. We are going to use the Advanced REST client. The following screenshot demonstrates the API execution:

As you can see here, we've uploaded the MS Office document file and received the response in JSON format with all the text data present in the uploaded file. Mission accomplished.

Summary

Finally, we have implemented the solution for developing an application with a custom dependency. With the help of Docker containerization, we have built the binary of the required `catdoc` library, which is configured against the Docker container, and the results are similar to those we would expect with AWS Lambda, thanks to LambCI's Docker image and the `build-Python3.6` tag. This is how we resolve the custom dependency problem with AWS Lambda.

Questions

1. How does a Docker container work?
2. What is the difference between a Docker image and Docker container?

Assessments

Chapter 1, Amazon Web Services for Serverless

1. Deploying your application on serverless architecture is nothing but handover your application to Amazon infrastructure. Hence, there are the following benefits:
   - Amazon will take care of auto scalability
   - No server management process is required
   - It also makes a huge difference in terms of cost, you pay as per usage which is based on the execution time
   - It provide high availability

2. **Amazon Simple Storage Service** (**S3**) is a storage service provided by Amazon. AWS Lambda supports inline code execution, where you can directly write your code from its web interface. It also supports fetching the code base from an Amazon S3 bucket, where you can put your code base as a build package in ZIP format. Zappa has a command to generate the ZIP package of your application.

Chapter 2, Getting Started with Zappa

1. It's an open source tool developed by gun.io (`https://www.gun.io/`) to automate the manual process of creating a serverless environment on AWS infrastructure.

2. Zappa provides an easy way to configure the AWS **VPC** (**Virtual Private Cloud**) by adding the AWS VPC subnets and security group ID in `zappa_setttings.json`.

Chapter 3, Building a Flask Application with Zappa

1. Amazon API Gateway is a service to connect with other AWS services. API Gateway provides a RESTful application interface for mobile and web applications to connect with other AWS services. In our case, Zappa configured the API Gateway interface with proxy requests to invoke AWS Lambda.

2. Zappa performs the deployment operation based on the `zappa_settings.json` file configuration. Zappa uses the `function_name` to point the Flask application object in order to configure the application on AWS Lambda and API Gateway.

Chapter 4, Building a Flask-Based REST API with Zappa

1. **JWT (JSON Web Token)** provides an easy way to secure an application from unauthorized access. Access to the API can be authorized based on the JWT token provided in the authentication header.

2. The `function_name` indicated the module path of Flask application object. It helps Zappa to configure the Flask application and its routes with API Gateway.

Chapter 5, Building a Django Application with Zappa

1. Amazon CloudFront is managed web service that delivers static and dynamic web content with high speed over the internet. Amazon has various data centers located worldwide, these data centers are referred to as edge locations, hence AWS CloudFront uses these edge locations to deliver the web content with minimal latency and boost the application's performance.

2. Pipenv is a packing tool used to manage Python packages. It is also recommended by the **Python.org** (https://www.python.org/). It helps to maintain the packages and dependencies along with their versions. Thus it helps to develop and maintain a stable version application.

Chapter 6, Building a Django REST API with Zappa

1. Django Rest Framework is a library for developing RESTful APIs with Django based application. It has a standard pattern to implement APIs over Django Models. It offers many features to developers for implementing and managing APIs in a simple way.

2. Django-storage is a library for implementing custom storage for your Django application. It follows Django's standard in order to persist data.

Chapter 7, Building a Falcon Application with Zappa

1. Falcon frameworks have a great benchmark as compare to other Python frameworks. It is intended to write RESTful API in a very optimized way.

2. Peewee library follows Django's model patterns to create database tables and performing the CRUD operations. It offers many features such as high performance, lightweight, and less complexity. SQLAlchemy has a little learning curve and complexity. Peewee can be considered a small/medium size of application or microservices.

3. Scheduling is a defined mechanism for executing a program at a particular time period. Hence it used with many scenarios where we required to execute a program or script to perform a specific time. For example, updating a weather information, sending a notification alert, and more.

Chapter 8, Custom Domain with SSL

1. AWS Route 53 is a managed service of Amazon. It offers services for domain registration, routing internet traffic to your AWS resource for a specific domain, and creating a health checkpoint for your running AWS resources.

2. **Domain name servers (DNS)** is a mechanism to maintain and translate the domain names into **Internet Protocol (IP)** because computers communicate with each through IP addresses and it is hard to remember. Hence DNS helps to manage domain names against IP addresses.

3. ACM generates the SSL certificate against a domain name. If you use an SSL certificate along with your domain name, it enables HTTPS protocol for transitioning through your domain. HTTPS is a secure protocol that encrypts the data over the internet and provides a security for your confidential information transfer through your domain.

Chapter 9, Asynchronous Task Execution on AWS Lambda

1. AWS SNS is a web service provides a messaging implementation as a publish and subscribe pattern. It supports various resources to subscribe over a channel and get published messages. It can be used to manage and implement a notification service for your application. There are many other features, which can be considered to AWS SNS service for your application development.

2. AWS SNS works on to publish and subscribe pattern. As it supports AWS Lambda to be registered as a subscriber. It can invoke the AWS Lambda function with the published message context.

Chapter 10, Advanced Zappa Settings

1. AWS Lambda is designed to provide a serverless infrastructure. It instantiates the context on invocation request and then destroys itself after serving the request. AWS Lambda adds a little time delay for the initial startup and setting up the context. To avoid it, you can keep the Lambda instance in a warm state by setting up the schedule trigger using AWS CloudWatch. Zappa provides this feature by default and you can turn off this feature by setting the `keep_warm` attribute to `false`.

2. **Cross-Origin Resource Sharing** (**CORS**) is mechanism that allows a domain to access restricted resources from the different domain.

3. Zappa provides an easy way of managing large size project as AWS Lambda has a limitation of uploading the build package with 50 MB but also have an option to service bigger size build packages from Amazon S3. In Zappa setting, you can `slim_handler` to `true` which will upload the build package on Amazon S3 and then configure the AWS Lambda against the uploaded build package on Amazon S3.

Chapter 11, Securing Serverless Applications with Zappa

1. API Gateway authorizer is a mechanism to secure API resources. API Gateway authorizer generates an API Key that can bind with any resource. Once you bind the API resources then API Gateway will restrict any HTTP request with the API key in the `x-api-key` header.

2. AWS Lambda has a feature of **Dead Letter Queue** (**DLQ**), which enables developers to monitor the unknown failure. It can be configured against the AWS SNS or SQS as a DLQ in the AWS Lambda function. AWS Lambda will publish the failure event over the configured AWS SNS or SQS ARN.

3. AWS Virtual Private Cloud creates an isolated virtual network layer where you can configure all your AWS resources. AWS VPC will restrict the access from a outside the VPC network and enables the security layer.

Chapter 12, Zappa with Docker

1. A Docker container is a virtual instance of a basic Linux system that enables you to perform operations in an isolated environment. Docker container has all basic configurations such as networking, filesystem and OS level utilities.

2. A Docker image is an actual OS image with the required packages. You can also create your own image and publish it on the Docker repository. A Docker container is an instance of the Docker image. You create N number of containers using a Docker image.

Other Books You May Enjoy

If you enjoyed this book, you may be interested in these other books by Packt:

Python Microservices Development
Tarek Ziadé

ISBN: 978-1-78588-111-4

- Explore what microservices are and how to design them
- Use Python 3, Flask, Tox, and other tools to build your services using best practices
- Learn how to use a TDD approach
- Discover how to document your microservices
- Configure and package your code in the best way
- Interact with other services
- Secure, monitor, and scale your services
- Deploy your services in Docker containers, CoreOS, and Amazon Web Services

Building Serverless Applications with Python
Jalem Raj Rohit

ISBN: 978-1-78728-867-6

- Understand how AWS Lambda and Microsoft Azure functions work and use them to create an application
- Explore various triggers and how to select them, based on the problem statement
- Build deployment packages for Lambda functions
- Master the finer details about building Lambda functions and versioning
- Log and monitor serverless applications
- Learn about security in AWS and Lambda functions
- Scale up serverless applications to handle huge workloads and serverless distributed systems in production
- Understand SAM model deployment in AWS Lambda

Leave a review - let other readers know what you think

Please share your thoughts on this book with others by leaving a review on the site that you bought it from. If you purchased the book from Amazon, please leave us an honest review on this book's Amazon page. This is vital so that other potential readers can see and use your unbiased opinion to make purchasing decisions, we can understand what our customers think about our products, and our authors can see your feedback on the title that they have worked with Packt to create. It will only take a few minutes of your time, but is valuable to other potential customers, our authors, and Packt. Thank you!

Index

www.ingramcontent.com/pod-product-compliance
Lightning Source LLC
Chambersburg PA
CBHW080624060326
40690CB00021B/4800